ORGANIZATIONS
IN MODERN LIFE

Cities and Other Large Networks

Herman Turk

ORGANIZATIONS IN MODERN LIFE

Jossey-Bass Publishers
San Francisco • Washington • London • 1977

ORGANIZATIONS IN MODERN LIFE
Cities and Other Large Networks
by Herman Turk

The Jossey-Bass
Behavioral Science Series

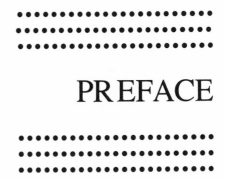

PREFACE

*I*t is my intention to reformulate broad perspectives on stability and flux in collective life, so that they may be applied to all kinds of large and complex social units. These macrosocial units shall be defined as patterns of conflict and support among organizations—using, in this work, comparisons among central cities in the national context of the United States.

People affect the city and are in turn affected by it through organizations. I have endeavored to show that this is no empty abstraction, but rather that these interorganizational networks constitute much that is significant about modern life. And it is further my intention to show that a theory of such macrosocial units pertains also to larger units, such as nations, and to such nonterritorially specified complexes as multinational industry, scientific establishments, and mass communication.

The germ of an interorganizational perspective has existed for some time. Chapter One shows that it is possible to draw together strands of thought now in the macrosocial and organizational literature and that the explication of such a perspective does not constitute too radical a departure from mainstream social thought.

Classic models of social units are capable of restatement as propositions, some of which are only implicit in these models, about units in which the actors are organizations. Models of differentia-

ix

tion and interdependence, of consensus and solidarity, of dominance and centralization, of political pluralism, of the interplay between external and internal relations, and of dialectical conflict are, in this book, interwoven with abstract interorganizational theory as the catalyst—a kind of theory that has experienced rapid development over the past several years.

Contributions made by all manner of community and societal studies may be taken into account in the formulation of our interorganizational propositions—not only propositions about cities and nations, but also about macrosocial units in general. The interorganizational approach is shown to be empirically relevant to some of the major issues and problems in community theory: how the locality—here, the metropolis—is patterned by its external (corporate, governmental, and associational) relations; the effects of such patterning on local solidarity (expressed by voluntary associations), on local government (scale and diversification, centralization), and on how decisions are made; and the consequences of all this for community conflict, for the mobilization of community effort, and for the responsiveness of such effort to local and national interests. The last chapter outlines the implications our findings have for certain popular conceptions about the United States and its cities, and the interrelationships between the two.

I have taken anecdotes, case materials, and research findings having to do with recent events in the United States as examples of interorganizational phenomena or of phenomena that lend themselves to the interorganizational analyses toward which the theory points and on which it rests. These materials have been drawn from the areas of health, welfare, municipal politics, urban economics, and voluntary associations. Illuminating these areas are the published studies reviewed and original data presented that have to do with "export economies," "reformism," fluoridation controversies, the War on Poverty, Model Cities programs, relations among hospitals, health and welfare planning, and community chest campaigns.

These four kinds of content appear throughout the book. The first two, being the most abstract, are intended mainly, but not exclusively, for theoretically oriented social scientists. Introduced in the form of a rough sketch in Chapter One, a formal system of defined concepts and of propositions relating these to one another—linearly, and as sums, or conditionally—is developed in Chapters Two through Five. The theory is eclectic in that it emphasizes interfaces among traditional models rather than stressing any specific one of them. The figures placed at the ends of chapters show the elements of this theory, identifying the portions that were related to measurable attributes of cities and those that employed hypothetical constructs. That the latter are required (although they sometimes have some anecdotal validity) means that the reader can substitute his or her own constructs in stating alternative theory, or may uncover faults in my logic. Such challenges will help to further refine the theory presented here.

The second two kinds of content refer specifically to the urban scene and should therefore appeal to community scholars and investigators in national economy and urban politics, on the one hand, and planners, policy makers, practitioners, or community activists, on the other. The general theory avoids the debate, for example, about whether local decisions are monolithically or pluralistically made, by specifying the external conditions that affect the extent to which a city's structure tends towards the one or towards the other mode. Similarly, it considers the translation of economic resources into power—rather than equating the two—in terms of organizational theory. The inseparability of local and national interorganizational relations, as well as the simultaneous tendencies towards pluralism and the search for predictability among multiple organizations, are used not only to account for the absence of centralization and polarized conflict in organizationally complex cities, but also to predict locally dominant coalitions, rather than just to say that coalitions will occur. The concluding speculations having to do with these contents are likely to arouse sorely needed controversy.

Intercity comparisons are conducted through multiple regression analyses of data that are mainly secondary. The inevitable choices among alternate strategies were necessary. These have been made explicit in the lengthy methodological statement of Chapter One, so that their effects may be evaluated on each specific finding. The book's appendix figure and appendix tables provide the critic with the materials for evaluating my empirical claims on the basis of any personally more favored procedure. More importantly, they also provide critic and noncritic alike with the means for further hypothesis testing, constituting a tertiary data source of no little value in and of itself.

There is no question that the task I have undertaken is ambitious (hopefully, not presumptuous)—hence, provisos are not out of place. Complex agendas are subject to change, but seldom require total repeal. Nonetheless, it would not only be vain but sheer folly to claim that all errors, even major ones, have been avoided in an undertaking of this scope. The logic is complex, the relevant literature inexhaustible, and data management problems can never fully be solved. As in all large sample studies of urban units, documentation has been limited to anecdote in some cases and to crude indicators of basic city characteristics in others. What I have attempted to draft is a superstructure—based on the major concepts used in the social sciences—for ordering fact and allegation and for identifying commonalities among discretely different macrosocial units. The substantive findings are subject to challenge, and any part of the formal theoretical agenda subject to modification. I will feel that the book is a success if it merits constructive critical attention.

Acknowledgments

I cannot hope to recall all of the help by students and professional colleagues of all kinds and from many different places and might, had I attempted a list, have offended persons left out, who deserve much better from me. Therefore, only those individuals and organizations that had some formal and substantial connection with the book or with the six years of investigation that preceded its writing are acknowledged by name.

The investigations were supported at various times by faculty grants from the University of Southern California as well as by the National Institutes of Health—National Library of Medicine and the National Center for Health Services Research and Development (U.S. Public Health Serivce [USPHS] Grant Number HS00541). The sponsors or editors of *Sociological Inquiry, Administrative Science Quarterly, American Sociological Review,* the *Arnold and Caroline Rose Monograph Series* of the American Sociological Association, and *Sociological Focus* gave their kind permissions to incorporate portions of my previously published works (Turk, 1969, 1970, 1973a, 1973b, 1975) into the present volume. (Although this book is new, and not a collection, the reader may recognize a number of passages where efforts to improve my earlier wording failed.) The University of Southern California's Computing Center and the Health Sciences Computing Facility (sponsored by the National Institutes of Health under Grant FR-3 to the University of California, Los Angeles) provided computing assistance. John Greg Getz, Stephen S. McConnell, Shirley Fisk, and Elizabeth Kleffel granted helpful technical assistance.

Terry N. Clark and William H. Form provided a wealth of imaginative suggestions after very careful readings of much earlier drafts. John W. Foley, William E. Henry, Victor Jones, James R. Lincoln, Peter H. Rossi, and Anselm L. Strauss made helpful comments. None of these persons have seen the major changes in orientation that were made afterward; they must be both thanked and held blameless for the current edition.

And, finally, the extensive footnotes and text references in this book offer my acknowledgment of equally extensive scholarly debts.

Los Angeles HERMAN TURK
March 1977

CONTENTS

THE AUTHOR

HERMAN TURK has been professor and director of the Laboratory for Organizational Research in the University of Southern California's Department of Sociology since 1966. His abiding interest in all manner of general theory and research methodology has led to more than fifty scientific publications on topics that include sociological theory, social psychology, small group dynamics, formal organizations, communication, statistics, computer applications in social science, and urban communities. Among his books are *Clinic Nursing: Explorations in Role Innovation* (1963); *Institutions and Social Exchange* (senior editor and contributor, 1971); and *Interorganizational Activation in Urban Communities: Deductions from the Concept of System* (1973), selected by the American Sociological Association as a Rose Monograph. He has held office or served on steering councils in several international, national, and regional scientific bodies, including the national presidency (1968–1970) of Alpha Kappa Delta, the National Sociology Honor Society. He has edited the journal, *Sociological Inquiry* (1964–1967) and currently serves on five editorial boards.

Holding a bachelor's degree in electrical engineering from the University of Nebraska, Turk received his M.A. in sociology from Columbia University (1952) and was employed by its Bureau of Applied Social Research (1950–1952). Subsequently, he joined

George Washington University's Human Resources Research Office (1952–1957), and rose to the position of research scientist. After brief association with the National Institute of Mental Health (1957–1958), he began his academic career at Duke University, where he taught sociology and was principal investigator on several projects in the sociologies of health and aging (1958–1963).

Awarded the Ph.D. in sociology by the American University (1959), Turk joined the University of Nebraska (1963–1966), founding its Bureau of Sociological Research. Recipient of a Health Sciences Scholar Award from the National Institutes of Health–National Library of Medicine (1968–1970), he has also held visiting appointments at the universities of Cologne, Kiel, Stockholm, and Wisconsin–Madison and serves major federal and academic research organizations in various ways. This book signifies the culmination of a gradual shift in scholarly emphasis from micro- to macrosocial.

For my sons, Gregory and Norman,
who not only helped with the project
technically, but also accepted my
preoccupation with it

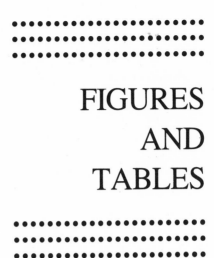

FIGURES
AND
TABLES

Tables

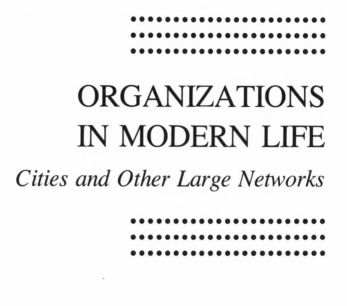

ORGANIZATIONS IN MODERN LIFE

Cities and Other Large Networks

Chapter One

••••••••••••••••••••••
••••••••••••••••••••••••
•••••••••••••••••••••••

ORGANIZATIONAL MODELS OF MODERN LIFE

•••••••••••••••••••••••
••••••••••••••••••••••
•••••••••••••••••••••••

*H*uman life has become organizational life. The fortunes, both good and ill, of modern populations depend on schools, churches, gangs, fire departments, governments, labor unions, courts, cartels, consulates, armies, hotels, political parties, television networks, football teams, insurgent groups, airlines, and countless other associations. The actions and interactions of organizations such as these form the affairs of cities, nations, and still larger social units—and even constitute their identities.

*Inter*organizational relations are everywhere in evidence. Corporations forge ties with banks, supply houses, and law firms; banks are linked to one another by clearing houses; armies establish liaison with one another; professional societies grant or withhold support of educational enterprises; revolutionary groups form alliances; and federal agencies concur with or oppose organizations from society's several institutional sectors. Moreover, organizations band into coalitions, federations, councils, congresses, and chambers. Indeed, granted the prevalent belief among social scientists that associations are the ubiquitous form of urban indus-trial or postindustrial society, the attempt seems warranted to view such a society or any one of its major subdivisions as a patterned aggregate of organizations.

This multiorganizational perspective will manifest itself, in this book, in restatements and partial syntheses of classic models of social order and change. Applied mainly to metropolis and na-tion here, such restatement is intended as a guide to the analysis of *macrosocial units in general.* These macrosocial units, which will be defined more precisely in Chapter Two, *are large but nonautonomous complexes of interdependent organizations.* The present application of the multiorganizational perspective to territorial units will fol-low from—and sometimes produce—general propositions about the ways in which the macrosocial unit's structural properties of external linkage, organizational complexity, internal coordination, solidarity, and centralization are interrelated, and also proposi-tions about the ways in which these properties influence responses, whether of conflict or accord, to internal issues, solutions of macro-social problems, and overall adaptation to the external social en-vironment. Such an undertaking requires a merging of materials from human ecology and other approaches to community study, urban politics and economics, human geography, organizational analysis, and such other special areas of inquiry as voluntary asso-ciations, urban planning, welfare systems, and the delivery of health services. It involves, as well, the comparative analysis of data from 130 of the largest American cities.

This introductory chapter is intended to provide a freehand sketch of our subject matter in its social scientific context, as well as a statement of methodology and a preamble to the more sys-tematic development of formal theory and its empirical referents in the chapters to follow.

First, this chapter introduces an interorganizational level of macroanalysis. Second, it briefly indicates that level's congruence with classic models of organizational complexity, pluralism, con-sensus and centralization, dialectical conflict, interplays of external interdependencies with internal solidarity, and organizational theory, including analysis of contexts within which formal orga-nizations emerge. Third, it describes the logical method of assessing the utility of the intended level of analysis by assessing the possibility of its being confounded by nonorganizational variables. Fourth, it describes the empirical procedures to be used in comparative analyses of the 130 American metropoli. Fifth, it introduces the form of the arguments of the chapters to follow by describing the three categories of interorganizational propositions to be discussed, in descending order of abstraction: (1) the macrosocial in general, whether or not it is territorially organized, (2) urban structure and process, and (3) operationalizations, using data from our 130 metropoli.

The Interorganizational Level

Modern society is constituted, not by persons and populations, but by their organizations. These organizations can vary from totalitarian agencies, business enterprises, garden clubs, and security councils to underground forces, reform groups, and criminal bands. *What all organizations have in common is that they tend to be formally constituted by plans and rules (but acquire informal structure), emerge in the light of specific purposes, (which may later proliferate and become ambiguous), have proper names, and be graded in authority (which can come to be challenged or to be plural in nature).* These structures of contemporary society are frequently invented; often they result from directives or legislation. Thus they stand in contrast to spontaneous collective behavior, which may or may not develop into new organizations.

Any city, society, or other macrosocial unit (especially one that is *not* territorially based—say, an entire international industry and other social sectors with which it is interdependent) consists of constellations of organizations. It is logically possible for such constellations to range from loose aggregates of autonomous associations that in no way respond to one another, through interorganizational systems of economic or ecological conflict, competition, or cooperation, to actual sociocultural *unions* of organizations, which may themselves range from loose federations and solidarities to legally sanctioned and politically coordinated networks. Two or more such constellations can logically exist in conflict or in accord with one another or somewhere in between.

The properties of such multi- and interorganizational complexes (including their simple presence or absence), we shall argue, are often the ones actually measured by such indicators of the organization of macrosocial units as external linkage, social complexity, social regulation and coordination, solidarity and consensus, social resources, centralization, dialectical conflict, structure of decision making, collective activation, and activation in response to internal demands. Such correspondences suggest a level of investigation in which organizational variables can be used as the principal means of studying cause-and-effect relations within macrosocial units such as metropoli, or others not spatially defined, while variables depicting rates of individual persons as the actors assume secondary importance.

The pattern of relationships within any densely constituted set of organizations has been said by some to generate its own "field," whose properties cannot be inferred from any simple description of the individual organizations, let alone from descriptions of the organizations' members or clients. (See Emery and Trist, 1965; Warren, 1967b, Turk, 1969; Warren, Rose, and Bergunder, 1974.) An independent level of analysis is needed in which characteristics of the interorganizational situation may be used to predict and explain other characteristics of the same situation without reference to more conventional and microscopic objects of inquiry such as persons or positions, or to population rates that such objects may comprise. These assertions require support.

Any effort involving broad sectors of any macrosocial unit depends on local organizations. Being mainly composed of organizations, such modern urban settings as large American cities, entire nations, or even cross-national complexes that are not spatially defined may be studied at the interorganizational level of analysis. At this level of abstraction, large-scale social settings are examined without explicit reference to such nonorganizational or suborganizational units as populations and categories of persons.

Our rationale derives from the assumption that individual behaviors depend on the presence of organizations that encourage or accept them, and that organizations are thus primary determinants of regularities and uniformities in human potential for such behaviors. Organizations can be assumed to be both the formulators and the means of individual action: Organizations are the actors that comprise any large and complex structure.

Persons or the populations and subpopulations they form are seen in terms of their effects on large-scale social settings through the various organizations that they generate or join, that they serve, for which they are targets, from which they acquire their personal values or receive their statuses, and that can act on their behalf. Populations are thus clienteles and electorates, "organization men," repositories of specialized knowledge such as occupational skills and bureaucratic talent, recruitment reservoirs, and diffuse sources of ideological backing or protest. They may also be viewed as undifferentiated means of disposal or support, acting through such mechanisms as consumption, donation, taxation, and investment. These various behavioral and attitudinal potentials of the population are themselves assumed to be organizationally determined and, in turn, can result in collective behavior from which new organizations emerge.

Once certain more conventional ways of thinking are put aside, it becomes difficult to identify entities like "community roles" or "revolutionary roles" within large urban settings that are not already defined by such enacted formal groups as voluntary associations, government agencies, churches, militant groups, commissions, or the public relations departments of large corporations. It proves to be even more difficult to conceive of roles in the broader society—which are often located in divers urban places—outside the context of national or international organizations. The less spatial propinquity is the basis for social interaction, the more likely is such interaction to occur between organizations and *via* organizations that connect them with one another.

Power positions within larger cities and nations appear to rest heavily on organizational memberships; prestige may also depend on organizational memberships.[1] Organizations with differing degrees of influence on particular social issues may embody "public opinion" and affect its source (Blumer, 1948; Form and Miller, 1960). Even diffuse ways of thinking, feeling, and acting toward the broader setting are acquired and exercised through contact with organizations of all kinds, and not only those specializing in the transmission of influence.[2] Further, macrosocial units marked by cleavages might also be expected to include a variety of organizational proponents for each point of view or organizational means of implementation. Indeed, large-scale conflicts require organizations, even networks of organizations, to pursue the conflicting aims.

The occupational structure appears to pervade contemporary society, perhaps all society, including within it even such manifestly nonbusiness roles as artist, priest, teacher, and volunteer. And organizations do indeed seem to absorb an ever-increasing number of occupational roles, including some that in the past have been craftlike or professional.[3]

From the interorganizational perspective, then, contemporary human life *is* organizational life. This is not to say that individuals are helpless in the face of omnipotent organizations, but only that effective action by any set of persons depends on their choice and utilization of existing organizations or their creation of new ones. Nor is the question of "freedom" germane: On the one hand, organizations, like any other form of social group, require conformity; but on the other hand, the multiorganizational society provides the individual with a "mix" of standards and choice among alternative standards to which to conform, whereas the undifferentiated tribe or commune does not.

Perhaps some difficulty in maintaining an analytic distinction between interpersonal and interorganizational relations has stemmed from the homily that, after all, organizations are composed of people, and organizational actions are composed of nothing more than the acts of persons. This difficulty is resolved by the concept of "group representative" or "representative role." Save perhaps for certain team sports, each member of each organization seldom interacts with each other one. Rather, there are certain organizational roles—not always at the highest level, as some writers have assumed—whose incumbents are given *a mandate to act on behalf of the organization.* Ambassadors, shop stewards, and public relations officers constitute ready examples. The failures in this role are sometimes called *traitors.* Representation, we may note, is as important a concept for interorganizational relations as authority or leadership is for *intra*organizational relations.[4]

If mass responses to the broader setting are both formulated and enacted by organizations, it is reasonable to redefine the setting in terms of such organizations and the relations that exist among them. This is not to say that rudiments of an interorganizational framework have been lacking in specific empirical arenas. One has only to read about collective bargaining, change in land use, education, community conflict, community development, community disasters, and delinquency in order to put the lie to any such claim. (See respectively, Harbison and Coleman, 1951; Form, 1954; Coleman, 1957; Form and Nosow, 1958; W. Miller, 1958; Moe, 1959; B. Clark, 1965.) It is only to say that recognition of its more universal applicability has, for the most part, not been made quite as explicit as this book seeks to do by merging social, political, ecological, economic, and organizational perspectives into the interorganizational perspective. Any interorganizational macrotheory cannot limit itself to just one of these, for its propositions grow out of all of them and out of their articulation with one another.

Recently, social scientists have used such familiar concepts as consensus, conflict, differentiation, and coordination to generalize about interorganizational relations within broad settings. (Pioneering attempts to examine relations among organizations in such terms have been made by Levine and White, 1961; Litwak and Hylton, 1962; Turk and Lefcowitz, 1962; Levine, White, and Paul, 1963.) Such concepts will be used in the chapters that follow to describe the setting itself interorganizationally. Here conventional variables of macrosocial structure—for example, linkage, diffusion, conflict, and complexity—will be defined as multi- and interorganizational patternings and applied in the special case of the United States metropolis—including its external relations.[5]

In short, such complex macrosocial units as nations or cities or even ones not territorially defined might more appropriately be conceived as aggregates of interacting organizations than as aggregates whose main components are persons, roles, or personal statuses. People generally link themselves to society by way of the organizations they join or establish; many of their more important roles can only be played within organizational settings; and many of their more important statuses are determined by their positions within organizations. There undoubtedly are limits to this interorganizational formulation of macrosocial structure and process. But note that when federal agencies contact a city, they contact its organizations. Private practitioners are less often approached to institute medical innovations than are health associations, medical schools, and hospitals. And when municipal governments formulate alternatives, they are more strongly influenced by the actions of organized interest groups such as minority leagues, political parties, taxpayers' associations, labor unions, educational associations, corporations that "pay the taxes," or citizen committees that can "deliver the vote" than they are by the opinions expressed by private individuals who represent only themselves.

Classic Thought and Interorganizational Analysis

The sampling of the main organizational properties mentioned in this section introduces the idea that interorganizational analysis cuts across the perennial problems and issues that have engrossed macrosocial scientists, and is not incongruent with any one of them. Only a smattering of the relevant writings—not a history of social thought—is necessary in the following discussion to suggest the theoretical scope of what is to be considered more systematically in the subsequent chapters.

Organizational Complexity. Although failing to pursue the full implications of his insights, Emile Durkheim, in his classic treatise on the division of labor in society ([1893] 1933), recognized the rise of organizations that accompanied increasing social complexity. He noted that small employers became foremen and formerly independent merchants accepted employment (pp. 269–270). He also posited the substitution of occupational associations for the now defunct communal society as mediators between individual and state in the emerging mass society (in the preface to the 1902 edition). Even further, he recognized cities as parts of regional and interregional divisions of labor and cited studies that classified them by their principal organizations, much as urban inquiry does today: as university cities, government cities, manufacturing cities, and so forth (pp. 188–189). His observations about the *correlates* of social differentiation, it will be shown later, also can readily be translated into interorganizational propositions. And the location of different numbers and kinds of organizations in different cities will lead to our variables of external linkage and organizational complexity.

Pluralism. Cultural pluralism aside, Durkheim observed further that "functional diversity induces a moral diversity that nothing can prevent, and it is as inevitable that the one should grow as the other does" (Durkheim, [1893] 1933, p. 361). Indeed, later he echoed and expanded William James' "each" form contrasted with the monistic "all" form of human substance and, like James, discussed society in terms of links among plural groups (James, 1909, p. 34; Durkheim, [1914] 1964, pp. 412–420).[6]

Political scholars defined the pluralistic versus monistic question as a question of whether (1) the state is some kind of super body that coordinates other bodies that are differentiated from one another by function or whether (2) the state is but one among many other forms of human association that pursue values as compelling as those of the state (Coker, 1921, citing Lasky). The historical model of pluralism was taken from the Middle Ages: from the interplay between church, king, feudal lord, chartered town, and Roman Empire (Coker, 1934, pp. 498–499). Every nation was considered to be something of a federal society containing different nationality groups, different churches, and different economic organizations (Follett, 1918, p. 262, citing Barker). Clearly, organizations have figured heavily in classic pluralistic models.

Consensus and Centralization. Thomas Hobbes ([1651] 1881) answered the tentative question of how social order can exist at all, even briefly, by positing political centralization through mutual consent for purposes of regulating mutually destructive impulses. It would appear that this monistic view clashes with the view of the pluralists, who saw the political state to be codominant with other organizations. Actually, political domination through consensus—however ambivalent such consensus may be—might well be *the limiting case for interorganizational theory: one in which few organizations exist.*

This idea is not incongruent with Durkheim's discussion of the repressive nature of undifferentiated society (which he appeared to have taken from Comte's theological-military type) or with Michels' description of the production of leaders by mass consensus but their inevitable organization into a self-interest group in opposition to the unorganized masses (Durkheim, [1893] 1933, pp. 70–85; Michels, [1915] 1958, pp. 400–408).

Indeed, Durkheim suggested the changing character of the political state as society moves from repression under consensus to its more complex form. He speculated that the state might eventually become a vast and decentralized system of occupational associations, which together articulate certain diffuse standards that each of them specifies in its own terms. Consensus does not disappear with social complexity, he said, it just becomes weaker and more abstract (Durkheim, [1893] 1933, p. 283; Durkheim, preface to the 1902 edition).

Dialectical Conflict. The Hobbesian repressive state and Michels' corrupted power elite suggest what Marx, Pareto, and their successors have made explicit (partly in organizational form): that where there is any clear-cut division into organized power wielders and power yielders, a polarization of interests occurs (Marx and Engels, [1888] 1959; Pareto, [1916] 1965, pp. 130–139, Dahrendorf, 1958, 1959, pp. 179–240). Marx took the organizational view of the primacy of production enterprise. Pareto saw that the units of society could either be individuals or "communities" (a concept he left undefined). Under these conditions, it remains only for the yielders to recognize their common interests and to organize, in order for dialectical conflict to occur. Lenin's revolutionary strategy in such conflict was to make explicit use of the machinery of formal organizations (Selznick, 1952).

But the preceding discussion of the inverse effect of social complexity on centralization suggests that *repression will be greatest where organizations are fewest.* Further, where organizational complexity is low, therefore *where organized pluralism is low, the possibility of consensus among the yielders against their oppressors is greatest.* From this we shall later deduce an empirical hypothesis that the less centralized and more pluralistic a macrosocial unit is, the less likely is dialectical conflict to occur within it.

External Interdependencies and Internal Solidarity. The threads of Durkheim's discussion of the mass society can easily be pulled together in contemporary language. The broadening division of labor increased interdependence with external organizations, thereby reducing the internal cohesion of communal units. From a dialectical perspective, the greater the estrangement from higher levels, the more organized are the lower levels likely to become. For not altogether different reasons, both approaches suggest an inverse relationship between the external links of subunits and internal solidarity within them. This connection, carried to the external and internal relations of macrosocial units, will be discussed in greater detail later; because the literature on relations between systems and subsystems is extensive, continuing from Sumner and Simmel through Parsons and including investigators of small groups as well.

Organizational Theory. From Durkheim's theory of change from monistic to pluralistic society, one might infer, as Durkheim failed to do fully, that increased spontaneity accompanied by social heterogeneity, and consequently reduced consensus, meant that specific forms of social relationships based on clearly articulated rules and procedures, namely formal organizations, had the best chance of surviving. For diffuse relationships require more similarities of outlook than generally exist among modern persons, and informal understanding can no longer be relied on to coordinate actions. Formal organizations, then, fulfill needs to shape the networks of interaction within large, complex social systems.

Using data not unlike those drawn on by Durkheim, Weber ([1904] 1958, pp. 105–106, 122, 160–181) carried this argument further. His monograph on the rise of Western industrial bureaucracy suggested that a new kind of moral worldliness and emancipation from tradition, as well as the inner isolation of the individual, contributed to the segmental forms of association that characterized formally organized business enterprises. Thus, the very scarcity of pervasive social bonds may have made the existence of formal and specialized social groups both necessary and possible. (See Udy, 1962, for cross-national support of parts of this argument.)

Weber provided an essentially monistic view of the large-scale organization. Its pluralistic alternative awaited "human relations" approaches that considered areas of concord and discord between the formal and informal elements of all concretely organized groups, and other approaches that emphasized the multiplicity of interests, formal as well as informal, within them. (See, for example, Roethlisberger and Dickson, 1939; Selznick, 1949, 1952.) Eschewing concepts of motives, attitudes, and values, urban ecologists also tended to emphasize the monistic view of large-scale organizations over its pluralistic counterpart (Hawley, 1950, p. 179, 1973b; Duncan and Schnore, 1959). *Yet, as will be shown later, large-scale but diversified (that is, plural-like) organizations play key roles in restructuring rapidly changing environments.*

From the standpoint of the individual person, the segmentalization and formal standardization of human relationships arising from the multiplication of persons in interaction and the consequent diversification of activities and outlooks means that urban dwellers and members of other kinds of macrosocial units are dependent on a far greater number of organized groups than are rural dwellers, but less dependent on particular persons. And whatever dependence on others exists is confined to highly fractionalized aspects of the others' rounds of activity (Simmel, [1908] 1950, p. 415, Wirth, 1938, p. 71).[7] Thus formal organizations might also be means by which modern persons can immunize themselves against the certain personal claims and expectations of others, which may be unlike their own; but this debatable aside is not worthy of pursuit in the light of our main arguments.

The inability of persons to know, let alone interact with, all of those who belong to the macrosocial unit necessitates standardized and non-person-bound means of need satisfaction. In large cities, for example, one no longer learns of other checker players through word of mouth; rather, it is necessary to find a checker club, perhaps in the classified directory provided by the telephone company. In short, the modern urban dweller is unlikely to find out who shares his or her interests, dispositions, or needs, until the appropriate organization comes into being (Goldhamer, 1942). Even intimacy may be produced through, say, the activities of "singles" organizations and computer matching agencies.

Up to this point in our discussion, the proliferation of organizations in macrosocial units has been congruent with changes in the social environment—its forms as well as its contents—and with the needs of the individual as well.

Application of the Modified Classics. Guided by these broad and varied theories, this book seeks to apply, adapt, and modify general social science theory by using interorganizational properties of the macrosocial unit in analyses of urban structure and process and, in so doing, to assess the robustness of those properties in the face of more conventional ways of describing the urban scene. Perhaps convergences and interfaces among the classical perspectives can also be shown, even if not to everyone's satisfaction.

Macrosocial Research at the Interorganizational Level

If certain aspects of the constellation of organizations that constitute the macrosocial unit may be employed to account for other aspects of that constellation, the interorganizational level of inquiry is useful. If such prediction cannot be confirmed, apart from the confounding influences of demographic and other non-organizational variables (although these themselves may simply be proxies for organizational phenomena), the utility of this level must be questioned.

Organizational Variables. To conduct one such examination of utility, we seek to construct a formal macrosocial theory partly guiding and partly based on the interrelations among indicators of the following organizational properties and their consequents in American metropoli: namely, external linkage, organizational complexity, scale and diversification of the internally regulating and coordinating organizations, organizational representation of solidarity and diffuse consensus, externally provided resources, centralization of the macrosocial unit, availability of internal linkage, and the activation of interorganizational networks. (Each of these concepts will be defined in the chapters to follow.) In addition to explaining one another, these properties shall also be used to explain partly person-based events of dialectical conflict, decentralization of decision making, and the translation of "need" for interorganizational activation into demand.

Population Variables. Four main population (demographic) variables shall be employed throughout, for purposes of control. These variables have been widely used in urban research. Although human ecologists have tended to view formal demographic process as secondary to organizational process, they have nonetheless used population variables, and not without success. (See Park, 1925, 1936; Duncan and Schuore, 1959. Hawley [1973b] even goes so far as to say that population problems are essentially ones of adjusting the size and characteristics of populations to the personnel requirements of a social system.) The introduction of demographic variables into each analysis tests the robustness of our interorganizational hypotheses without necessarily placing the independent utility of these variables for research in question. Because they can be interpreted in several ways (so can geographic region, also to be introduced by way of control), their use assures very demanding tests of the hypotheses to be stated, by serving to control effects that could not be measured directly. Other population variables (dealing with ethnic minorities) have been adopted as surrogates for organizational ones, but are to be viewed quite cautiously.

Population size is a key variable that will receive major attention in Chapter Two. Here it suffices to say that number of inhabitants and organizational complexity are closely associated with one another, because populations provide for the staffing needs of formal organizations and, to somewhat lesser degree, constitute their clienteles. But here we also wish to guard against the possibility that population size *in and of itself* might account for the correlates of organizational complexity.

Population density is the second variable of interest. First taken by Durkheim as an indicator of the density of social interaction, it is also considered by Hawley to have been made possible in urban centers by the development of organization. He views density as productive of economies for organizations, at least in the cost of certain public services, and as supporting specialization by placing it within reach (Hawley, 1971, pp. 132–138). Density might also mean, however, a city whose space is taken up by organizations rather than by residents, or it might signify residential crowding. It can also distinguish between the older high-rise cities and the newer ones that are more spread out. For all of these reasons, consideration of this variable guards against spurious attribution of cause in testing association between other variables.

Annexation aside, migration, the third variable, accounts for the major part of urban population growth. Once local organizations have met their staffing needs, migration can be controlled by the actions of local governments (Hawley, 1950, pp. 374, 338–339; Form and Miller, 1960). Even when industry locates on the basis of a ready labor market, this market very likely has been generated by preexisting industry that encouraged migration (Thompson, 1965, p. 39). Contrary to out-migration, heavy rates of in-migration could conceivably overload organizational facilities and thereby precipitate social disorganization.[8] Further, migration rates could indicate changes in the organizational composition of the city or of its possibly residential character. This variable, like the others, constitutes a necessary control.

Socioeconomic status is the final, fourth, broad demographic control to be employed; its measurement by median education and by the poverty rate is explained in Chapter Two. This variable may signify not only the types of organizations in the city but also the quality of its residential facilities. Its alleged association with attitudes and values allows us to assess whether certain macrosocial outcomes are determined by organizations, as we claim, or by some form of status ethic. The question is moot, because the higher strata participate in more and in different organizations than do lower ones (as will later be documented).

All or most of these four variables (or factors to which they make major contributions) have recently been featured in several major comparative studies of urban units, for varying purposes and with varying results. This grants some additional confidence in the demographic rates that, together with other kinds of variables, have been chosen for control throughout the various analyses described in Chapters Two through Five.[9]

The 130 Large Cities Compared. Theory will be applied to urban and interurban problems throughout this book by means of systematic comparisons among all 130 incorporated United States metropoli—central cities that had more than 100,000 inhabitants in 1960 (defining *metropolis* as central city of a metropolitan area is taken from Theodorson and Theodorson, 1969, p. 254). I have chosen to begin the macrosocial task by comparing large United

States cities to one another, for the most is already known about these. It should prove possible for future research to test or specify the resulting propositions in larger units (such as metropolitan area or nation), in smaller ones (such as subsections of the city), under other sociocultural conditions, or in different political and economic settings, or even in macrostructures that are not defined by location or spatial proximity.

Domestic comparisons may now be drawn over so large a number of cities thanks to a "critical mass" of organizational censuses, directories, and data files, not to mention the powerful information-processing techniques that have become available. The 130 cities' fundamental characteristics were measured in the early 1960s, so that certain theoretically crucial events of the middle and late 1960s could less questionably be assumed to be effects rather than causes of these characteristics.

The decision to limit intensive discussion to just these cities is based on several concerns. First, these are the American cities about which the most is known by urban specialists[10] (especially by myself, for I have been assembling and analyzing the relevant data for more than eight years). This means that allegations about them are especially amenable to the close, critical examination that is particularly necessary where new approaches are first attempted. Second, the data were assembled with interorganizational analysis in mind, and therefore bear most directly on the theoretical issues considered and the specific urban problems to be investigated in their light. Finally, the several comparative analyses we will present can be interrelated through our theory, although many of them predated its formal and detailed statement. Using the same cities and drawing from a common pool of metropolitan characteristics also make it possible to point out interrelations among variables through data and allow critical evaluation by the reader, to whom the raw materials for doing so are available in the Appendix.[11]

Large-scale, multiorganizational urban settlements are important topics of inquiry simply—if for no other reasons—because of the increasing monopoly they have gained, and probably will continue to gain, over all social life, and because they have become the loci of some of the world's most crucial problems. Certain issues appear to defy solution more than others, and certain actions defy execution more than others, except on a local territorial basis. For example, government, politics, employment, certain business activities, and volunteer action—important aspects of community— still appear to have primarily territorial bases. So do matters concerning the concentration of population, the state of the natural environment, and human health and welfare in general. These considerations make it important to emphasize not only the business, municipal, political, and voluntary organizations in various aspects of urban life but also how these organizations may be considered in conjunction with the rich data available from, say, the health and welfare arenas for identifying the interorganizational foundations of urban communities.

The decision to select incorporated central cities, or metropoli, for discussion rather than other urban areal units such as standard metropolitan statistical areas (SMSA's), urbanized areas, or counties is based on theoretical as well as more pragmatic reasons.

It appears quite clear that the American metropolis is no longer, if it ever was, independent of its social environment (Park, 1925; Hawley, 1971, p. 9). It has increasingly become a place of intersection among various regional, national, and international forces. Nonetheless, cities vary in this respect; and, not only political activities and organizations, but also other organizational phenomena—both voluntary and nonvoluntary—are coterminous with political boundaries. So are subjective aspects of organizations such as the collective symbolism inherent in incorporating a city's name into that of an organization located within it or into the organization's communicative behavior (for discussions of the symbolism of cities, see Strauss, 1961). Moreover, such boundaries constitute a major means of establishing uniform lines of demarcation between the local and extralocal structures and processes whose interplay concerns us. (For a protypic discussion of such interplay, see Stein, 1960, pp. 94–114.) Finally, central cities within the stipulated size range are the ones most capable of containing elements of many of the institutionalized sectors of society. Indeed, the extent to which they do so is one of the constructs of our theory. And one of our chief concerns is to investigate the relationship between a city's external linkage and its internal structures and processes.

Most important, having a set of precisely defined units of analysis enables use of *degree of boundedness*—that is, the *extent* to which each city constitutes a system—as a variable for study. We do not confuse the empirical unit (here the central city) with system. Rather, we seek to measure how much of a system each one is. The word *system*, in its generic sense, implies interconnectedness of parts and covariation among properties, thus suggesting not only harmony, but also conflict. Revolution is as much a system attribute as is governance, because both involve analyzable processes within a macrosocial unit (which is both a generic term for Leviathan as well as for a unit of the political economy).

Subsequent interorganizational studies having different emphases might well make use of other regional units; but the central city is the most appropriate for the problems at hand. Both the need to eliminate complexity in an empirical arena not previously investigated and the need to rely on secondary data, many of which are most readily available for the aforementioned cities (for example, one of the analyses is of the Model Cities program; there is no "Model SMSA"), also contributed to the selection of these urban centers for discussion. What is lost by such selectivity is our ability to speak of entire metropolitan regions that form economic and social units of which the city is but a part. Such selectivity restricts what we can say about such processes as intra- and interregional divisions of labor, or suburbanization, or regional dominance, or spatial decentralization. Yet all science requires comparability through selectivity and abstraction, and our theory can still be implemented using central cities and the external networks to which their organizations belong.

Comparisons Among the 130 Cities. In this book, each application of the comparative method to our 130 metropoli will be little more than showing all of the city's characteristics—economic, political, cultural, or social; organizational or demographic—that have been found to account for some other characteristic of the city. Specific contemporary issues, some related to health and welfare,[12] will be used in developing knowledge about matters that concern the city as a whole and that activate its several organized sectors—its government agencies, organized protest groups, business enterprises, voluntary associations, hospitals, and so on. Generating knowledge in these concrete instances of how organizations appear, disappear, change, merge, compete, or form coalitions or networks of relations with one another is necessary, according to our theory, to account for how macrosocial units structure themselves or act in the light of environmental influences or internal issues.

Multiple regression analysis will constitute the basic comparative tool. Using it, we will seek to answer questions about the extent to which certain aspects of variation in the social organization of the metropolis or its change can be accounted for on the basis of several other characteristics of the metropolis—characteristics whose overall, mutually independent, and combined effects have been assessed.

A Methodological Note. It bears repeating that the main characteristics used in predicting the organizational and interorganizational characteristics of the United States metropoli are themselves organizational and interorganizational substitutes for demographic indicators of urban structure and process such as population size and density, migration, and socioeconomic status. This substitution enables assessment of utility of the interorganizational approach to large-scale social systems. However, more conventional demographic variables that have played prominent roles in research reports and other statements about cities are included for purposes of control. Although themselves often proxies for underlying organizational phenomena, the inclusion of such variables enables preliminary assessment of the robustness of organizational and interorganizational variables in the face of potentially confounding influences, and provision of controls that lessen chances of spuriously imputing direct effects of what are here the theoretically most interesting variables on one another. In order to err conservatively, the controls *and only the controls* are applied in "shotgun" fashion where alternative hypotheses cannot be stated, but are applied in a more systematic way where they can be. Organizational variables are only applied in terms of our rationale. This approach maximizes chances of disproving any favored hypothesis.

All variables used repeatedly are listed in Appendix Figure A. The reader might find it convenient to refer to that figure from time to time.

Although not necessary for the comprehension of the comparative analyses reported in this book, certain prior statistical adjustments must nonetheless be reported here—not to suggest that any one of them is without responsible precedent, but rather to permit the methodologically oriented reader to evaluate their combined use.

All continuous variables were transformed into 130-point ordinal scales, so that they could be used in computing product-moment correlation coefficients, r, without ad hoc adjustments for individual peculiarities of distribution.[13] These coefficients are estimated by biserial r (r_b), where one of the variables is a dichotomous approximation of a continuum—and all dichotomies except geographic region are, in this research—and by tetrachoric r (r_t), where both variables are represented by such dichotomization.[14] Matrices of these three kinds of estimates of Pearsonian product-moment coefficients representing all intercorrelations among the main variables appear in the Appendix.

All multiple regression analyses are computed from such matrices throughout, because our interest lies in the intrinsic relationships among theoretically meaningful properties, rather than in the practical predictive value of their frequently crude dichotomous indicators, which heavy reliance on secondary data and empirical uncertainties force us to employ. Descriptively, these adjustments enhance comparability among analyses, and parsimony of reporting without sacrifice of relevant information. (For statistical defenses of such a parametric strategy in multivariate analysis over its ordinal alternative, see Kim, 1975, and Allan, 1976.) Nor is there any problem in assessing significance of the three kinds of zero-order coefficients, despite their different sampling distributions. Yet each such analysis is accompanied (in parentheses) by more conventional, undermeasured "dummy variable" analyses, in order to satisfy the skeptic. The corresponding zero-order matrices are in the Appendix. For the greater part, conclusions remain unchanged.

Significance of higher-order coefficients is conservatively based on the conventional analyses—that is, as though each coefficient were based on continuous variables, while in fact dichotomous indicators had only the values of 0 or 1. This procedure tends to depress the "real" value of the coefficient relative to its standard error.[15] "Not significant" describes chance expectations greater than 10 percent. Critical zero-order magnitudes are in the appendix.

Both versions of the zero-order correlation matrices may be used to test the reader's own hypotheses. Although my preference to work exclusively with estimates of product-moment coefficients is obvious, the skeptic is invited to use the unadjusted matrices.

Unless specifically noted otherwise, independent variables are substituted for, rather than included with, other independent variables or sets of such variables with which their correlation is more than .60. Where multicolinearity exists, according to this conservative criterion, the multiple correlation coefficients produced by the alternative equations are compared.

The exception to this rule is when redundance or repetition among independent variables would produce *conservative* conclusions, as when a theoretically deduced effect remains even after introduction of a colinear control. If such an effect were to disappear and the new variable were other than a substitute measure of the same theoretical property, the possibility must be considered of spurious attribution of cause. Allowance should be made for such possibilities in any kind of nonexperimental research.

It bears repetition that the means chosen here is to introduce, singly, every conceivable "control variable"—fully thought out or not, in the quest for spuriousness. This means of seeing whether a favored argument can withstand even the most severe test is not to be viewed as using a "shotgun" to produce questionable theory but rather as a way to maximize chances of proving oneself wrong.

The combined effect of variables is summarized by the multiple correlation coefficient, R, in favor of its square, the proportion of variation explained (which the reader can readily calculate), because variance was not partitioned, and R appears more congruent with the r's and *betas* with which the effects of individual variables are described.[16]

Summing Up and Looking Ahead

It is my intention, in this book, to provide propositions about large-scale and complex social units, called *macrosocial units,* which exist in even larger-scale social environments. To do so, I seek to proceed *as though* the social actors that comprise both unit and environment were formal organizations rather than individual persons or any simple aggregates or subaggregates that persons may constitute. Clearly, organizations are composed of interdependent roles enacted by people or of people with common or complementary interests; but aggregates of persons are here viewed as labor pools, audiences, clienteles, consumers, depositors, electorates, investors, adherents, "latent interest groups," and similar necessary kinds of "raw materials" required by formal organizations for their genesis and survival. People affect the macrosocial unit and its environment by affecting its organizations; the person's way of thinking, feeling and acting are in turn affected by those same organizations—such ways are often the products of the organization.

The present formulation of macrosocial phenomena is an exaggeration and attempted integration of ones already suggested in sociology, political science, economics, and in such combinations of these fields as human ecology. Although the temptation to reify has proven irresistible in certain cases, as the reader will note, the true intent is only to see how far the multi- and interorganizational view of macrosocial units and of their social environments can carry us.

The general definitions of main concepts to be provided and their subsequent linking into theoretical propositions are couched in language that does not refer to spatial distance or territorial arrangements. Yet most of the empirical literature referred to, and my original data analyses (to be described) emphasize local concentrations of social actors and the extralocal influences between these actors and other social actors that constitute the environment. This means that the general formulations are partly inductive. Although the skeleton of formal propositions that introduces each chapter is a priori, unless otherwise stated, the full formal theory must in all honesty be stated at the chapter's end. Yet it may be frustrating for some to read without knowing to what end; such a reader is encouraged to begin each chapter by examining the causal diagram of each concluding summary.

But the process is also one of deduction, because the social scientists who studied localities and their relations with region and nation, as well as myself, were not unaware of classic as well as modern conceptualizations of social differentiation, centralization, internal-external relations, consensus, pluralism, and dialectical conflict. Indeed, these conceptualizations guided what I have deemed important to attempt to review or to investigate at the multi- and interorganizational level of analysis. Classic frames of reference have not always avoided vagueness and obscurity. Yet I have sought to state, wherever I could, how these frames of reference have affected my thinking, even where the effect was only one of sensitization to a conceptual issue rather than of a directive to hypothesize. It is as important to provide the full rationale that influences the doing of science as it is to be as systematic in such doing as personal wit and the state of the art permit.

Such a mosaic does not make for easy reading, and it may be skipped—as may be the general macrosocial propositions—in favor of the comparative analyses of what have been the 130 largest central cities of the United States. It is here that the empirical utility of our multi- and interorganizational perspective may be assessed. In several cases, we speak of utility with caution—because validity has not been established.

Chapter Two takes as one of its points of departure that competition and other kinds of interdependence among organizations—an idea foreshadowed in the general works of Adam Smith, Spencer, and Durkheim, and carried on more specifically by human ecologists, urban geographers, and location economists—affect the tendency of organizations to cluster with one another and to attract or to generate other organizations. This approach resulted in finding intercorrelations among several indicators that measured partly different aspects of externally oriented organizational complexity. Extending the same argument, but specifying it with Hobbes' solution to the problem of social order, amended by interorganizational theory, we assume that larger-scale regulating and coordinating bodies arise where the number of organizations is large and varied. However, beginning with the classic philosophical and political pluralism of James and Lasky, which started to recognize government as codominant with other organizations, and continuing with the interorganizational idea that organizations would merge if their interests did not in part conflict, we assume also that diversified and decentralized regulatory bodies arise where the number of organizations is large and varied. Together, these assumptions led to the confirmed hypothesis that the scale *and* (not "or") diversification of municipal government is associated with (but also clearly contributes to) the city's organizational complexity.

Proceeding with Hobbesian ideas, but continuing with the theories of ingroup-outgroup relations of Marx and Sumner, carried to the present with theories of mass society, we find externally oriented organizational complexity to be inversely associated with the extent to which organizations signify local solidarity and consensus—in the data employed, the degree to which local voluntary associations are uncontested and city-wide in their impact. Yet, from the economists' and human ecologists' emphases on extra-locally acquired resources and from the Marxian idea that intra-societal regulation is followed by consensus (whatever the reason and however temporary), we note, belatedly, that the externally enabled scale and diversification of municipal government has a positive effect on how uncontested and city-wide in their impact are the local voluntary associations. And from general sociological assertions since Comte, too numerous to mention, about the association between consensus and the duration of relationships (assertions that were not hypothesized), we find that the independent effect of the city's age is how uncontested and city-wide in their impact are its voluntary associations. Theories of cultural pluralism suggest why the effect of foreign minorities (which may be organized) on this organizational variable is inverse.

The idea, which goes back to Durkheim and Weber at least, that cities are differentiated from one another in terms of their main types of organizations, together with the human ecologists' observation that organizations in cities exchange coordination of the hinterlands for sustenance, provides a special case of more general economic and sociological theory of exchange. Such theory accounts for the finding that externally oriented organizational complexity is associated with the flow of certain resources (here federal funds) to the city. Not surprising, but not fully predicted, is the added specification that internal relationships among organizations can be a prerequisite for the flow of external resources.

Chapter Three states a major premise on which this book is based. At the level of individual persons, it can be traced to Simmel's idea of the web of group affiliations, and more recently, to pluralistic models of urban power structure. At our level, interorganizational theory has stated it as follows: Organizations, more so than other social actors, exist in partial states of competition, conflict, and cooperation with one another. From this premise, it follows that organizations will also exceed other actors in the extent to which they resist their stratification and their domination by any one or a few of their number. Thus, centralized (that is, monistic or elitist) macrosocial units are likely either to be weak or to exist in organizationally barren environments, in which it is possible for what few organizations there are to be treated as "haves" and "have-nots," and for whatever dissent there is not to be organizationally represented. Consonant with this monistic or elitist framework are the findings that "reform" government varies positively with the extent of prestige-based support to the city's hospitals and with the degree to which local voluntary associations are uncontested and city-wide in their impact (that is, codify the degree to which organized pluralism is lacking), and varies inversely with externally oriented organizational complexity, as well as with an organizational measure of ethnic heterogeneity. The correlation between "reform" government and the community's socio-economic status (measured by the median education of its inhabitants), not anticipated directly by our interorganizational theory, might be interpreted as the effect of the city's residential, rather than productive character—therefore, of its lack of organizational complexity.

Chapter Three continues along lines foreshadowed by the classical conflict theory of Marx but divested of its economic primacy, that is, the existence of an organized elite over an undifferentiated nonelite (whatever the overall quality of the latter's life chances) is a precursor of polarization (dialectical conflict). To this proposition is added a modern derivation of pluralist theory, that the more cross-cutting lines of conflict and cooperation there are, the less likely is such polarization to occur. Fluoridation controversies did indeed prove to be more likely in the centralized, organizationally barren and *manifestly* consensual "reform" government cities than in others, and did indeed vary inversely with the organizational complexity of the city's export economy as well as with the scale and diversification of municipal government, which also constitutes an alternative, negative measure of centralization. These results appeared confounded by diffusion of this conflict model from one city to the next, obtaining most strongly among the cities where the question of fluoridation first arose.

Finally, in Chapter Three we note that the macrosocial unit's organizational structure (here using only the *de*centralization measures of "nonreform government" and municipal scale and diversification) is capable of predicting a person-based measure of decentralization in actual decisions that had been made, and also capable (as described in this and subsequent chapters) of explaining that measure's effects on various kinds of new interorganizational arrangements or the activation of old ones. Thus, organizational centralization-decentralization predicts day-to-day process in the macrosocial units studied.

Chapters Four and Five address the question of how one can predict such outcomes. The answer does not only depend on the organizational characteristics that affect capacity for the altered interorganizational arrangements. It also depends on extending the pluralist model of coalitions provided by political scientists to show that these same characteristics affect the process by which the arrangements are decided on. Clearly, in pluralist thought, decisions are specific to issues and are made by coalition rather than by fiat; but how does one predict coalitions—let alone the decisions that are reached—among the welter of cross-cutting interests in the multiorganizational city? A return to Durkheim's pluralism is instructive. He showed that with increasing social differentiation the nature of consensus changes from monistic concreteness to abstractness, but that consensus does not fully disappear. From this, and from organizational theory, it can be deduced that common, abstract standards and interests accompany the joint search for predictability by organizations in an organizationally complex environment. That these consensual states are external (here, national) in their origins follows from the inseparability between organizational complexity and external linkage. Provided that internal (here, local) organizational means exist for articulating such abstractions—through organizations that are visible, uncontested, and diffuse in the interests and standards they pursue (measured here by the extent to which local voluntary associations are city-wide and uncontested)—they will not only affect the capacity for interorganizational relations but also will form the basis of "winning" coalitions that determine what these relations will be. But the actual forging of such coalitions and of the interorganizational arrangements that they advocate is not only a *consensual,* but also a *political* process of bargain, threat, promise, or coercion. Here the organizations that are large and diversified and can resolve their inner conflicts are important. In the United States, great municipal scale and diversification measures this second attribute.

Following this argument, Chapter Four shows—with modest success—that one or both of these organizational indicators of the capacity for internal linkage and/or ones of external linkage can predict over time the activation of new interorganizational relations or the reactivation of old ones in the War on Poverty, the Model Cities program, health planning, cooperation among hospitals, and community chest campaigns.

In most cases, organizational variables are shown to operate independently of population characteristics or other rates and acts among individuals in predicting macrosocial outcome in terms of such interorganizational activation. This, too, adds confidence in the utility of our interorganizational level of macrostudy. So does the aforementioned finding that decentralization of actual decision making, defined in terms of number and variety of persons involved, fails to have any direct effect on these five outcomes, once the organizational variables are taken into account. Also notable is the much more pervasive influence on variability in outcome of the capacity for interorganizational relations, compared to the need for them.

Chapter Five further explores the latter finding, arguing that the internal decision process is the pluralist and decentralized one of producing a "winning" coalition, and that in modern society such coalitions not only depend on the availability of internal linkage, but also form around standards of the broader setting (here, the nation) within which the macrosocial unit (here, the city) is contained. Thus, the more internal linkage there is, the more likely will be the demand for interorganizational activation as well as for the manner and level of meeting demand to be defined in terms of the standards of the broader setting. From this it is hypothesized and predominantly confirmed that the extent to which each of the five forms of interorganizational activation discussed in Chapter Four is a *correlate* of preexisting "need" (defined by national standards) is a function of the amount of internal linkage available. The same generic organizational correlates of the capacity for linkage apply here as before: organizational scale and diversification, given means of conflict resolution; or diffuseness of goals, given visibility, noncontroversiality, and broad impact on the unit. Thus, again in the United States, the larger the scale of local government and the more diversified it is, *or* the more uncontested and city-wide the local associations are, the closer was the correlation hypothesized and found to exist between poverty and the complexity of antipoverty networks; between poverty and Model City status; between local welfare burdens and Model City status; between the death rate and health planning; between municipal health costs and health planning; and between number of hospitals and cooperation among them.

Chapter Six summarizes our interorganizational agenda for macrosociology as well as the findings among the 130 largest United States cities that support its utility and place in question certain popular assumptions; indicates the manner of its application within other sociocultural and other political settings and at other levels of macrosocial scale; hints at its policy relevance, and suggests the broader implications of our theory for macrosocial units that are not necessarily territorially or otherwise spatially determined. Isomorphisms between our macrosocial findings and the more general social theory that prompted them encourages the supplementary search for *non*macrosocial applications.

Notes

1. These inferences were drawn—and in some cases virtually echoed—from such varied materials as those reported by Rostow (1953), Mills (1956), Galbraith (1958), Babchuk, Marsey, and Gordon (1960), Freeman, Fararo, Bloomberg, and Sunshine (1962), Hawley (1963), Stinchcombe (1965), Freeman (1968), and Perrucci and Pilisuk (1970).

2. This phenomenon has been accounted for in several complementary ways. For example, see Parsons (1956), Eisenstadt (1965), Stinchcombe (1965), Turk, Smith, and Myers (1966).

3. See, for example, Bidwell (1961), Ladinsky (1963), Miller (1967), Engel (1969). The term *occupation* is a loose equivalent for *activity*, it is claimed by modern human ecologists; activities are seen as the atoms that are arranged in *overlapping* and *interpenetrating* activity constellations or *groups* (Duncan and Schnore, 1959, italics mine). Relatedly, the effective unit of the community is some combination of individuals (based upon corporate interdependence or, as in occupational associations, common interest) rather than the individual himself; such units can form relations with one another (Hawley, 1950, pp. 206–222, 1971, p. 130).

4. For discussions of representation and the relevant literature, see Turk and Lefcowitz (1962) and Pitkin (1967). Familiar to political scientists and—in somewhat more limited degree—to nonecological sociologists, the concept would seem to be crucial to human ecologists in discussing functional relations among groups. The latter employ the term *functionary* (Duncan and Schnore, 1959; Hawley, 1963), frequently without formal definition. Hawley measured the concentration of power in the city as one minus the number of managerial functions relative to all functions in the labor force (1963, 1971, pp. 210–211). For some human ecologists, *role* is defined as a pattern of observable activity devoid of "subjective" role expectations by self or by organized others (Duncan and Schnore, 1959). For others of their colleagues, rules, rituals, and symbolism are admissable concepts (for example, Hawley, 1950, p. 218) as are prescribed roles and responsibilities (Hawley, 1971, p. 201). It is quite likely that increased concern with the concept of *functionary* will bring the issue of culture and other forms of intersubjectivity to the fore as human ecologists encounter exceptions to their classic paradigm.

5. Other general treatments of urban communities have assigned a prominent place to formal associations, functional units, or corporate and categoric units—as organizations have variously been called. See, for example, Hawley (1950, 1963, 1971), Form and Miller (1960), Duncan (1961), Banfield (1961), Warren (1963). But now it is possible to develop the field exclusively from the vantage point of organizations and to make full use of comparative investigations in the service of that end. The interorganizational level of community analysis has already begun to be explicated in the comparative study of cities. See Turk (1969, 1970, 1973a, 1973b), the conclusion of Aiken and Alford (1970), and Warren, Rose, and Bergunder (1974). Throughout the book, it will be apparent that such analyses follow from what has gone on before in all of the social sciences.

6. Also note that Almond (1960) suggested that, for reasons such as these, contemporary Communism and other authoritarian systems might also develop plural interest groups.

7. From my backgrounds in social action theory and formal organizations, I have independently reached conclusions similar to those of

Hawley, a human ecologist (1971, p. 203). This speaks well for convergences among different perspectives.

8. Alford and Scoble (1965) have taken in-migration to signify population instability that affects governmental structure. Our data suggest this to be an artifact of organizational complexity, as Chapter Three will show.

9. Population size and socioeconomic status were the first two factors that emerged out of Berry's (1972, pp. 11–57) analysis of 97 variables that described the 1762 American urban places with 10,000 or more inhabitants in 1950 and 1960. The third, having to do with age of population, appeared meaningless for present purposes. The fourth was most highly loaded with proportion of nonwhites, which appears throughout our analyses, as does proportion of foreign stock, which contributes heavily to the seventh factor. Migration contributed modestly to a weak fifth factor having to do with population growth. Only two of the remaining factors were relevant: an organizational one having to do with manufacturing for which our own measure (described in detail in the next chapter) was not used; another (factor 8), having to do with growth in employment, for which we have no measure. Hadden and Borgatta's (1965) analysis of cities with 25,000 or more inhabitants yielded similar factors, but included one that is highly correlated with population density. Bonjean, Browning, and Carter's (1969) analysis of the 3,101 contiguous counties in the United States produced similar factors that were represented by our own measures in each case, save for age of population and (possibly) the organizational one of wholesale and retail trade. All of the discrete independent variables selected (out of many) by Clark (1971) for the study of voluntary association activity, decentralized decision making (see our Chapter Three), and policy outputs—or ones much like them—are routinely employed throughout this book. In addition, we make far more systematic use of region here than did any of the researchers just cited.

10. The other comparative urban research known by the author to touch this book's topic is at least mentioned in the text that follows or is cited in the sources mentioned.

11. See Appendix, as well as the author's larger Urban Data File available as "Data on 150 Incorporated Cities with Population Greater than 100,000 in 1960," Herman Turk, Principal Investigator, through the Inter-University Consortium for Political and Social Research, Ann Arbor, MI 48106.

12. Studies of community organization and social action in the health and welfare arenas are not only useful in their own right but also are strategic to more general formulations about the community and its interorganizational relations. First, because health and welfare outputs flow to individuals and not to organizations, accounting for these flows

in terms of relations among organizations places exacting demands on the interorganizational approach. Second, although generally matters of concern at the level of community, the nature of the needs for local delivery systems of health and welfare services and their characteristics are considered nationally. The societal organizations that define need in these respects also provide relevant models for interorganizational relations. This means that cities tend to be like one another in the types of interorganizational relations they endeavor to establish in the fields of health and welfare, but differ from one another in their relative capacities or needs to do so. According to the theory to be developed in this book, what holds true for health should also hold true for welfare; and this may account for an observation sometimes made (for example, by Hunter, Schaffer, and Sheps, 1956, pp. 226–240 and by Robert Wilson, 1968, pp. 83–98), namely, that the manner in which a community goes about solving its health problems, for example, follows its pattern of problem solving in other areas. The health and welfare structures and processes to be described were most likely to be subject both to national definition and the particular city's capacity for interorganizational relations. With a few, relatively untroublesome exceptions, the material resources required were either trivial or provided externally; therefore, the effect of capacity could be assessed relatively independently of the viability of each city's economy.

13. That rectangularly distributed variables such as these rank orderings provide best estimates of underlying properties whose distributions are open to question is strongly suggested by findings reported by Labovitz (1970). Moreover, the use of ranks means that perfect control may be obtained over the mathematically induced relationship between population size and per capita rates. The use of ordinal data in multivariate analyses is discussed by Kim (1975).

14. Carter (1971) suggests expressing multiple correlation coefficients as proportions of their maxima, but this procedure leaves understated the association (r or *beta*) between independent and dependent variables. And R/R *max* yields magnitudes difficult to relate to those of *beta* or r. An excellent review of the main arguments for using polychoric series to estimate r in contingency tables and some supporting data are provided by Lancaster and Hambdan (1964). Also see Kim (1975).

15. These observations may be deduced from formulas provided by Guilford (1950, pp. 331–343, 434–436) and Blalock (1960, pp. 302–305, 346–358) and from the fact that even unskewed dichotomies can prevent product-moment calculations from yielding maximum absolute value of 1.00. For our 130 cases, the maximum is only .85 where one of the variables is such a dichotomy and the other is continuous.

16. Note that in multiple regression analysis the variables follow the same rank order according to the standardized partial regression

coefficient (*beta*) that they do according to variance uniquely explained. Clearly, reliance on biserial and tetrachoric estimates of *r* as "inputs" to multiple regression analysis makes the use of standardized rather than unstandardized partial regression coefficients unavoidable. Anyhow, lack of direct correspondence between indicator and underlying continuum would have caused the latter to mislead. Also, comparisons across statistical subpopulations of cities will mainly be made for purposes of control.

Chapter Two

●●●●●●●●●●●●●●●●●●●●●
●●●●●●●●●●●●●●●●●●●●●
●●●●●●●●●●●●●●●●●●●●●●

EXTERNAL
COMPLEXITY AND
MACROSOCIAL UNITS

●●●●●●●●●●●●●●●●●●●●●
●●●●●●●●●●●●●●●●●●●●●
●●●●●●●●●●●●●●●●●●●●●

*M*acrosocial analysis, as we have suggested, has been profoundly affected by the works of Emile Durkheim, especially by his classic treatise on the division of labor. Combining Spencer's emphasis on interdependence, as it did, with that by Comte on moral integration and hinting at philosophic pluralism, Durkheim's treatment of social order and change directly influenced contemporary human ecology, human geography, and local economics; at least foreshadowed the monistic-pluralistic issues in the social sciences of the 1900s; and anticipated the roles of large-scale organizations in linking the individual to mass society. Some of these aspects of his influences are exhibited in this chapter's solidification of the theoretical models and methodologies briefly sketched in Chapter One.

We begin with nominal definitions of *macrosocial unit* and of some of its properties. Using large cities for operational definitions, this chapter continues with a discussion of the near inseparability of *external (organizational) linkage* from *(internal) organizational complexity* and how the various aspects of such complexity affect one another. Empirical demonstration follows. Having drawn on theories of social differentiation in general, and human ecology in particular for this demonstration, we now add political monism and pluralism as well as organizational approaches to sources of power. The several effects of organizational complexity on the scale and diversification of *internal regulation and coordination* by organizations are specified in the case of municipal (governmental) scale and diversification in the metropolis. Continuing in the same order from broad theory (adding sociocultural perspectives) to the urban case, the effects of these several properties are examined on the organizational representation of macrosocial *solidarity and diffuse consensus,* measured by the extent to which local voluntary associations are uncontested and city-wide in their impacts. We conclude this chapter with the effects of internal and external organizational linkage on *externally provided resources* for the macrosocial unit. These last two problems permit specification within metropoli of some classic issues between the solidarity-inhibiting versus resource-providing effects of relationships between social units and their social environments. Formal definitions, propositions, and hypotheses will be stated as these four main problem areas are encountered.

Organizational Complexity and External Linkage

By the term *macrosocial unit* is meant *patterns of interdependence among any large and diversified set of social actors* (here, organizations). In this book, the American metropolis is taken as the empirical referent for macrosocial unit. (Note that competition and conflict constitute interdependencies no less than do cooperation, coalition, and unity. The word *interdependence* just means *affecting one another.*) The word *link* means *any connection of communication, exchange, cooperation, agreement, or solidarity between one organization or network of organizations and another.* The word *internal linkage* means *the number and variety of links within the macrosocial unit.* The word *external linkage* means *the number and variety of links between the macrosocial unit or its parts on the one hand, and its social environment, on the other.*

Implied by our definition of macrosocial unit, *organizational complexity* means *the number and variety of relatively large organizations that comprise the macrosocial unit.*

For the theoretical and empirical reasons that follow Durkheim (in the work of human ecologists, human geographers, planners, and location economists), the following empirical assumption may be made: *The external linkage of any macrosocial unit defines that unit's organizational complexity.* Implied by our nominal definitions, this assumption is a logical outgrowth of longstanding views of the metropolis.

Already in 1925, Robert E. Park suggested describing the "community" by the number and variety of organizations within it and by the dependence of these organizations on the "larger community" that always exists. It remained only to make explicit the covariation between those two variables.

Seen to varying degree by urban historians and sociologists, human ecologists, and scholars in related fields, the larger and more complex the social unit, the more important it is to define organizations as its smallest consequential subunits. (See Park, 1925, 1936; Mumford, 1938, Hawley, 1950, pp. 207–211, 1971, pp. 217, 236, 240; Philbrick, 1957; and Duncan and Schnore, 1959. Also see the perpetuation of Park's theme by Chicago sociologists Burgess, 1925; Wirth, 1938; Blumer, 1948; and Hauser, 1965.) Not only do organizations compete with one another to constitute locally interdependent urban networks (see also Quinn, 1950, pp. 154–182, 471–488; Schnore, 1965, p. 22), but also—following Durkheim ([1893] 1933)—they compete to become units of participation in regional and national interdependencies within a larger division of labor. This last point is illustrated by the ubiquity of large-scale national corporations, federal agencies, national voluntary associations, and other kinds of parish, chapter, or branch types of organizations (suggested in parts by Park, 1925; McKenzie, 1933, pp. 313–314; Hawley, 1950, pp. 225–228, 1971, pp. 236, 240; Gist and Fava, 1964, pp. 247–248; Schnore, 1965, pp. 10–11; and H. Turk, 1970).

Here we view the nation as organizations and organizational processes, some of which congregate in certain places called *cities*. This is not to say that the locational decisions of organizations are unrelated to one another, or that cities containing organizations that coordinate region or nation in certain respects do not also contain other organizations that coordinate in other respects; indeed, much of what follows indicates the contrary. It is only that the inquiries we propose at this point make it unnecessary to face such questions as whether different organizations within the city coordinate organizations in quite different cities or whether a given region is coordinated by organizations located in different cities (Pappenfort, 1959, has shown the latter to occur).

The ingenious methods required to classify relatively small numbers of metropolitan places according to their establishments' memberships in urban hierarchies or in regional and interregional divisions of labor[1] attests to how complex a task we avoid, but also— more importantly, for present purposes—to the pertinence of the interorganizational view of urban nations. Entire cities may or may not be linked to one another as, for example, Galle (1963) and historian Lampard (1965) theorize they are, but at least some of their respective organizations are. Thus, the question of urban hierarchies and intra- or interregional differentiation will be avoided here by viewing metropoli as a set of nodal points that outline a national society in which large-scale organizations are the basic units. Nevertheless, any *failure* of national organizations to cluster only in certain cities might be considered the main distinguishing characteristic of traditional, agrarian, or rapidly developing societies (suggested in varying degrees by Durkheim, [1893] 1933, chaps. 3–8; Eisenstadt, 1957, 1968; Huntington, 1966).

The outlines of the national society may be identified not only by the natures, varieties, and numbers of nationally dispersed organizational components located within each city's boundaries, but also by relations between locally oriented organizations of one city and those of the next. Municipal governments compete with one another, for example, in attracting nationally controlled industrial organizations (Netzer, 1968, pp. 435–474), thereby affecting the national economy.

But exactly why should certain organizations concentrate near certain other organizations and be connected with yet other organizations elsewhere? Clearly, because with specialization—

and organizations do specialize—goes interdependence. Sociologists, economists, and geographers agree that industrial plants and other establishments locate themselves near natural resources, labor pools, transportation routes, markets, and the like. Having done so, they require, establish, or attract more industrial or other kinds of organizations, including banks, schools, government agencies, and recreational facilities. This no doubt partly competitive process leads to regional and interregional specialization (see such works of location scholars from various disciplines as Isard, 1956; Philbrick, 1957; Quinn, 1950, pp. 164–182; Duncan and others, 1960; and Thompson, 1965. Also see general sociologists Form and Miller, 1960, pp. 19–30). It also follows that, in order to "colonize," organizations require more than simply markets and the mere factors of production. They also require preexisting organizations: transit lines, public utilities, police departments, office supply houses, and so on. Otherwise the original organizational "colonists" would *not* have had to go to *exactly* the same places. Interdependence among organizations is the first main theme of this entire chapter. The second one is that no macrosocial unit can be understood except in the context of the larger unit or units of which it is a part.

Organizational Complexity as Organizational Coexistence

In sum, organizations locate themselves or are established near one another for various reasons. Their respective markets; natural resources; labor, member, or client pools; and transportation links may exist in the same territory. Or they may simply *require* proximity, even if only to keep a watchful eye on one another. Moreover, such interdependence may be direct, as when factories depend on municipal departments of water and power; or it may be indirect, as when attracting clients or employees depends on the availability of nearby organizations for housing development or of certain educational, recreational, or health establishments (Thompson, 1965). Furthermore, even competing organizations often find advantage in clustering as a "specialty center" (Philbrick, 1957; see also our discussion of health centers in Chapter Four, this book).

But whatever the reason for their proximity, neighboring organizations—public as well as private, voluntary as well as non-voluntary—frequently also have to take one another into account in such matters as local labor markets, land use, the cost of local business services, government regulations or municipal service delivery, and local goodwill. Other organizations ensue. Classic definitions of the community as locality-relevant relationships are congruent with the human ecological idea of community as organizational interdependencies. The general implication that stems from these observations is that geographic concentrations of organizations with external linkage may be expected to exceed chance and, consequently, various aspects of the quality and degree of organizational complexity covary and may be quantified.[2]

The Measurement of External Linkage and Organizational Complexity

Organizational complexity may be measured, first of all, by the presence of and transactions among organizations oriented to a national economy. Next, such external orientation should betoken the presence of various kinds of national headquarters, including those of voluntary associations considered in this study. Then, with less certainty, we seek contributions made by industry and by ethnic groups to such complexity. Finally, our measures are evaluated in terms of the more traditional, less conceptually rooted ones of population size and age of city.

Economic Complexity. The 130 United States cities with over 100,000 inhabitants in 1960 were ranked, in turn, according to the number of establishments in 1963 within each of the following twelve business categories that might have at least some *export emphasis*—that is, that might serve nonresident persons and non-local organizations: manufacturing; lumber; building supplies and hardware; automotive dealers; apparel and accessory stores; eating and drinking places; wholesale merchants; wholesale trades; hotels, motels, and tourist camps; motion picture theatres; other amusement and recreational establishments; and hospitals. The degree of similarity among each city's twelve rankings (formula in Gibbs and Martin, 1962) constituted its index of diversification among export organizations. The fact that the correlation between the diversification index and the arithmetic mean of all ranks for each city was at least moderate and highly significant ($r = .44$) implies that the more organizationally diversified a city, the larger the absolute number of export establishments, whatever their type. Note that, at least partly extralocal in their outputs, the kinds of establishments named could also often be extralocally controlled. Also note that these tend to be reasonably large-scale establishments, potentially capable of having measurable impacts on the city—either individually or in sets.

Although the export economy may be expected to vary from city to city, depending on the city's location and whatever else it has to offer, the maintenance economy—composed of establishments (mainly smaller ones) whose primary outputs serve resident persons and local organizations—depends more on the city's spatial layout and the characteristics of its population.[3] Thus, any valid indicator of export diversification may be expected to be, and in the present case was found to be, only weakly correlated ($r = .19, p < .05$) with a similarly constructed 1963 index of diversification among the following maintenance establishments: general merchandise establishments, food stores, gasoline service stations, drug stores, personal services, auto repairs and services, and garages.

The level of *banking activity* within a city not only reflects how favorable its location is for the export by organizations of *financial* services to region or nation, but also the number and sizes of transactions involving other locally based organizations.[4] For both of these reasons, substantial correlation was expected and was found among the 130 cities ($r = .52, p < .001$) between the 1959 per capita dollar volume of bank deposits and diversification among export organizations. Banking was virtually uncorrelated ($r = .09, p > .10$) with diversification among maintenance establishments, indicating either a small or—as previously noted—a uniform effect of the latter on the economies of large cities. Nor did the city's relevant *population* characteristics of wealth and poverty have any significant effect on banking ($r = .08$ and $.05$, respectively, with proportions of families with 1959 incomes of $10,000 or more and with proportions having incomes under $3,000).

Thus the banking index constituted a second indicator of organizational concentration. It was added to the indicator of diversification among export establishments to yield a reliable overall *organizational indicator of economic complexity* (the correlation of each component with the sum is $r = .87$), for three reasons. First, the two organizational indicators show remarkably similar correlations with the other thirty variables discussed in the book (the two sets of correlations differed by only .01 in their means, but were correlated with one another at $r = .96$), and therefore appear to reflect a common underlying dimension. Second, each might be more sensitive to a different portion of that common dimension (for example, Hoover and Vernon [1962, pp. 84–109] suggest that corporate headquarters and financial establishments have an affinity for one another). Third, the combined indicator yielded a satisfactory and highly significant correlation ($r_b = .49$) with a 1950 measure of whether or not the city was located within an economically diversified or financial region (measure adapted from Nelson, 1955, by Clark, 1968b).

National Headquarters of Voluntary Associations. Inquiries into "metropolitan dominance" suggest that the preceding indicators of external linkage are associated with other ones (see Hawley, 1971, pp. 219–240). The organizations discussed so far export goods and services from the city. But other organizations export national and regional integration (Kornhauser, 1959; Shils, 1962)—much as organizations located in county, state, and national capitals export power and as incorporated residential units might assist in the export of labor.

Of particular importance among such national integrative organizations—indeed, also among local integrative organizations, as we shall see subsequently—are voluntary associations that act as diffuse communication belts between different sectors of the society and with the governmental agencies that are removed from them. These crystallize, promote consensus among, express, and enforce the wishes of their members through processes such as publicity and lobbying (Goldhamer, 1942).

According to our general model, national headquarters of voluntary associations, like other organizations, may be expected to locate themselves either where they are needed or near the organizations to which they require access. But there are several advantages to focusing on this particular kind of organization. First, each association cuts across the specific enterprises or other acting organizations that comprise the class that it represents. Therefore, emphasizing voluntary groups is a useful way of avoiding idiosyncracies or accidents that affect the appearance and nature of more discrete organizational units. In short, each national association has within it the diffuse content of what is *common* to the more specific organized units that it links to one another or represents.

Second, to identify the nature and the number of headquarters of national associational units within a city appears to be the best way not only of approximating the nature and number of that city's activities on the national scene, but also, as shall be shown, of *approximating the number and variety of other organizations* within the city that determine its organizational complexity. Third, unlike those of other organizations, the locational decisions of voluntary associations are, in the main, free of such extraneous factors as land values, specific natural resources, the physical plant, or specialized labor; and for this additional reason they can more faithfully reflect the already-mentioned organizational composition of each city.

Finally, although industry might be moving out of the metropolis, headquarters and related organizations of all types might well be continuing to move in, because of their dependence on rapid exchange of information.[5]

Evidence already exists that, completely apart from the extent to which it affects the other organizations within a city, the very presence of the national headquarters of a given voluntary association signifies something about the types of other organizations in that city whose presence cannot always be measured directly. An important but infrequently cited empirical study (Lieberson and Allen, 1963) showed strongly that these national headquarters of associations locate themselves on the basis of which other organizations, possibly which other kinds of headquarters, exist within the city. Thus a disproportionately large number of headquarters of associations that lobby in dealing with the federal government were found to be located in Washington, D.C., while New York, the main locus of stock exchanges, led other cities by far in the number of headquarters of business associations. Taking sixteen of the very largest metropolitan areas, the authors of the study found, with very few exceptions, that the business and trade associations of any one of a number of *industries* tended to locate their headquarters in places where the percentage of all of the cities' employees in that industry was disproportionately high. Thus, for example, although Detroit had about 7 percent of the employed population of the cities studied, it was found to have nearly 25 percent of the labor force for those industries that had association headquarters within the city. We might suggest that labor force data are only crude indicators of organizational data in these instances; because, by and large, labor takes place within organizations. Another finding was that headquarters of the associations *in any particular ethnic category* tended to distribute themselves among the same sixteen areas in much the same way as that in which particular ethnic population was distributed among them. Here one is more hesitant than in the case of employment to assume that association headquarters indicated the presence of local organization; but the possibility cannot be ruled out, because sheer numbers of persons allow ethnic businesses, schools, newspapers, or churches to be feasible undertakings and perhaps to serve as magnets for the attraction of national headquarters.

If the voluntary associations do indeed locate their headquarters near organizations that they represent or with which they must interact, then the *sheer number* of national headquarters within any given city should *indicate not only that city's external linkage but also its organizational complexity*—economic as well as noneconomic— even though its own direct contribution to such complexity is very likely minimal. Using twenty-one categories, which range from business and health associations through religious and patriotic, the *Encyclopedia of Associations* (1961) listed the number of such headquarters in each of our 130 study cities. The underlying dimensions of external linkage and overall organizational complexity that the number is claimed to indicate constitutes the real interest of our study and, unlike its indicator, is applicable to divers societies. Our present claim, however, requires further verification.

Association Headquarters and Economic Complexity. Our indicator of economic complexity, it will be recalled, consists of diversification among organizations that have export emphasis, combined with the level of banking activity. One would expect the number of national headquarters of voluntary associations to vary with this first, partly external indicator of complexity, because the latter signifies, roughly, not only the number and size of organizations *within a given category* that are likely to affect the *presence or absence* of association headquarters in that category, but also the *number of categories* at each level of number and size that will affect the number of association headquarters.

This expectation was confirmed among the 130 cities. Crude though it is, the indicator of economic complexity varied with the number of national headquarters of voluntary associations at the substantial and highly significant level of $r = .60$. Such covariation suggests that external linkage and the organizational complexity that it produces tend to be single dimensions to this point, and—because they also include voluntary associations with noneconomic goals—that these dimensions are not strictly economic.

Industrialization. Industrialization has not only been used as an indicator of structural differentiation within cities (Aiken, 1970) and therefore a potential alternative indicator of organizational complexity; it has also been viewed as a revolutionary influence on the whole of collective life; its introduction, therefore, permits the control of a variety of influences that might otherwise have led us to false conclusions, but that cannot directly be assessed. The per capita value added by manufacturing in the city in 1958 is our indicator of industrialization.[6] It measures the total output of each city's manufacturing firms, standardized for the city's size.

Industrialization proved to be significantly associated, but only slightly, with our original banking and export indicator of economic complexity ($r = .22$), and even less with the number of national headquarters of voluntary associations ($r = .17$). However, it must be noted that the industrialized cities tend to be concentrated in the northeastern and east north central states, while urban concentrations of other kinds of economic organizations and of national headquarters of voluntary associations are more widely dispersed.[7]

Taking these regional differences into account shows that the overall correlations with industrialization are misleading. In the northeastern and east north central cities, industrialization tends to vary *inversely* with our indicator of economic complexity ($r = - .26$, $p. < .01$) and with the number of association headquarters ($r = - .14$,

$p < .10$), while such correlation is substantially more positive ($r = .42$ and .30, respectively) in the southern and western cities.

These regional differences may be confirmed by reorganizing the results of a study of the fifty-six largest standard metropolitan areas (SMA's) that included fifty-five of the present study cities but used data from 1950 rather than mainly from 1960 (Duncan and others, 1960, p. 217). Fifteen of the twenty-four northeastern and east north central areas classified as manufacturing fell into that category alone, while all five areas so classified in other regions were also identified as having at least some metropolitan significance.

Moreover, the low correlations between industrialization and the other measures of external linkage are in accord with the aforementioned literature that suggests that while producing activities were moving away from the metropolis, administrative and related activities might well be moving toward it. They also confirm our argument that externally linked organizations that do not settle on the basis of land, labor, or natural resources are more sensitive indicators, than are those that do, of both external linkage and organizational complexity. (Hawley, 1971, p. 229, has also observed that industrial concentration is not the best indicator of metropolitan ascendancy.)

It is also possible that although heavy manufacturing may be leaving the older metropoli of the highly industrialized regions, or may never have been established in large central cities elsewhere, whatever manufacturing activity the latter may have is due to the small production organizations that are even seen as constituting metropoli such as New York City. These, like financial and commercial organizations, cannot afford to provide certain costly or rarely used services for themselves, for which they can, however, contract within an organizationally diversified city (Hoover and Vernon, 1962, pp. 45–63; Vernon, 1972).

The covariation between economic complexity and headquarters remains high, both within and outside the regions in which the highly industrial cities are found: $r = .64$ and .56, respectively. It appears that these two indicators do in fact measure external linkage. That they are associated with one another is further evidence of interdependence as a factor in the locational decisions made for organizations. Cities in the two regions we have considered do not differ from one another in this respect.

Association Headquarters and Ethnic Complexity. Three somewhat primitive, but available measures of population heterogeneity may be considered possible indicators of complexity among ethnic-group- or class-differentiated organizations, such as certain churches, nationality groups, and minority businesses. At the very least, they will serve as demographic controls in subsequent analyses. The first of these is proportion of elementary pupils in private schools as of 1960. Clearly organizational, this measure reflects the presence and power of church-affiliated schools, mainly Catholic; and, perhaps to only a slight extent, educational facilities for the upper class. The second measure, the proportion of adults in 1960 who were native-born but who had at least one foreign parent, is less clearly a measure of complexity among ethnic organizations—but is more so than the proportion of foreign-born, on the assumption that it takes time for migrants to organize. Finally, the proportion of nonwhites—referring mainly to blacks in 1960, who were relatively less organized during the 1950s than were other class or ethnic categories[8]—was the least likely indicator of complexity among class and ethnic organizations.

To the extent that national headquarters of associations locate themselves near the other class or ethnic associations that they represent, and to the extent that our three measures of population heterogeneity vary in their power as indicators of complexity among class or ethnic organizations, one would expect the following sequence of correlation coefficients: highest between national headquarters and private school enrollment; then between national headquarters and first-generation Americans; and lowest between national headquarters and nonwhites.

The observed correlations did not fully meet expectations: They were significantly .28, .17, and .19, respectively. Yet ethnicity varies in both type and numbers from one region to the next. The northeastern and east north central cities have the highest private school enrollments, the Northeast also having the highest proportion born of foreign parents, and the Southeast having the

largest nonwhite populations. Further, the western Spanish sur-
name minorities are probably not as highly organized as are eastern
groups with European origins. Finally, the migration of blacks
from the South to the inner cities of the metropoli that national
headquarters indicate might yield high correlation between nonwhites and headquarters, but *not* for reasons of ethnic organization. The relatively low values of the three correlation coefficients
suggest deferring their further discussion until after some of these
intruding considerations can be dealt with more systematically.

Complexity by Age and Size of City. Older and larger cities have
been considered likely to surpass others in the degrees of their
overall differentiation.[9] This could mean that age or size of a city
indicates its organizational complexity. It takes time for organizations to locate or to be established near other organizations that
demand their services or provide advantage, as we have argued
they do. And the number of inhabitants signifies the number and
variety of organizations there are to attract people by soliciting
their participation or by being able to serve and support them.

The longer a large central city has existed as such, the more
organizationally complex and the more intimately and elaborately
interwoven with the broader society its organizations may be expected to be. The commercialism that accompanied early urbanization very likely led to the proliferation of external economic
linkages in the search for markets or for sources of supply, and
the organizations of the older cities might well have established
outside linkages and become external objects of attention at a time
when competition with organizations elsewhere for such advantages was less intense than later. Or else the organizations around
which the older cities formed *were* the nation. Or these were among
the few places that organizations with national aspirations had available to them as potential sites.

But a city's age may also signify how stable relations among
that city's organizations have become, or how prevalent certain
old organizational forms are. It may even mean the city's obsolescence or physical deterioration. And size may be cause as well as
outcome of organizational complexity:[10] It may signify labor pools
and clienteles that attract new organizations. For example, opera
companies, mass transit lines, professional athletic teams, and fire

departments require minimum population sizes in order to be financially advisable; otherwise, their "products" must be "imported" from elsewhere. Or size may generate need for organizations that channel and mediate human interaction, such as dating bureaus, real estate brokerages, and the classified advertising departments of newspapers. Thus, a city's age, measured by the number of censuses taken since it first had 50,000 inhabitants, and its size, measured by the number of its inhabitants in 1960, not only indicate extralocal linkage and organizational complexity, but also serve to control potentially confounding influences of other variables that could not be measured directly.

Age and size are indeed correlated at high levels of significance with both the number of national headquarters of associations ($r = .69$ and $.71$, respectively) and with the combined export and banking indicator of organizational complexity ($r = .51$ and $.36$), as one might expect. It is noteworthy, regarding our main thesis, however, to observe that the initially reported correlation of .60 between association headquarters and economic complexity remained substantial (partial $r = .40$) even when age and size of city were held constant.[11] These interrelations among headquarters, economic complexity, age, and size are sufficiently compelling to further suggest a single dimension of extralocal linkage and organizational complexity. The number of national headquarters of voluntary associations best represents this dimension, yielding the highest correlation of all with the other three variables taken simultaneously (multiple $R = .83$ compared to .72, 71, and .63 in the respective cases of size, age, and economic complexity). And another analysis, using somewhat different methods, also found our national headquarters measure to be a good indicator of external linkage.[12]

Remember that the number of national headquarters of voluntary associations is only a convenient indicator of organizational complexity in the large cities of the United States. Thus, its ability to predict other attributes of the city—which shall later be demonstrated—is not necessarily to be taken as the result of what these headquarters do per se, but rather as the effects of the city's organizational composition, which is measured by the number of headquarters. For example, we have seen the headquarters measure to do better at reflecting industrialization's contribution to organizational complexity in the nonindustrial than in the industrial parts of the country.

Still, size and age do *not necessarily* indicate number, size, or variety of organizations, as we have already noted. Hence, their high correlations with the number of association headquarters should not be taken uncritically as further evidence only of the latter's validity as an indicator of organizational complexity. For example, although some headquarters tend to abound in the cities that are more organizationally complex in the economic sector, others might also seek the visibility that location in the older and larger, and therefore better known cities could afford. Thus *age and size of city will continue to be employed for purposes of control wherever the headquarters measure is applied.*

Anatomy of External Linkage and Organizational Complexity. Table 1 summarizes all of the correlates of the number of national headquarters of voluntary associations that have been discussed until this point. In addition to number of inhabitants, it introduces other

Table 1. Accounting for the Number of National Headquarters of Voluntary Associations on the Basis of Other Indicators of External Linkage and Organizational Complexity as well as Demographic Variables Used for Purposes of Control (N = 130 Cities).

Predictor of Number of National Headquarters of Voluntary Associations	Zero-Order Correlation Coefficient, r	Standardized Partial Regression Coefficient, *beta*
Economic Complexity	.60[b]	.28[b]
Age of City	.69[b]	.30[b]
Population Size	.71[b]	.45[b]
Multiple Correlation, *R*	.83[b]	
Industrialization	.17[a]	−.01[c]
Private Schools	.28[b]	−.03
Foreign Stock	.17[a]	.05
Nonwhite	.19[b]	−.03
Democratic Vote	.12	−.02
Population Density	.40[b]	.07
Migration	−.24[b]	.18[b]
Education	−.04	.20[b]

[a]Significant at the .10 level.
[b]Significant at *at least* the .05 level.
[c]The variables on the lower half of the table were alternated into the regression equation one at a time. Unless mentioned, their introduction did not alter rank ordering of the *betas* on the top half of the table.

conventional population characteristics (demographic variables) that—as discussed in Chapter One—will be used for purposes of control throughout this book. The independent contributions made by specific organizational variables will have to remain intact *despite* these population variables, if the idea of an interorganizational level of analysis is to be retained.

The top half of the table repeats, in the form of standardized partial regression coefficients (to be used throughout the book), the mutually independent effects of age and size of city and of the city's economic complexity on the headquarters proxy for external linkage and overall organizational complexity.

Turning to the lower half of the table, we see that this outcome failed to be disturbed when the aforementioned indicators of industrialization and of ethnic heterogeneity were included, one by one, in the analysis. The proportion of Democratic votes in the county's two-part election for president in 1960, a possible additional indicator of minority or industrial labor organization, also failed to make a difference.[13]

For reasons given in Chapter One, and to err on the side of caution, also included (here and in the rest of the book) were the 1960 effects of the frequently used demographic indicators of population density (population per square mile), migration (percent who lived in a different county five years earlier), and socioeconomic status (measured by median years of school completed by those twenty-five years of age or older).[14] It can be seen that none of the three variables, also included one by one, materially affected the outcome.[15] Thus there is no reason to this point to doubt the validity of the number of national headquarters of voluntary associations as an indicator of the city's underlying organizational complexity, complexity that appears to be based on the export by organizations of economic, social, and cultural goods and services—organizations that lend the city its external linkage to region or entire nation.

Regional Differences in Complexity

Specialization by region has already received attention in our discussion of the concentration of manufacturing output among northeastern and east north central cities and of the greater tendency for what manufacturing there is elsewhere to be associated with other kinds of extralocal linkage. Clearly, the possibility of other regional differences must be entertained: not only economic or geographic ones, such as transportation access or natural resources, but also ones that are social, cultural, and political in their contents, whose origins may be a mix of lawlike social forces and historical accident. Regions constitute complex and spongelike variables that often defy theoretical interpretation and do not enter into the formulations that constitute the substance of this book. Yet it is necessary to consider whether hypotheses are supported for reasons other than those of our theory and also whether outcomes hold for at least most parts of the country. In other words, investigators are obligated to try to invalidate their attributions of cause and effect, and to identify the boundaries of the universe to which their generalizations apply. The broad variables formed by region are useful in both tasks. But how should they be used?

One way would be to test each assertion within each region. Were it not for the small numbers of cases available for each test that affect both sampling error and the number of variables that may be considered at one time, this method would have a certain surface appeal. However, given organizational linkages that may transcend regional boundaries, what theoretical justification is there for failing to compare, say, the number of national headquarters of voluntary associations and the economic activities of *any* pair of cities—just because they might be located in different parts of the country?

A frequently used attempt to circumvent some of these problems is to consider each region—however broadly or narrowly defined—as a dichotomous ("dummy") variable that gives each city a score of 1 for location within it and 0 for any other location. Region may then be introduced in the analysis for purposes of control in the same way that the demographic variables were in the analysis whose results have been reported on Table 1. As our example concerning industrialization illustrates, however, this method controls only the possibility that the cities in a given region surpass others with respect to some variables, but not the possibility that region affects the direction and degree of association between variables. Further, if the cities in a given region are high or low with respect to some variable as well as some other variable used to account for the first—for example, the northeastern cities tend both to be industrialized and have relatively many pupils in private schools—the results of the analysis are inconclusive, for statistical as well as substantive reasons. The statistical problems have already been well discussed elsewhere.[16] The substantive issue rests on whether two variables are correlated with one another because of region, or because the cities high (or low) in one variable that causes them to be high (or low) in another happen to be concentrated in a certain region. Whatever the method of control, the question is a difficult one to resolve.

Nonetheless, the method selected here not only allows for sufficient numbers of cases, but also allows complete control of regional effects on variables as well as on *correlations among* variables, while at the same time avoiding the previously mentioned statistical sources of inconclusiveness and minimizing the substantive sources. The method simply consists of seeing the extent to which a given result or set of results is altered by *removing* all of the cities located within a given region, and of repeating the analysis for those that are left. The generality of a result that depends on only a handful of cities may be questioned, although, as we have suggested, not entirely ruled out. Confidence is encouraged, however, in the generality of a result that remains after various relevant handfuls have in turn been removed. This procedure for dealing with regional differences will apply throughout the book. Intraregional comparisons will only be made where their inclusion helps to resolve ambiguities detected in the data.

The northeastern and east north central subregions have already been considered, without explicit reference to their composition; to these we now add the western, southwestern, and southeastern subregions. Combining these also into larger regions has the twin advantages of producing categories that are homogeneous for certain purposes—for example, the industrial region, the South—and of diminishing skepticism about where certain states were assigned. One might wonder, for example, whether the District of Columbia of 1960 should be considered northeastern or southeastern.[17] Table 2 provides the first illustration of our method of determining to which degree, if at all, region confounds theoretically based generalizations about large United States cities.

The first line of Table 2, however, shows the average national

Table 2. Accounting for the Number of National Headquarters of Voluntary Associations on the Basis of Other Indicators of External Linkage and Organizational Complexity, Independently of the Effects of Region.

Number of National Headquarters of Voluntary Associations	All Cities	Cities Located *Outside* of							
		NE	ENC	W	SW	SE	NE & ENC	W & SW	SW & SE
Mean Rank of City[a]	65.5	66.9	66.4	67.6	63.4	63.5	68.5	65.2	60.5
Standardized Partial Regression (*beta*) on:									
Economic Complexity	.28	.26	.25	.28	.22	.28	.26	.23	.28
Age	.30	.31	.35	.36	.32	.26	.38	.34	.17
Size	.45	.42	.45	.41	.46	.49	.36	.45	.53
Multiple Correlation, R	.83	.82	.83	.84	.83	.84	.82	.85	.82
Number of Cities	130	101	106	95	113	105	77	78	88

[a]Rank among all 130 cities, 1 representing the largest number of national headquarters of voluntary associations, and 130 the fewest.

rank of cities according to number of voluntary association head-quarters, for the entire country, and then *exclusive* of each designated subregion or region (see the Appendix for means *within* regions of all variables used in this book). A small number indicates a large average number of such headquarters. Thus, the average remains relatively constant, regardless of which region or subregion is ignored.[18] This suggests that, on the national scene at least, no one region is ecologically dominant over the remaining ones in all respects. Interregional differentiation is the probable reason for this. More than half of all the headquarters were located in the New York, Washington (D.C.), and Chicago metropolitan areas (Lieberson and Allen, 1963); yet reducing the number in these areas to ranks has suggested that, although certain cities in certain regions may dominate nationally, this says little about the national dominance of the other cities in these regions. It seems unlikely, for example, that many associations representing the tobacco industry would be headquartered in Phoenix, or that those having to do with Italian Americans would concentrate in Columbus, Georgia. Any such association is national in the sense of its domain, but regional in the sense that it locates where its member organizations or populations occur in greatest number.

Substantively, this means that the number of national headquarters of voluntary associations reflects not only the organizational complexity of the city, but also the number of extralocal linkages it has to the differentiated national set of formal organizations. At this point, we have some support for the speculation that local organizational complexity varies with extralocal organizational linkage; later we will acquire more such support. Methodologically, these same observations underscore the difficulty of distinguishing between regional and national dominance by the organizations of any given city—a problem avoided through testing purportedly general findings by first removing the cities of one region or subregion from the analysis, then reentering them and removing those of the next.

Testing the theoretically meaningful parts of Table 1 in this manner shows, in Table 2, that the number of national headquarters of associations remains a good indicator of organizational complexity, regardless of which part of the country is ignored. Its multiple correlation with the alternative indicators, economic complexity, age of city, and number of inhabitants remains unchanged. Moreover, the initially observed partial association (*beta* = .28) with the one clearly organizational indicator, economic complexity, varies very little, considering the innate instability of such higher-level coefficients.

There is no reason, then, to doubt the adequacy of the number of national headquarters of voluntary associations as an indicator of both external linkage and organizational complexity within cities of the United States. Yet the other indicators will continue to be employed not only because of the control they offer, but also because they may reflect organizational complexity a bit more and external linkage a bit less than does the headquarters measure.

Scale and Diversification of Internal Regulating and Coordinating Organizations

Until this point, our discussion has centered on interdependence among organizations in general. Yet the very fact of organizational complexity has implications for the generation of further complexity among intertwined organizations internal to the macrosocial unit, organizations that not only provide specific services, but that also contribute to regulation and coordination within the entire unit.

Here we will attempt to organize and synthesize several strains of organizational thought. Organizational participation in regulating and coordinating bodies has been viewed as attempts to maximize gain and to minimize costly conflict (Litwak and Hylton, 1962; Hawley, 1950, pp. 209–221); as responses to resource needs and the absence of competitive disadvantage (Levine and White, 1961; Levine, White, and Paul, 1963); as political control and competitive advantage (Clark, 1965); and as mutual dependence (Form and Miller, 1960; Emery and Trist, 1965; Thompson, 1967, pp. 25–38). These ideas and findings may be recorded and expanded to refer to the following correlates of the scale and diversification of organizations that regulate and coordinate the entire macrosocial unit: (1) demands and resources, (2) mutual interest in predictability, and (3) plurality of interests and standards. Under these headings appear constructs leading to the proposition that organizational complexity affects the scale and diversification of regulating and coordinating organizations, operationalizing that proposition in the scale of municipal (governmental) diversification and case.

Regulation and coordination will be left undefined for the time being, because in subsequent chapters we shall argue at length that these are involved processes in organizationally complex environments. It suffices to say at this point that regulation and coordination make available local linkages around which coalitions can form, and from which solidarities and diffuse consensus emerge.

Demands and Resources. Within the United States, and in most other modern countries as well, at least some of this regulation and coordination is done by the departments of the municipal government. At this point, we shift somewhat from contributions made by human ecology and related disciplines to those made by students of urban politics. In one sense, our discussion of municipal government is nothing more than an extension of the idea of general interdependencies among organizations to include the public sector.

Municipal units, too, are established where they are both required and enabled by other organizations internally, but also where external demands for their services occur. City government may be viewed as an enterprise or set of enterprises that provides services to and acquires support from various organization (Thompson, 1965, p. 262; Eyestone and Eulau, 1968, Williams, 1968)—in the light of our previous analysis, as an enterprise whose extent and complexity depend on how externally linked (and therefore organizationally complex) the rest of the urban setting is. Further, a city's external linkage, when viewed only in terms of its governmental organizations, might also be measured in terms of services (say, fire protection) contracted for by smaller governments in nearby municipalities. But we have no means at hand for measuring this aspect.

These themes may first be summed into the following pair of postulates: *The greater the organizational complexity, the greater the magnitude and complexity of* demands *on internal regulating and coordinating organizations. The greater in magnitude and more complex these demands are, the larger in scale* and *the more diversified the regulating and coordinating organizations will be.* From this it follows, in the empirical case at hand, *that the greater the organizational complexity, the greater the municipal (government's) scale and diversification.*

The same hypothesis follows from a second, different, summarizing pair of postulates, based on the generally accepted idea of exchanges between exporting organizations and ones outside the macrosocial unit: *The greater the external linkage and organizational complexity, the greater the magnitude and complexity of resources available to internal regulating and coordinating organizations. The greater in magnitude and complexity these resources are, the larger in scale and the more diversified the regulating and coordinating organizations will be.*

Mutual Interest in Predictability. As complexity increases, so do the requirements for integration and administration. This has nearly become a truism among functionally oriented scholars. Yet *why* this requirement should ever be fulfilled is best described by organizational theories that are not very different from Thomas Hobbes' explanation of social order.

In spite of their respective pursuits of varying, often conflicting values, organizations do affect one another's fates through conflict as well as through alliance.[19] Interdependent organizations must come to terms with one another, even if their basic relation is one of contest. This requirement of mutual survival becomes more intense with increasing organizational complexity. We might deduce, from interorganizational theory, that with the proliferation of organizations there occurs for each organization a loss of control over the environment that it has helped constitute (Latham, 1952, pp. 27–33; Emery and Trist, 1965; Terreberry, 1968) and an attendant loss of predictability. To regain predictability—we might conclude—that it is in the common interest of all organizations to have organizations within the macrosocial unit that regulate and coordinate: to support a Hobbesian "Leviathan."

We restate these dynamics as two further postulates. *The greater the organizational complexity* the less the predictability *among organizations. The less the predictability among organizations, the larger in scale will the regulating and coordinating organizations be.* From this follows *only the first part* of our empirical hypothesis: *The greater the organizational complexity, the greater the municipal* scale.[20]

Plurality of Interests and Standards. From philosophical and political pluralism comes the idea that organizations like government and church in earlier eras are not only codominant with one another, but also pursue different interests and standards (see, for example, Durkheim, [1893] 1933, pp. 152–153, 347–348, 289; Latham, 1952, pp. 1–12, 31; Polsby, 1960; Dahl, 1961.)

Recent theories of interorganizational relations have emphasized the partial accord and partial competition or conflict, the *pluralism* that results from the pursuit of different interests and standards by different organizations. (Litwak and Hylton, 1962, provided the important statement—and its consequents—that organization identical in these respects would merge.) Competition and conflict occur because different organizations embody separate, specific, and often opposing standards and interests, sometimes even by decree. The very complexity and heterogeneity of contemporary social life means that it includes a variety of organizational proponents for each issue that it faces and a variety of organizational means for resolution and implementation. The consequent picture of any macrosocial unit, including urbanized society, shows a pluralist constellation of organizations that embody or pursue different values in part, both because some of them pursue separate roles within a division of labor (not only economic labor, be it noted), and because they represent remnants of divers cultures.

I am referring not only to, say, competition for customers, for religious converts, or for political partisans, but also to the conflict that can exist, for example, among various government agencies pursuing values that may in part be mutually antithetical under any political philosophy. Penology and rehabilitation, military spending and consumer goods, environmental health and industrial productivity, and fiscal solvency and public welfare provide a few illustrations. (Almond, 1960, suggests this is also true of Communist and other centralized societies.)

In other words, organizational pluralism means that attaining certain of the values that society deems necessary for its continuation—those promoting environmental adaptation, the mobilization of power, the integration of broader systems, and at least the minimal conformity of organizations to community or to macrosocial standards—may actually jeopardize attainment of the others. Any hotly contested interests or standards—be these economic, scientific, political, religious, or so forth—could not survive beside one another within the same organization without bringing about its total disruption.

Given the demand for large-scale regulation and coordination of the macrosocial unit, *but* given such pluralism, it would appear that diversification of the regulating and coordinating organizations into separate, but equally large subunits would provide a set of partly "countervailing powers." No single one of them, then, could fully dominate the others, nor is it likely to succumb.

Multiorganizationally induced pluralism, then, has the effect of opposing monolithic dominance by government or by any other organization. Thus, the fourth and final pair of postulates: *The greater the organizational complexity, the greater the* plurality *of interests and standards. The greater the plurality of interests and standards, the more diversified the regulating and coordinating organizations will be.* These postulates yield the second part of the empirical hypothesis: *The greater the organizational complexity, the greater the municipal diversification.* Thus the shared dependence on predictability that produces large-scale regulating and coordinating organizations is tempered by the pluralism that opposes monolithic regulation and coordination, resulting in the "tradeoff" or "satisficing result" of large organizational scale *but* diversification of these organizations.

The reader will note a certain ambivalence here as to whether government should be defined as one organization or as several. This issue cannot, and perhaps should not, be resolved at this "state of the art." Whether one thinks of the municipal government as one organization with internal conflicts or as a federation of agencies, it is still—compared to, say, "business," as it shall later be argued—a *relatively* enduring structure. This same definitional problem exists in other kinds of entities that have "chapters" or "departments": conglomerates, "the Catholic Church," the "Democratic Party," and so on. Failure to resolve the question does not affect the theory developed in this book. If anything, the world might be even more multiorganizational than we are painting it. (In either case, the municipal government as a whole *does not fit the concept of bureaucracy* in the sense of a clear-cut hierarchy of offices.)

An indicator that reflects not only the *diversification* among levels of municipal services provided by the city, but also the overall *scale* of municipal government, then, should vary with the non-municipal aspects of the city's organizational complexity, and—to the extent that space and time mean that the organizations of a city have overlapping "export markets" (say a nighttime population that flocks into town for entertainment)—also more directly with its external linkage (see Kasarda, 1972).

A second objective was anticipated in constructing such an indicator. This was the assessment of the extent to which each metropolis approximated the New York City prototype of *vast public bureaucracies,* each a "core organization" in its own activity area, linked to the other bureaucracies and to private organizations in various coalitions (Sayre and Kaufman, 1960). The indicator to be described appears to fulfill this need, and the full purpose will become apparent in the discussions of linkage and coalitions, introduced in this chapter but fully explicated in Chapters Four and Five. First, the *number of municipal employees* per capita measured the *scale* of each municipal government. Second, the *degree of similarity among its rankings*[21] *in 1960 across budget categories* of expenditures per capita for education, fire protection, health, highways, police protection, sanitation, and welfare indicated *the degree of its diversification.* Per capita numbers of municipal employees could have been used in this second measure, instead of budget items, had they been available in all service categories; but the fact that those available yielded strong correlations with expenditures lends confidence to the substitution.

The thirty-seven cities above both *respective medians—in total number of employees* and *in diversification—*were defined as *both* large in scale *and* diversified, compared to the remaining ninety-three cities. Using the respective measures of scale and diversification *jointly* in this dichotomous indicator of a theoretical continuum guarded against undue effects of single municipal programs that might have been idiosyncratically large or small. By using such a broad measure, we are also responsive to questions raised by urban economists as to comparability among specific budget categories from one city to the next.

The diversification portion of this indicator bears some resemblance to a separately developed measure of scope of municipal government (Liebert, 1974). For example, all things equal, municipalities with no welfare or health departments would receive lower scores in diversification (would be narrower in scope) than ones that have them. Yet the alternative indicator of scope only considers whether certain kinds of municipal activities are authorized, not whether they occur, without assessing their magnitudes relative to one another or relative to activities, such as police and fire protection, that were not considered. Nor does scope address itself to how potent government is in general; that is, is it "big" or "small"? Constructed for different purposes, scope is not to be confused with our indicator of a continuum of diversification *and* scale. (Other discussions of diversification appear in Turk, 1973a, 1973b, 1975, 1977. Also see Lincoln, 1976, for a comparison between our indicator of diversification and that of scope.)

It is to be expected, according to our hypothesis, that the greater the organizational complexity among the city's nonmunicipal organizations, the more likely its government is to be large in scale and diversified. This expectation is borne out by positive correlations (r_b) with our direct indicators of organizational complexity: coefficients of .39 with economic complexity, .39 with industrialization, and an impressive .64 with the number of national headquarters of voluntary associations—the last being the best complexity indicator discussed thus far. Older and larger cities are not only likely to surpass others in reflecting organizational complexity, as we have already noted, but they are also more likely to reflect the *effect* of this complexity on municipal scale and diversification.[22] Here the respective coefficients (r_b) with municipal scale and diversification are .66 in the case of the city's age and .47 when the number of inhabitants is considered. As for the more questionable indicators that are purported to measure ethnic organizational complexity, the correlations of the municipal indicator are .42 with private schools, .39 with foreign stock, .20 with nonwhite, and .36 with Democratic vote. Although these measures of ethnic heterogeneity had not been found to have an effect on the voluntary association headquarters indicator of organizational complexity (see Table 1), it will be shown, once other influences are taken into account, that the same does not hold in the case of municipal government. Here it has been suggested that special-interest organizations of voters can affect the number of programs and departments created by local governments (Clark, 1971)—an effect that foreshadows our subsequent discussion of municipal politics.

Table 3 summarizes the correlations just reported and provides the end result of a series of analyses that tested the effects of each predictor of municipal scale and diversification, independently of the influence of other predictors. Beginning with an examination of the mutually independent effects of the five most persuasive indicators of organizational complexity, it was found

Table 3. Accounting for Municipal Scale and Diversification on the Basis of Other Indicators of Organizational Complexity as well as Demographic Variables Used for Purposes of Control (N = 130 Cities).

Predictor of Municipal Scale and Diversification	Estimated Zero-Order Correlation Coefficient, r (association before estimate)		Standardized Partial Regression Coefficient, $beta$ (before estimate of r's)
National Headquarters of Voluntary Associations	.64 (	.48)[c]	.48 (.36)[c]
Industrialization	.39 (	.30)[c]	.17 (.13)[b]
Foreign Stock	.39 (	.29)[c]	.40 (.30)[c]
Nonwhite	.20 (	.15)[b]	.32 (.24)[c]
Multiple Correlation, R (before estimate of r's)		.77 (.58)[c]	
Economic Complexity	.39 (	.29)[c]	−.01 (.00)[d]
Age of City	.66 (	.49)[c]	.15 (.11)
Population Size	.46 (	.35)[c]	.07 (.05)
Private Schools	.42 (	.31)[c]	−.01 (.01)
Democratic Vote	.36 (	.27)[c]	.12 (.09)
Population Density	.51 (	.38)[c]	.05 (.03)
Migration	−.42 (−.32)[c]		.07 (.06)
Education	−.29 (−.22)[c]		−.07 (−.06)
Poverty[a]	−.11 (−.08)		.00 (.00)

[a] Adopted as a possible indicator of high municipal costs (for example, for welfare) relative to municipal revenue, measured by percent of families with less than $3,000 income in 1959 (U.S. Bureau of the Census, 1962a).
[b] Significant at the .10 level, based on association before estimates.
[c] Significant at *at least* the .05 level, based on association before estimates.
[d] The variables on the lower half of the table were alternated into the regression equation one at a time. Unless mentioned, their introduction did not alter rank ordering of the *betas* on the top half of the table.

that economic complexity and population size ceased to make a difference that even approached significance, while the number of national headquarters of associations, industrialization, and age of city continued to do so. (Throughout this book, a finding simply described as *not significant* failed even to approach the .10 level.) The last of these, namely age of city (being also the least clear-cut in its meaning), became insignificant once the foreign stock and nonwhite indicators of ethnic heterogeneity were introduced (private schools failed to make a significant difference).

The headquarters indicator of organizational complexity, taken together with industrialization, foreign stock, and nonwhite, account for 60 percent of the variation in municipal scale and diversity, estimating a multiple correlation coefficient of .77. Reintroduction of each indicator that had previously failed to have a significant effect, and introduction of the remaining ones adopted as controls (for reasons given earlier), each singly, failed to alter this coefficient significantly.

Table 4 shows that, with conceptually trivial exceptions, the findings tend to remain the same when the effects of geographic region are taken into account (in the manner previously discussed), even though the five subregions differed from one another in rates of large municipal scale and diversification ($p < .01$ by chi-square).

The proportion of the nonwhite population failed to affect municipal diversification and scale once the cities of the South were removed from consideration. Southeastern cities rank highest in proportion of nonwhites, compared to the cities in the remaining four regions, but are average in scale and diversification of municipal government. The "separate but equal" municipal facilities of the 1950s might account for the nonwhite effect there. There is also some variability in the effects of foreign stock from one set of cities to the next, especially when the ethnically diversified cities of the Northeast are ignored. It is not only likely that racial and ethnic minorities are the most organized, thus having the greatest effect on municipal activities in regions where they are most numerous, but it is equally likely that different minorities with different degrees of organization reside in the cities of different regions. But this is speculation.

The effects of industrialization on the scale and diversification of municipal government, however, are greatest once the cities

Table 4. Accounting for Municipal Scale and Diversification On the Basis of Other Indicators of Organizational Complexity, Independently of the Effects of Region.

Municipal Scale and Diversification	All Cities	Cities Located Outside of								Cities Located in
		NE	ENC	W	SW	SE	NE & ENC	W & SW	SW & SE	NE or ENC
Precent of Cities with Large and Diversified Government	28	21	29	31	32	29	19	37	33	42
Standardized Partial Regression (beta) on:[a] National Headquarters of										
Voluntary Associations	.48	.40	.47	.52	.52	.52	.35	.63	.65	.73
Industrialization	.17	.14	.27	.13	.17	.13	.29	.09	.20	.18
Foreign Stock	.40	.32	.46	.37	.36	.48	.50	.31	.50	.34
Nonwhite	.32	.46	.44	.26	.27	.11	.67	.17	-.03	-.17
Multiple Correlation, R[a]	.77	.71	.89	.72	.76	.82	.87	.76	.84	.76
Number of Cities	130	101	106	95	113	105	77	78	88	53

[a]Betas and R are based on estimated r's.

of the most highly industrialized regions are removed from consideration. Quite possibly this is because of our previously reported finding that industrialization is a better indicator of nonmunicipal organizational complexity when these regions are ignored. This may occur both because the specialized manufacturing cities (therefore, ones that are not complex) tend to be located in the northeastern and east north central states, as we have observed, and because the metropoli in which relatively smaller production enterprises accompany organizational complexity, as we have also noted, are likely to be located elsewhere.

Our best indicator of nonmunicipal organizational complexity, number of national headquarters of voluntary associations, continues to be the best predictor of its municipal counterpart, irrespective of the effects of region.

Thus, organizational complexity in the private sector is closely associated with organizational scale and diversification in the public sector, as hypothesized, and both kinds of complexity very likely reflect the city's external linkage. Two reasons are given for why organizations locate themselves, emerge, or are formed near other organizations: (1) demands for their services, and (2) resources to support them. Two other reasons are that organizational complexity is associated with (1) the mutual search for predictability among the city's organizations through regulation, and, at the same time, (2) their resistance to monolithic coordination. Insofar as diversification may mean decentralization in the twin senses of loose control over various municipal agencies and the provision of special client-dominated facilities (for example, schools in minority neighborhoods), large-scale but diversified municipal government may constitute the compromise between need for predictability and resistance to central coordination and may therefore be permitted to exist.

Important to note is that a city's governmental characteristics seem to depend on its other organizational characteristics, especially those having to do with the economic and other exports that provide its external linkage. The manners in which industrial establishments and racial or other forms of ethnic organizations play a part remain an open question, but age and size of city fail to make a difference once the more direct indicators of organizational complexity and of ethnic heterogeneity are taken into account. It is noteworthy that the failure of number of inhabitants to account directly for the scale and diversification of municipal government was echoed by similar failures in the cases of the other demographic variables—population density, education, poverty, and migration—although these are among the variables most frequently used in comparative studies of urban structure and process in general and urban complexity in particular.

Organizations That Represent Consensual Solidarity

We shall assume, along with Durkheim ([1893] 1933), that consensus does not disappear with increasing social complexity—it only becomes weaker and more diffuse in its content. By *the organizational representation of diffuse consensual solidarity* is meant *the degree to which certain kinds of organizations signify the interests and standards that the macrosocial unit's organizations share*. In the United States, certain voluntary associations can vary in the degree to which they display this characteristic—as shall be shown. Elsewhere, other kinds of organizations might come into question.

External Linkage, Organizational Complexity, and Consensual Solidarity

One set of general theories about relations between system and subsystem suggests the integration of the one to be at the expense of the integration of the other. (Considered at various levels by Marx and Engels, [1888] 1959; Simmel, 1908, pp. 96–98; Sumner, 1906, pp. 1–121; Parsons, 1951, pp. 293–320; Riecken and Homans, 1954; Collins and Raven, 1959; Dohrendorf, 1959, pp. 179–240; Gouldner, 1959; Turk and Lefcowitz, 1960; Ramsöy, 1963; Starbuck, 1950).[23] Speculation about what is now called "mass society" incorporates this idea (see, for example, Warner and Low, 1941; Vidich and Bensman, 1958; Kaufman, 1959; Kornhauser, 1959; Stein, 1960; Mott, 1965, pp. 165–184; Warren, 1966; Walton, 1968). Gains in the integration of the mass society are at the expense of integration into the local community. Theory already provided in this chapter allows specification: *The greater the external linkage, the greater the dependence on the outside, and consequently, the less flexibility of organizations in mutual adaptation.* Also, *the greater the external linkage,* as we have already claimed, *the greater the organizational complexity and therefore the greater the plurality of interests and standards.* To these propositions we may add that *the less flexible organizations are in adapting to one another and the greater the plurality of interests and standards, the less*—almost by definition— *the organizational representation of diffuse consensual solidarity.*

From these postulates, it follows that: (1) *The greater the external linkage, the less the organizational representation of diffuse consensual solidarity,* and (2) *The greater the organizational complexity, the less the organizational representation of diffuse consensual solidarity.* Not apparent until after the fact, the linkage made available by the scale and diversification of regulating and coordinating organizations should facilitate solidarity and consensus. Thus: (3) *The greater the scale and diversification of regulating and coordinating organizations, the greater the organizational representation of diffuse consensual solidarity.*

City-Wide Associations. Such representation was measured in the metropolis by the extent to which local voluntary associations are uncontested and city-wide in their impact. Some cities suggest organizational representation of consensual solidarity, to the extent that their local voluntary associations pursue diffuse goals and avoid conflict by advancing abstract and uncontested values purportedly oriented to the interests of the entire city.[24] Insofar as these attributes of civic or service organizations fail to be coupled with opposition by government agency, political party, or by any of the city's other organizations, local voluntary associations reflect solidarity and whatever consensus exists among organized sectors of the city—even though this may mean ignoring, possibly overriding, prevailing sentiments in the local unorganized sectors. Indeed, that members of higher socioeconomic strata join voluntary associations in disproportionate numbers (see, for example, Wright and Hyman, 1958; Williams and Adrian, 1959; Greer and Orleans, 1962; Hyman and Wright, 1971) affects the likelihood, be it noted, that certain values and interests are not represented Belonging to a general class of structures believed to have integrative import for broader social contexts,[25] the extent of these locally oriented associational patterns represents what is held in common by the community's other organizations, much as the locations of extralocally oriented national headquarters of voluntary associations represent what is held in common by other organizations nearby within specific national spheres of activity. Henceforth called *the extent to which local voluntary associations are city-wide,* the former shall later be discussed in terms of their local significance.

Yet it may not be assumed that local voluntary associations are not without their external aspects; for their prototypes exist in other cities and are known. Also, their representation of what is held in common by the city's other important organizations, externally linked as they are, is often what is held in common among such organizations nationally; and the failure of local associations to become city-wide may reflect local occurrences of conflicts between organizations that are actually manifestations of conflicts at a national level.

Indicator of City-Wide Associations. Form letters were mailed early in 1961 (by Joel Smith and myself) to the incumbents of each of the following positions: mayor or city manager, city planner, city editor, head of school board, Chamber of Commerce official, fund drive organizer, and urban sociologist (or to their respective designates). The letters elicited essay answers by one or more of these knowledgable informants to broad questions about citizen participation, civic pride, cohesion, conflict, and the distribution of power. Although phrased in terms of "persons," "groups," and "kinds of people," the questions yielded unsolicited but explicit mention, in 76 of the 130 cities, of one or more voluntary associations that either implemented or supplemented their manifest purposes by symbolizing, serving, coordinating, influencing, or acting on behalf of the community itself. Such city-wide associations, as we have already called them, included broad-based fraternal organizations, booster groups, community chest organizations and other fund-raising groups (not just drives), boys' clubs, a labor council, a taxpayers' association, Chambers of Commerce, and various business and professional clubs. These reports were unaccompanied by any reference to the organized representation of contested and enduring special interests. Presumably the respondents did not consider contested organizations to be oriented toward the community.

Thus, whether or not the city was one of the seventy-six having such organizations became the indicator of the extent to which its voluntary associations were uncontested and city-wide.[26] It might be argued that the unqualified mention by informed persons of publicly oriented organizations that they and others found to have integrative significance,[27] and their failure to speak of organizational contestants, constitute evidence that city-wide associations occurred in the sense that we view them in this book. Nonetheless, there is another means of assessing the validity of the indicator; namely, 70 percent agreement occurred between informants in voluntary mention (or nonmention) of at least one such association in cities providing more than one reply.[28] This means that, guided by their separate experiences, individual observers concurred on the degree to which certain of the city's organizations were broadly oriented and uncontested.

Organizational Complexity and City-Wide Associations. Any investigation of the association between organizational complexity and the extent to which the city's voluntary associations are uncontested and city-wide must perforce be speculative and exploratory. On the one hand, local voluntary associations tend not to enter into coalitions or otherwise to take sides in controversy, for fear of losing members, because the latter's ties to their organizations, being voluntary, can readily be severed (see Coleman, 1957, p. 26; Banfield, 1961, pp. 297–301; Banfield and Wilson, 1963, pp. 254–256). This means that city-wide associations can play mediating roles among the organizations in an organizationally complex environment, which, as we have already suggested and shall discuss in detail later, seek to maximize predictability in turbulent surroundings— but not at the cost of autonomy that decentralization supports. From these standpoints, the more organizationally complex a city is, the more likely are its voluntary associations to be community-wide. That the membership of voluntary associations is disproportionately composed of occupational elites has already been hinted. Very likely these are the elites of other organizations, which they might represent in the mutual search for predictability that can take place within the context of community-wide associations. It is within this context that shared, abstract standards and interests can be articulated and supported thus increasing predictability without threatening any one organization's domain. These shared elements are likely to be national. Indeed, however much social scientists disagree concerning the involvement in community affairs of extralocally oriented organizations—especially absentee-controlled corporations—most sources imply or refer directly to either the formal or the informal participation of their representatives in noncontroversial civic associations (for example, see Pellegrin and Coates, 1956; Fowler, 1958; Form and Miller, 1960, pp. 310, 327–329; Schulze, 1961; Banfield and Wilson, 1963, pp. 249–261; Mott, 1970). National standards and interests are most likely to be the ones held in common among these extralocal and cosmopolitan organizational elites, who may come from anywhere, and their counterparts, who may come from local enterprises and from other local organizations. The very types of associations listed by our knowledgable informants in the 130 large cities suggest standards, interests, and prototypes that are not unique to any one American city.

Our first two propositions, however, have suggested that the greater the external linkage (with or without the organizational complexity it constitutes), the greater are the number and variety of conflicts—a possibility that would impede uncontested and community-wide states of a city's voluntary associations.

The unexpected finding (stated as our third proposition) that city-wide associations are correlates of municipal scale and diversification points the way out of this dilemma, as we shall see, by showing that the direct effects of external linkage and organizational complexity are inverse, while their indirect effects might well be to promote the implementation of external interests and standards that are also shared internally.

External Complexity and City-Wide Associations. Predominantly insignificant correlations between the indicators already discussed, and the extent to which each of the 130 cities' voluntary associations were uncontested and city-wide, would ordinarily have discouraged further analysis. However, although the effects of the clearly organizational indicators of external linkage and organizational complexity were inverse ($r_b = -.08$ in the case of national headquarters of voluntary associations and $-.05$ and $-.10$ in those of economic complexity and industrialization, respectively), that of their more local counterpart, the scale and diversification of municipal gov-

ernment was positive ($r_t = .08$). Because the latter indicator was positively correlated with each of the former to a substantial degree
(see Table 3), this reversal of effect was not inconsequential, and
"suppressor" relationships were considered to be at play. Indeed,
simultaneous consideration of the four effects on the city-wide
association indicator yielded a multiple correlation of .26, with
the independent effect of economic complexity becoming nil.[29]

The possibility that the three apparently independent effects
were further confounded by the operation of other variables was
considered, one additional predictor at a time. Only age of city and
the proportion of its inhabitants who were of foreign stock significantly affected the extent to which local voluntary associations were
uncontested and community-wide and—save for industrialization—only served to sharpen the initially observed effects. Once
association with the other measures of organizational complexity
was held constant, the direct effect of foreign stock was, as expected
under pluralist theory, to make community-wide associations less
likely. The result, shown in Table 5, is a multiple correlation of .40
($p < .10$), which is constituted by the positive (presumably link-
strengthening) effects of the municipal and city age measures and
the inverse (presumably pluralist) effects of national voluntary
headquarters, industrialization, and foreign stock. (Reintroduction
of the predictors that had failed to make a difference before did
not alter the results.) These findings clearly leave much of the variation in our organizational measure of community unexplained.
This is partly the result of how this measure was constructed,[30] but
also suggests the operation of other variables or idiosyncratic events.

There are two tentative conclusions to be drawn from what has
been explained. First, according to Propositions 1 and 2, the effects
of ethnic heterogeneity and of the extralocal orientation of a city's
organizations are negative *to the extent* that they have not brought
about large-scale and diversified municipal government, but, as
described by Proposition 3, were unexpectedly found to be indirectly positive to the extent that they *have* done so (see Tables 3
and 4). This hints at a theme already suggested, but to be developed in detail later, in Chapter Four, namely that such municipal
government is instrumental in the provision of all manner of local
linkage, which in the present case seems to have a positive influence

Table 5. Accounting for the Extent to which Local Voluntary Associations Are Uncontested and City-Wide on the Basis of Indicators of Organizational Complexity as well as Demographic Variables Used for Purposes of Control (N = 130 Cities).

Predictor of City-Wide Associations	Estimated Zero-Order Correlation Coefficient, r (association before estimate)	Standardized Partial Regression Coefficient, beta (before estimate of r's)
Municipal Scale and Diversification	.08 (.05)	.35 (.13)[a]
National Headquarters of Voluntary Associations	−.08 (−.06)	−.42 (−.26)
Industrialization	−.10 (−.08)	−.19 (−.12)
Age of City	.04 (.03)	.30 (.28)
Foreign Stock	.20 (−.16)	−.31 (−.22)
Multiple Correlation, R (before estimate of r's)	.40 (.27)[b]	
Economic Complexity	−.05 (−.04)	−.07 (−.06)[c]
Population Size	.02 (.01)	−.02 (−.00)
Private Schools	−.07 (−.05)	.09 (.04)
Democratic Vote	.05 (.04)	.06 (.08)
Nonwhite	.08 (.07)	−.19 (−.09)
Population Density	−.14 (−.11)	−.17 (−.12)
Migration	.04 (.04)	.01 (.02)
Education	.02 (.01)	.20 (.13)
Poverty	.14 (.11)	−.08 (−.04)

[a]The intercorrelations among independent variables are so high relative to their respective correlations with the dependent variable that significance tests of the individual *betas* would be misleading; so would any attention to their values be, except for sign.
[b]Significant at the .10 level, based on association before estimates.
[c]The variables on the lower half of the table were alternated into the regression equation one at a time. Unless mentioned, their introduction did not alter rank ordering of the *betas* on the top half of the table.

on how uncontested and community-wide the city's voluntary associations are. Second, the independent effect of the city's age is *positive* on this community variable once the former's high correlation with the pluralism implied by extralocal linkage is controlled. Barring its pluralism, the older a city is, the more chance, it appears, have its broader and more abstract structures had to become stable. It might also be the case, however, that some city-wide associations were established during an earlier and organizationally less complex era and somehow managed to survive. (See Meyer and Brown, in press, for a suggestion about the effect of era on the attributes of urban organization.)

Regional effects on correlates of city-wide associations. There is
no significant variation from any one of the five subregions to
the next in the proportion of cities having at least one such city-
wide association ($p > .10$ by the chi-square test). Nevertheless, Table
6 shows that the *effects* on this indicator reported in Table 5 do vary
among regions and subregions. The most striking result is the multiple correlation coefficient of .73, attributable almost entirely to
large-scale and diversified municipal government, and not at all
attributable to age of city, once the relatively older and more heavily industrial cities of the northeastern and east north central regions are excluded. Note, however (see the last column), that—save
for industrialization (which, as already mentioned, may be an urban
specialization there)—the general predictive pattern remains, even
when these excluded cities are examined separately. That this pattern is weak might result from the greater differentiation among
them according to type of external linkage, alluded to in our earlier
discussion of the inverse correlates of industrialization within this
region (also suggested by Table 6), and the resulting difficulty of
measuring organizational complexity. It might also mean that,
given time, municipal governments grow large and diversified
without necessarily producing the linkage required for local voluntary associations to be uncontested and community-wide,[31] or
that the older community-wide associations owed their existence
to linkage other than that provided by local government.

Community-wide associations do appear to be especially capable of occurring in cities rich in interorganizational linkage,
provided that such linkage is predominantly local. Unlike municipal
diversification and scale, community-wide associations are not very
likely to depend on external resources and therefore to be more
subject to the pluralizing effects of external links than to their
resource-providing effects.

Externally Provided Resources

Inverse association between system integration and subsystem
integration is not invariant. Cases can be imagined in which such
association is positive (Turk and Simpson, 1971), as when the system rewards, depends on, or makes possible the integration of the
subsystem, or when integration of the subsystem is contingent on

Table 6. Accounting for the Extent to Which Local Voluntary Associations Are Uncontested and City-Wide on the Basis of Indicators of Organizational Complexity, Independently of the Effects of Region.

Number of City-Wide Associations	All Cities	Cities Located *Outside* of								Cities Located in
		NE	ENC	W	SW	SE	NE & ENC	W & SW	SW & SE	NE or ENC
Percent of Cities with at Least One City-Wide Association	58	61	60	55	60	55	65	56	57	49
Standardized Partial Regression (beta) on:[a]										
Municipal Scale and Diversification	.35	.54	.54	.44	.25	.17	1.02	.35	.08	.14
National Headquarters of Voluntary Associations	−.42	−.54	−.41	−.72	−.34	−.31	−.53	−.64	−.21	−.51
Industrialization	−.19	−.26	−.20	−.04	−.21	−.16	−.26	−.03	−.19	.06
Age of City	.30	.39	.12	.57	.27	.24	−.02	.54	.15	.42
Foreign Stock	−.31	−.15	−.32	−.58	−.30	−.19	−.14	−.55	−.18	−.29
Multiple Correlation, R[a]	.40	.55	.40	.60	.36	.23	.73	.55	.23	.36
Number of Cities	130	101	106	95	113	105	77	78	88	53

[a]Betas and R are based on estimated r's.

that of the system (see Shils and Janowitz, 1948, for an example of this condition). Subsystems may in part maximize their integration by establishing optimum relationships with the broader system that constitutes their environment. These latter linkages, though called *adaptation* from the viewpoint of the subsystem, may be called *integration* from the viewpoint of the entire system. The twin properties of adaptation and integration have been cited among those most crucial in understanding small social systems (Bales, 1949) as well as larger ones (Parsons, 1951), and have been generalized to systems of all kinds (Parsons, Bales, and Shils, 1953, 1955; Parsons and Smelzer, 1956; Parsons, 1960, 1961, 1968). Adaptation does not only mean the procurement of environmental elements that clearly constitute subsystem facilities, as in the case of revenues of economic goods and services; it also means the incorporation of information, standards, symbols, and segments of broader institutional structures. In both cases, the materials necessary for subsystem integration may be "procured" from the environment. To the same extent that procurement promotes subsystem integration, it is likely to promote total system integration, either as a planned or an unplanned consequence of system-subsystem interaction. In the case of the family, for example, integration among its roles, and the viability of society as well, may be in part maintained on the basis of successful transaction between household and economy (Parsons and Smelzer, 1956) and also of kinship role definitions that are provided by society itself.

Turning now to macrosocial units, one might suppose, from the concept of adaptation, an effect the reverse of that implied by the concept of mass society; namely, either internal or external linkage might provide organizational *resources*—flows of standards, persons, money, and materials, for example—*defined as requirements for survival or achievement,* the result being positive association between integration of the macrosocial unit and with its integration into the external system of organizations that contains it as a subsystem (this possibility is hinted in such works on the economic structure of cities as Duncan and Reiss, 1950; Nelson, 1955; Netzer, 1968, pp. 435–474). Indeed, our foregoing discussion of national standards and national prototypes as bases for community-wide associations points to this conclusion.

From the empirical standpoint, the external linkage of cities may be essential for their local integration, as in the case of external markets or inputs of needed goods, services, or regulatory mechanisms. On the other hand, their external linkage may either make local integration superfluous, as in cases where internal sources of facilities have been replaced by external ones, or it may make local integration difficult, as our propositions about consensual solidarity have suggested, because of the intrusion of divers or conflicting national standards, divers or conflicting interests, and divers or conflicting sources of external control. Which of these possibilities will overshadow the other is a question whose answer will depend on the particular kinds of internal integration and external linkages under consideration and the constraints that they place on one another.

Thus one might expect positive association between the two kinds of linkage where internal integration depends heavily on national values that support local linkage, or on other resources that encourage it or make it possible, and one might expect negative association where such dependence is slight and therefore outweighed by the fragmenting effects of external influences, as we have found to be the case for organizational representation of diffuse consensual solidarity (city-wide associations). Formally stated, *the greater the external linkage, the more the externally provided resources.* The unexpected corollary, found to hold in one special case but not predicted, is, *The more the specific internal linkage, the more the externally provided resources.*

External Relations with the Federal Government. Thus, from the fragmenting effects of extralocal linkage, which have just been emphasized, we turn to its resource procuring effects. The case to be described seems to meet the conditions we have suggested to be necessary for this effect to occur.

The external distribution patterns of influence, power, and value commitments have eluded direct assessment in comparative urban research to date. The flow of federal monies to the other organizations in a nation's cities[32] does not suffer from these restrictions. More than that, however, it enables description of the relationship between "private" aspects of the national system (voluntary associations) and its "public" (governmental) aspects.

The political state appears to have replaced the church and other central institutions as the main repository of society's values and as its major symbol. Government not only represents the state, but serves in many other institutional sectors as well. This means that any processes involving national government are likely to be society-wide processes, both in terms of their impact and in terms of the degree to which they involve the main structures of social system. Little documentation of this point is required beyond simply noting that urban communities even constitute the central concern of a separate federal Department of Housing and Urban Development (also see Wilson, 1966b). Federal intervention in the provision of community services within United States cities has been wide in scope (Schottland, 1963; Morris and Rein, 1963).

The specific community organizations having had linkages with various federal agencies are legion. Notable among these interorganizational linkages, however, are ones having to do with welfare, education, and health. One of their major sources is the U.S. Department of Health, Education and Welfare; another has been the U.S. Office of Economic Opportunity. However, the processes of several other federal organizations—for example, ones having to do with commerce, agriculture, and labor—also articulate with these institutional arenas. The three arenas, as we have noted in part, are local in their application, and therefore strategic to the study of cities as multi- and interorganizational structures.

Interorganizational Transactions in the War on Poverty. Clearly then, transactions between national governmental agencies and various organizations—both public and private—that are located within the large cities that we are discussing deserve special attention. The early years of the federal War on Poverty yield valuable data in this light, both here and elsewhere in the book. Based on the Economic Opportunity Act of 1964 and its amendments, activity in the poverty program—unlike urban renewal and hospital construction—clearly followed various indicators of fundamental metropolitan characteristics in time, thus allowing us to predict over a four- to six-year period. The act authorized several federal agencies coordinated by the U.S. Office of Economic Opportunity to encourage, negotiate, enter into contractual relations with, and fund the antipoverty efforts of local organizations or local federations. Unlike the case of urban renewal (Guttenberg, 1964; Glazer, 1966; Wilson, 1966b, pp. 489–558)—and possibly (by association) the latter phases of the Model Cities program,[33]—massive public resistance did not appear to be a complicating factor requiring ad hoc special consideration, at least not during the period covered by the data to be discussed. The cutoff date is April 1, 1966, because subsequent urban unrest and requirements of "participation by the poor" might have reduced the program's status as a relatively pure instance of interorganizational relations. At least until the cutoff date, the per capita number of poverty dollars that flowed into a city provided a very useful indicator of activity level between federal agencies and the organizations within each city (U.S. Office of Economic Opportunity, 1966).

Although—as will later be seen—the formation of elaborate local networks of organizations was encouraged under the poverty program, unaffiliated organizations such as schools, welfare agencies, municipal departments, legal aid societies, and labor councils could also receive funds. This meant that the extralocal aspect of interorganizational relations was not as likely to be affected by the presence or absence of local linkage or of local fragmentation as were, perhaps, Urban Renewal and the Model Cities programs. Indeed, the latter programs required explicit interorganizational coordination before funds were allowed. The fact that health facilities construction (Hill-Burton) monies were allocated at the state level, and only allocated to rural areas during the early years, made that program unsuitable for any study of interurban flow (*intra*-urban flow is another question, as will be seen later).

External linkage and poverty dollars. As suggested earlier, the amount of linkage between organizations in the city and one sector or set of sectors of the national networks of organizations can constitute the means of effecting linkage in other sectors where neither the fragmenting effects of extralocal linkage nor the possibility of a local instance of national conflict among organizations are at issue. Such was the case in the War on Poverty.

Accordingly, one would expect positive correlation between (1) the number of War on Poverty dollars received by the organizations within a city and (2) its external linkage measured by its economic complexity, the degree of its industrialization, and the number of national headquarters of voluntary associations. These expectations are partly confirmed by significant ($p < .02$ or better) product-moment coefficients (r) of .19, .21, and .31, respectively. However, correlations with the more local indicators of organizational complexity are sometimes even higher: They are .45 in the case of municipal scale and diversification and .32, .29, .38, in those of private schools, foreign stock, and Democratic voting, respectively.

The multiple regression analysis sought the effects of extralocal linkage by "holding constant" the values of the more local indicators of organizational complexity. For this reason, the results reported in the center columns of Table 7 provide a conservative test of the hypothesis. They include both the external headquarters measure and the more local indicator of municipal scale and diversification, in spite of more than moderate correlation (colinearity according to our methodological note in Chapter One and allowed only where conservation claims result) between the two: $r_b = .64$. This makes the observed contribution of each to the flow of federal poverty funds all the more compelling.

One cannot tell from these findings, however, whether municipal scale and diversification reflect unmeasured aspects of external linkage or whether their relationship to government funding merely indicates that larger and more diversified governments exceed others in their capacities to forge new links with outside organizations (one popular view is that big local government has easy access to big national government). Nevertheless, the number of national headquarters of voluntary associations had the predicted independent effect, one of uncertain magnitude (because of colinearity). Also, this is the only major case in which the more conservative results in parentheses constituted a substantive departure; here the effect of national headquarters is clearly the higher of the two, as predicted by the first of the two propositions about externally provided resources.

These ambiguities are capable of resolution if one recalls that certain federal poverty funds were granted *in response* to the formation of locally complex antipoverty networks. (See Chapter Four for detailed description of Community Action Agencies and their sponsorship of Neighborhood Youth Corps projects.) The two far

Table 7. Prediction over Time of Per Capita Federal Poverty Funding on the Basis of External Linkage, and on the Basis of Indicators of Organizational Complexity, "Need," and Demographic Variables Used for Purposes of Control (*N* = 130 Cities).

Predictor of Per Capita Federal Poverty Dollars to the City during 1964–1966	Estimated Zero-Order Correlation Coefficient, *r* (association before estimate)	Standardized Partial Regression Coefficient *beta* (before estimate of *r*'s)	
National Headquarters of Voluntary Associations, 1960	.31 (.31)[b]	.12 (.21)[b]	.19 (.20)[b]
Democratic Vote, 1960	.38 (.38)[b]	.22 (.25)[b]	.18 (.23)[b]
Education, 1960	−.34 (−.34)[b]	−.21 (−.24)[b]	−.02 (−.16)
Municipal Scale and Diversification in 1960	.45 (.34)[b]	.24 (.12)[a]	−.05 (.05)
Complex Local Antipoverty Network, 1964–1966	.61 (.44)[b]	— —	.52 (.26)[b]
Multiple Correlation, *R* (before estimate of *r*'s)		.55 (.53)[b]	.65 (.58)[b]
City-Wide Associations	.08 (.06)	.08 (.02)	−.13 (.01)[c]
Economic Complexity	.19 (.19)[b]	−.01 (−.01)	−.06 (−.03)
Industrialization	.21 (.21)[b]	−.03 (.00)	.01 (.01)
Age of City	.40 (.40)[b]	.00 (.04)	−.12 (−.03)
Population Size	.22 (.22)[b]	.00 (.00)	.02 (.00)
Private Schools	.32 (.32)[b]	.06 (.07)	.09 (.08)
Foreign Stock	.29 (.29)[b]	.06 (.09)	.11 (.11)
Nonwhite	.13 (.13)	−.03 (−.02)	−.11 (−.06)
Population Density	.33 (.33)[b]	.01 (.04)	.02 (.03)
Migration	−.32 (−.32)[b]	.09 (.07)	.08 (.09)
Poverty	.06 (.06)	.00 (−.02)	−.06 (−.05)

[a]Significant at the .10 level, based on association before estimates.
[b]Significant at *at least* the .05 level, based on association before estimates.
[c]The variables on the lower half of the table were added, alternated one at a time, to those that showed significant effects on the upper half. Unless mentioned, these additions did not alter the rank orderings of the *betas* describing the latter.

right columns in Table 7 show the effects of the number of national headquarters of voluntary associations to be strengthened, and that of municipal scale and diversification to *disappear,* once the presence or absence of these local networks is held constant. As in the case of community-wide associations, and as Chapter Four will claim, large-scale and diversified municipal governments are instrumental in providing local linkage for these networks. Thus, it is the *local* influence of municipal government that affected the external flow of antipoverty funds. And the city's external linkages contribute to such flow directly. The last of these effects was predictėd;.the first, though not in opposition to our theory, was not.

Of the other measures of organizational complexity, only the proportion Democratic in the county's two-party Presidential vote in 1960 had an effect. This could signify an ideological commitment to the War on Poverty or (as considered earlier) signify deprived ethnic minorities seeking federal assistance through their organizations. Indeed, low levels of education, *not poverty,* predicted poverty dollars; it might be that this variable also measured the presence of interested minority organizations, or even political patronage—itself a form of extralocal linkage.

Be that as it may, the lack of relationship between poverty (measured as reported in the footnote to Table 3) and poverty *funding* ($r = .06$; *beta* $= .00$) suggest that "demand" does not have much to do with what happened to the city. But several of the significant relationships on Table 7 suggest that organizations do.[34]

Regional aspects of organizational links and poverty dollars. The mean number of poverty dollars shown on Table 8 varied significantly among the five subregions ($p < .01$ by the Kruskal-Wallis test), being highest in the northeastern United States. It is in this subregion that correlation between number of national headquarters of voluntary associations and municipal scale and diversification proved to be the highest ($r_b = .89$); and the latter's association with poverty dollars also proved to be high (.63). Such colinearity (allowed only because it affects our hypotheses adversely) might account for the positive effect on the top half of Table 8 of the headquarters indicator of extralocal linkage everywhere but east. Note at the same time, however, that the municipal measure had *no effect* once the northeastern cities were ignored. Again, the lack of correlation in that region between industrialization and other extralocal indicators`makes interpretation difficult. Note also that the effect of socioeconomic status measured by educational level diminished both within and outside the industrialized region, so that this effect can possibly be ignored for reasons in addition to those already given. At the least, poverty funding tended to be high in regions where the educational level was low; whether these two facts are

Table 8. Prediction over Time of Per Capita Poverty Funding on the Basis of External Linkage and on the Basis of Indicators of Organizational Complexity, "Need," and Demographic Variables Used for Purposes of Control, Independently of the Effects of Region.

Per Capita Federal Poverty Dollars, 1964–1966	All Cities	Cities Located Outside of								Cities Located in
		NE	ENC	W	SW	SE	NE & ENC	W & SW	SW & SE	NE or ENC
Mean Rank of City	65.5	72.1	65.5	62.2	62.6	65.2	74.2	57.3	61.5	52.9
Standardized Partial Regression (beta) on:[a]										
National Headquarters of Voluntary Associations	.12	.28	.02	.00	.16	.12	.24	.04	.14	−.07
Democratic Vote	.22	.22	.14	.21	.16	.33	.15	.15	.25	.33
Education	−.21	−.21	−.20	−.14	−.21	−.24	−.06	−.13	−.20	−.12
Municipal Scale and Diversification (Above, all 1960)	.24	.01	.42	.44	.22	.14	.11	.41	.10	.37
Multiple Correlation, R[a]	.55	.46	.61	.60	.51	.58	.49	.54	.53	.55
Standardized Partial Regression (beta) on:[a]										
National Headquarters of Voluntary Associations, 1960	.16	.13	.20	.15	.20	.11	.18	.22	.14	.10
Democratic Vote, 1960	.17	.15	.17	.21	.09	.24	.15	.11	.15	.25
Complex Local Antipoverty Network, 1964–1966	.51	.51	.54	.47	.53	.47	.57	.46	.49	.37
Multiple Correlation, R[a]	.65	.62	.69	.64	.64	.65	.68	.60	.62	.56
Number of Cities	130	101	106	95	113	105	77	78	88	53

[a]Betas and R are based on estimated r's.

causally connected is moot. The top half of the table is reported only because it refines the initial, superseded analysis.

The second set of analyses on the lower half of Table 8 confirm, by region, the favored analyses reported in the last two columns of Table 7. Education and municipal diversification and scale were removed from the equation, because their effects proved to be insignificant in the face of those of the local antipoverty networks. The general pattern is upheld, with prediction the least accurate (as often before) in the northeastern and east north central cities. The effect of Democratic voting was strong outside of the southeastern cities, quite possibly because of the historical accidents that created and preserved remnants of the "solid Democratic South," thereby lending idiosyncratic meaning to the voting patterns of that region.

What is important to note, in reviewing this case of process between federal and local organizations, is that external linkage and local aspects of organizational complexity have proven capable of predicting new transactions between the city's organizations and ones outside. Thus, considering also our analysis of community-wide associations, comparative evidence exists both of the locally solidarity-inhibiting and of the resource-providing effects of inter-organizational linkage within the national network of organizations. Comparative evidence is also available that the extralocal provision of resources can even *rest on the absence* of locally fragmenting effects. This last will be considered further toward the end of Chapter Four.

Summing Up

From the Spencerian idea of social differentiation and from human ecology, interorganizational theory, and related thought, comes the unifying theme of interdependence. Organizations are specialized actors, and, by the very meaning of the word *specialization*, they are not self-sufficient, and therefore depend on the actions of other organizations, whose actions are also dependent, for their viability and even for their survival. Whether these mutually contingent actions are by way of providing the means of viability in terms of exchange or whether they threaten survival through competition or conflict, they nonetheless do constitute *interdependence*.

Organizations cluster because of their interdependence. Thus we noted that where any one kind of organization establishes itself depends in large measure on which other organizations, among ones already in the cluster, require or are required by the specialties it provides. The organizations that comprise the cluster—called *macrosocial unit* and measured here by *metropolis*—locate themselves on the basis of participation in a broader context of interdependence—from the standpoint of the cluster, interdependence that constitutes *external linkage*. We have found different kinds of external linkage to coexist, so that the number and variety of certain kinds of external links of the metropolis is associated with the number and variety of other kinds. Moreover, the more these externally linked organizations proliferate in number and variety, the greater the *organizational complexity* (by definition) of the macrosocial unit. This is characterized in Figure 1, which summarizes our formal theory of Chapter One, by considerable overlap between external linkage and organizational complexity in terms of the urban indicators that the two properties have in common.

By their very clustering, however, by the ensuing organizational complexity, organizations become interdependent with one another even if they have not been established on that basis. From interorganizational theory, we assume that organizations collectively lose predictability, and require various services not already extant, and have to cope with the plurality of interests and standards (emphasized by political scientists) that emerge from specialization. These common requirements appear in Figure 1 as hypothetical constructs in dotted boxes to the immediate right of "organizational complexity." These emergent kinds of interdependence generate common, Hobbesian demands for large-scale organizations within the macrosocial unit that specialize in its regulation and coordination. And the internal resources enabled by external linkage (say, for example, by the wealth of a branch automobile assembly plant that pays taxes) provide support for these internal organizations—here the city's government or its agencies. The variety of interests that organizational complexity betokens produces resistance, classic political pluralists and interorganizational theorists tell

Figure 1. External Relations, Social Complexity, Pluralism, and Solidarity of a Macrosocial Unit (here, the Metropolis) from an Interorganizational Perspective: Summary of Chapter Two.

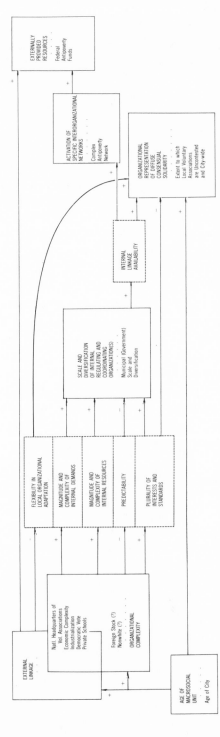

Key. Abstract properties of macrosocial units are in capital letters—in solid boxes if operationalized, in dotted boxes, if not. Lowercase letters are operational definitions of these properties in the special case of the metropolis. Arrows represent direction of causation. Plus and minus signs show direction of association.

us, to monolithic control, however; and the *scale* and *diversification of internal regulating and coordinating organizations* whose parts serve divers interests and add to complexity provides the necessary compromise. Hence, the four arrows drawn to this property on Figure 1.

Ingroup-outgroup theories, such as ones by Sumner and Marx, and theories of "mass society," suggest that external linkage is inversely associated with *organizational representation of diffuse consensual solidarity.* Here we say this occurs both because of the internal inflexibility of externally dependent organizations and because of the plurality of interests and standards that externally produced organizational complexity produces. Covariation followed prediction (see the respective arrows from "flexibility" and "plurality" to "consensual solidarity" on Figure 1). Quite unexpectedly, but consonant with the idea of regulation and coordination through the coalition-producing *availability of internal linkage* (this pluralist idea of decision and control by coalition will be developed further in subsequent chapters) the scale and diversification of internal regulating and coordinating organizations created by organizational complexity was found to be *positively* associated with the organizational representation of diffuse consensual solidarity. Also unexpected was the effect on the latter of the macrosocial system's age. This may betoken anachronisms from earlier times of Durkheimian mechanical solidarity, or may simply mean that it takes time for any social process to have its ultimate consequences.

External linkage, however, as the top line of Figure 1 shows, also provides resources other than those translated into the capacity for macrosocial power signified by internal linkage availability. These we call *externally provided resources,* which are employed in the macrosocial unit to solve what are defined as its problems. However, as our analysis of the effects of specific antipoverty networks shows, externally provided resources may also be contingent, indirectly, on internal linkage availability, which Chapter Four will show to be a function of scale and diversification of internal regulating and coordinating organizations as well as of the organizational representation of diffuse consensual solidarity.

The case for accounting for macrosocial structure and process on the basis of organizational patterings is strong to this point. With relatively minor exceptions, it has been possible (1) to elicit a broad dimension of organizational complexity on the twin bases of the locations of externally linked organizations and their covariant, the combined scale and diversification of municipal government; and (2) to assess the locally fragmenting versus the national resource-providing consequences of organizations that span the "mass society," as well as to introduce cases in which externally obtained resources were contingent on the absence of local fragmentation among organizations. Note the absence of strong, consistent, and pervasive confounding of all of this by the conventional demographic indicators that were employed. Although these latter indicators are widely discussed and employed in the contexts of urban sociology and comparative community research, the use of different indicators might, of course, have produced different results. So far, however, it would seem that to study urban society is to study its organizations.

Postscript: Interorganizational Perspectives on Social Consensus and Controversy

To recapitulate and develop a theme of this chapter that leads to those of the remaining chapters,[35] the organizations of an organizationally complex rather than barren macrosocial unit are interdependent (Dill, 1958; Emery and Trist, 1965; Form and Miller, 1960; Thompson, 1967; Warren, 1971; Warren, Rose, and Bergunder, 1974). Although organizations may have clustered according to unique, external, and noninterdependent interests—even to the extent that their primary orientations are toward some broader setting—they nevertheless probably have to take one another into account in some respects.

Such interdependence may take the form of a division of labor, in which the organizations are incapable of operating without one another; or it may be based on competition and conflict, in which one organization's attainment depends on another's nonattainment. Whatever the kind of interdependence, interdependent organizations require some form of regulation among them—either though interaction with still other organizations that control or mediate their relations with one another, or through the formation of such limited but direct affiliations with one another as federations.

Because conflict and competition, as well as cooperation, imply interdependence, in a certain sense these three forms of interaction among organizations of the macrosocial unit have more in common with one another than any one of them has either with organizational barrenness or with fragmentation (a state in which organizations exist in isolation and mutual nonresponse to one another). As suggested, however, the total fragmentation of a macrosocial unit is quite unlikely, unless it is so organizationally barren that its few organizations "rattle around" within it.

The very fact of plural interests that characterize interorganizational life can sometimes even promote harmony and consensus through the assurance that specialized and mutually interdependent goals may be realized without infringement by one (organizational) actor on the affairs of another. Yet, the multiorganizational macrosocial unit is mainly a *"fluid unit,"* characterized by shifting alliances, conflicts, and cross-cutting lines of mutual or opposing lines of specific standards and interests. It is also then a shifting mix of changing consensus and oppositions. Lest the discussion to this point be misleading, let us note that the fluid unit is not anomic, nor is it solely the system of competition and exchange one might later be led to believe from our pervasive emphasis on power, politics, and coalition formation. That organizational actors tend to be in partial conflict with one another does not belie the possibility of partial but enduring accord with respect to certain higher-level interests or standards. Certain of the reasons for such accord may now be made explicit.

Whatever broad interests and standards the community (*defined as locality relevant interactions*), the society, or any other macrosocial unit holds in common are mediated by organizations of all kinds, not only schools, mass media, and other socializing agencies. In a sample survey of a middle-sized city (Turk, Smith, and Myers, 1966), even casual or vicarious contacts with such of the city's organizations as its retail establishments, high schools, fraternal groups, mass media enterprises, and factories were taken as components of an index purporting to measure exposure to community standards. This index proved to be closely associated with the value-oriented act of voting in local elections (for when has an election ever been lost by one voter's staying in bed?). It has also been suggested that a high level of organizational complexity within a community, and therefore exposure to cross-cutting lines of conflict that tend to cancel one another out, means that common values may be mediated that mitigate the explosiveness of community conflict;[36] and it has further been suggested that the extent to which a community's values penetrate any one of its sectors is a function of the number and variety of organizations (Stinchcombe, 1965).

The very complexity of the organizational life of a macro-social unit may portend the extent of that unit's consensus about certain diffuse standards and interests; because each organization may carry within it a portion of the overall orientation of the total unit, which is likely to be *external* in its origins. That organizations can serve purposes other than those for which they are intended has generally been recognized. That they can play unexpectedly integrative, liaison, or value-mediating roles, has also been suggested (Maniha and Perrow, 1965). Other organizations—those that have been called "community decision organizations" (Warren, 1976b) such as health and welfare councils, health departments, antipoverty agencies, urban renewal authorities—may be deliberately constituted to provide integration among a set or sets of the community's organizations. Even though disparate interests and competition may characterize the organizations involved, it is still possible that they form coalitions or federations—those that are either permanent or transitory—that reflect the core of what they have in common (for example, see Moe, 1959). It is very likely that incorporation of these consensual elements constitutes the basis for any "winning coalition" that permits solution of problems at the level of community.

"Practicality" of Common Values. One kind of explanation for the association between organizational complexity and common standards and interests has its origins at least as far back as the social contract theory of the seventeenth century (Hobbes, [1651] 1881, pp. 91–96). Briefly stated: in order to prevent annihilation through the war of each organization against each other one, the organizational actors enter into "social compacts" in order that each may achieve its objectives at least in part. In this light, it may be suggested that—like other regulatory devices—common standards arise, with

increasing organizational complexity, that serve to increase predictability within an environment that no single organization is able to control (Emery and Trist, 1965; Terreberry, 1968); organizations have increasingly become aware of their lack of autonomy within the common setting and consequently of the obligations that arise out of their relations with one another (Form and Miller, 1960, p. 6). And organizational autonomy appears to vary inversely with the number of other organizations within the relevant environment (Evan, 1966). Generalizing from interindividual argument (Coleman, 1964), this self-interest approach to the problem of consensus also suggests that an enduring set of rules is most likely to occur amid shifting lines of conflict and alliance. Considerable diversification of interests, so that they may be distributed across organizations in several different ways, means that one organization can receive support of its own interest by another in exchange for supporting that other's interests. Perhaps only in this way can broad values such as "integrity" or "responsibility" arise to serve as rules that govern such exchange.

Cross-Cutting Organizational Affiliations and Diffuse Consensus. Overlapping memberships in organizations mean that participants are exposed to differing and sometimes conflicting points of view. This not only dampens divisiveness by creating cross-pressures within individuals, but also promotes their identification with the community (Coleman, 1957, p. 22, 1964; Parsons, 1959; Gamson, 1966). It also prevents organizations from attacking other organizations to which many of their members belong, and encourages them to emphasize what is held in common with these other organizations, or at least the rules of "living together" (Wilensky, 1958).

Organizational Mediation of Macrosocial Consensus. The production of consensus through social interaction is nearly a sociological truism at the interpersonal level. This may also be presumed to be true at the interorganizational level; namely, the greater the organizational density, the more extensive the interaction among the community's organizations, and therefore the greater the likelihood of consensus among them.

Perhaps the linkage among organizations that is most likely to promote their union into a "morally integrated" (Angell, 1947) or, alternatively, "oligarchic" community, however, is through the organization's governing body, which often conducts the organization's external relations. Boards of directors, trustees, regents, and the like are not only constituted on the basis of expertise in the affairs of the organization at hand, but they also feature political leaders, occupations of high prestige, and "leading citizens." This implies direct control over the organization by the macrosocial unit, by its external context, or by one of its subunits, which such powerful and prestigious persons represent (Parsons, 1960; Eisenstadt, 1965); and, from this, one might extrapolate that macrosocial standards pervade each organization that both prescribe and proscribe its relations with the other organizations of the social unit. In this manner, each organization may be assumed to mediate shared standards. A striking example has been provided in the case of a multi-hospital merger (Blankenship and Elling, 1962) that was approved by one of two hospitals best able to sustain themselves autonomously, because its board represented the leadership of the city, while the less representative boards of two fiscally precarious hospitals opted to stay out.

The Nature of Social Control. Specific organizations may not conform as much to the standards that they have incorporated in common with other organizations as they are *made* to conform by those others. Although tested only with persons as the social actors, this assertion is grounded at the macrosocial level in the implications of Durkheim's view of the symbolic significance of punishment and that by Weber on the legitimation of power (see Turk, 1965, for an exposition of these implications and of empirical findings to which they led). In brief, organizations act in terms of the unique and specific interests that each pursues and according to the respective standards of the unique constellation of interorganizational networks to which each belongs. Under these conditions, one might argue that each organizational act, although perhaps eminently "moral," may be the resolution of a unique and different set of standards; and the community values that are held in common might affect each organization's actions differently if the control that standards exercise is organizational *self*-control. Yet organizations tend to view *other* organizations only in terms of the specific standards that bind them together, and thus can unite with their fellows in concerted action, based on the same values, to control the potential deviate. Moreover, each organization's "investment" in self-control is far more costly, and therefore less likely, than the share of its "investment" in an "investment pool" to keep other organizations in line.

Collective Behavior and Interorganizational Relations. The public is characterized by discussion and controversy about an issue, while the mass is characterized by mutual isolation but similar reactions to a common object of attention (Blumer, 1939). Public opinion is formed within such organizational forums as the mass media or the Congress of the United States and has its impact on organizations—private as well as public—through its channeling via such organizations as polling institutes and election commissions. Mass opinion is ineffective, it has been found, unless there are organized means for its expression (Wiebe, 1952). A truly effective public opinion is formed where there are entities such as citizen committees, lobbies, interest groups, and clearinghouses to serve as organs for the channeling, mobilization, expression, and implementation of individual sentiments, however uniform and widespread such sentiment may be. The formation and expression of public opinion largely occurs through the interaction of formal groups, through leaders or officials that take stands on their behalf with reference to an issue. Much of the interaction through which public opinion is formed is through such clash of group views and positions (Blumer, 1948). And even the means of expression (for example, mass media, election machinery) are organizational.

A novel method has been devised for predicting the outcomes of community referenda (Form and Miller, 1960), which appears to have been influenced by an interorganizational interpretation of public opinion like the one just given. Arrangements among "the critically activated parts of the institutional power structure" (which appear to be organizational in the main) and the dispersion of stands taken by top influentials (who appear to stem from the community's various organizations, which range from business enterprise through church) provided the basic data. Thus, even the outcomes of referenda, which are organizationally enabled mass responses, also have organizational roots. A formal variant of this assertion will be discussed in the next chapter, in the form of protest against centralization of the macrosocial unit.

Notes

1. Such differentiation among cities and among the regions they comprise, has been discussed by Durkheim ([1893] 1933, pp. 188–189, 263). Duncan and Reiss (1950), Nelson (1955), Duncan, Scott, Lieberson, Duncan, and Winsborough (1960), Galle (1963), Winsborough, Farley, and Crowder (1966), Hawley (1971, pp. 220–231), Kass (1973). Also see note 9 (the discussion of population variables) in Chapter One. Hawley (1971, pp. 103–105, 224–227) considers each functional categorization of urban areas to be useful to only one or two problems, but he is still open to the idea of urban hierarchy in reviewing work by Vance and Sutker reported in 1954 and by Duncan and others, although anomalies were found.

2. Seeing similar implications in the work of Durkheim, Freeman and Winch (1957), have found complexity at the societal level to be, for the greater part, unidimensional.

3. Hawley (1950, pp. 104–105, 1971, p. 380) asserts that all cities are or tend to be alike in the distribution of goods and services to the local population as did Duncan and Schnore (1959) for communities of comparable size.

4. See Hawley (1971, pp. 219–240) for the use of banking activity in indicators of metropolitan dominance. Also see Vernon (1972) and Hoover and Vernon (1962, pp. 84–109) concerning the reasons that financial establishments settle in the metropolis.

5. Point made by Hoover and Vernon (1962, pp. 74–109) and Vernon (1972) with respect to corporate headquarters and financial establishments in New York City. Hawley (1971, pp. 169–170) suggests increasing concentration of organizations in central cities.

6. Confidence in this indicator is provided by correlations (r) of .89 and .87, respectively, with per capita number of employees in manufacturing and the per capita manufacturing payroll of 1958—also by its respective correlations of .74 and .40 with 1958 per capita employment rates in manufacturing durables and nondurables, rates that only yield an insignificant correlation of .11 with one another (U.S. Bureau of the Census, 1954, 1958). Using this measure, coded before later ones were available, serves to depress rather than inflate its correlations.

7. The mean industrialization rank of the northeastern and east north central cities was 35 compared to 86 (the lowest ranking city would have ranked 130) for the remaining cities, while the corresponding ranks

were 57 and 72 in the case of export and banking and 62 and 69 in the case of national headquarters. The first of these differences is highly significant (more than four times its standard error by the Mann-Whitney test), while the latter two fail even to approach significance (both are less than half their standard errors).

8. See, for example, Lineberry and Fowler (1967), Wolfinger and Field (1968), and Aiken (1970) for data-based assertions that nonwhites tended to lag behind other social categories as a political force.

9. Suggested to varying extent by Williams (1968), Dye (1968), Aiken (1970), and Aiken and Alford (1970). Elaboration of organizational ties within a community over time has also been suggested by Coleman (1957, 1966).

10. Isard (1956, pp. 57–58) suggests that the size of a city is partly associated with the number of activities within it. Citing Zipf (1949), in this context, the presence of every activity in each city is precluded by economies of scale; thus cities of different size emerge. Using different data, Hawley (1950, p. 203, 1971, pp. 135–136) suggests, without imputing cause, that the larger the place is, the greater is the amount of specialization that can be supported. Later (1973b), he explicitly viewed population size in general to be a function of the numbers of people needed to fill the growing diversity of (organizational) roles, and saw (federal) government action as meeting the needs of industrial society by increasing the number of consumers through improving living standards. Among generalization to which these observations point, as we have said, is Hawley's view of population problems as adjusting the population's size and its other characteristics to the personnel requirements of the social system. Also see Duncan and others (1960, p. 56).

11. A conservative estimate, considering the large correlations of the latter two variables with the headquarters measure. The corresponding partial r's with headquarters are .39 for age and .56 for size.

12. Note that the last three coefficients are only slightly higher than the zero-order correlations with headquarters. The independent effects of size and economic complexity on one another were even slightly negative; the partial correlation between size and age was only .12, and that between age and economic complexity (another organizational variable) .20. MacGillivray (1973) found our headquarters index to be almost perfectly correlated ($r = .96$), among 481 cities with 25,000 or more inhabitants, with a factor that was also based on wholesale receipts, retail receipts, value added by manufactures, bank deposits, population, and business services receipts. Also see Jiobu (1970, 1974), Freidman (1973 and in press), and Furnish (1975).

13. None of the standardized partial regression coefficients (*betas*) even approached the .10 level of significance; indeed, all of them, save in the case of foreign stock, were slightly negative.

14. Although there is ample literature defending the use of education as an excellent indicator of social status, pragmatic and empirical reasons are sufficient for present purposes. The first is that the special use made of the poverty rate later in the book opts against any income-based indicator here. Nevertheless, the poverty rate proved meaningful in this sense for so many of the subsequent analyses that it was included in all of them as an additional control. That rate did contribute heavily in socioeconomic status in the factor analyses described in Chapter One. Second, the multiple correlation (R) between education, on the one hand, and proportion of white collar workers in the labor force, median family income, and proportion of families with $10,000 or more income (U.S. Bureau of the Census, 1962a), on the other hand, is high (.88) and higher than that for each of these other variables with the remaining ones (.84 to .86).

15. In no case was the contribution of economic complexity (*beta*) altered by more than .01. Density yielded a *beta* that was not even significant and affected R only because of shared effects with age and size. Migration rates and education did produce moderate *betas*, but did not alter those for the three variables of theoretical interest—indeed, sharpened their apparent effects. High multicolinearity is responsible for these outcomes. Barring this, one might suppose that, controlling its economic complexity, age, and size, the city with national headquarters is a white-collar, part-bedroom city to which educated migrants are attracted ($r = .67$ between migration and education). Thus migration and the level of education may be consequences rather than causes. Whatever the case, these variables do not confound the main results.

16. For example, see Blalock (1963) and Gordon (1968). The problem of multicolinearity has been considered throughout the analyses reported in this book; explicit reference to it, however, will be reserved for cases in which it became relevant (see the methodological note in Chapter One).

17. Partly dictated by compromise between sociocultural homogeneity and the number of large cities, if any, in each state, the following groupings are used. *Northeastern:* Connecticut, Massachusetts, New Jersey, New York, Pennsylvania, Rhode Island; *east north central:* Illinois, Indiana, Michigan, Ohio, Wisconsin; *western:* Arizona, California, Colorado, Hawaii, Iowa, Kansas, Minnesota, Missouri, Nebraska, New Mexico, Oregon, Utah, Washington; *southwestern:* Arkansas, Louisiana, Oklahoma, Texas; *southeastern:* Alabama, District of Columbia, Florida, Georgia, Kentucky, Maryland, Mississippi, North Carolina, Tennessee, Virginia.

18. The chance expectation of the set of five subregional means is over .30 by the Kruskal-Wallis one-way analysis of variance for ranked data.

19. This observation has been made separately by Form and Miller (1960, p. 6), in writing about the industrialized community, and by Terreberry (1968), in writing about interorganizational fields.

20. In this sense government has attributes of what Hawley (1950, pp. 209–211, 216–221) called "categoric groupings." He failed to recognize the full implications of this in his discussion of dominance, which he attributed to the (sustenance-providing) unit that contributes most to the conditions necessary for the functioning of other units (Hawley, 1950, pp. 221–222). This unit may provide *resources* according to the previous pair of postulates, which then, however, must be translated into power by other units. See Parsons and Smelser (1956), *translated* to the case of the city in Laumann and Pappi's research (Laumann and Pappi, 1973; Laumann, Verbrugge, and Pappi, 1974). One must take into account here, among other factors, how much *interest* an organization has in regulating or coordinating the environment through its own efforts.

21. Formula in Gibbs and Martin (1962). This is a measure of dispersion that shows, *independently of how much* was spent, *how equally* expenditures were distributed across budget categories.

22. Suggested by synthesizing Williams (1968), Dye (1968), and Aiken and Alford (1970). The inverse association between a city's size and how narrowly specialized it is—claimed, among others, by Williams (1968)—suggests that the larger the city is, the more diversified are the services required of its government. Also see other references in our earlier discussion of population size in this chapter. Note that age and size of city have many other possible meanings and are used here only by way of control.

23. It bears repetition in that I use *system* (also *subsystem*) in its generic senses of interdependence among units and covariation among properties. Thus both conflict and harmony may be subsumed under this concept. See Turk (1973b).

24. Banfield and Wilson noted the existence of organizations like these (1963, p. 252), but failed to recognize their significance in this sense or, as we shall see later, the nature of their importance to community action.

25. For representative writings on voluntary associations and attendant literature review, see Goldhamer (1964), Babchuk and Edwards (1965). For voluntary associations as examples of categoric groupings according to common interests, look under the index entries for these terms in Hawley (1950, 1971).

26. Adopted to ensure comparability in the cases used from one analysis to the next, this scoring method tends to depress rather than inflate correlation with the other variables used as validating criteria, for some of the cities scored as having no community-wide associations—for

example, the twenty-six from which no replies were received or others where such associations just did not happen to be mentioned—might indeed have had them. But the bias is conservative in its effect, and resulted in understatement of regression results employing this indicator.

27. Consider Durkheim ([1893] 1933) and Freeman and Winch (1957) in conjunction with Greer and Orleans (1962), and review Note 25.

28. The mean response rate was 2.3 informants per city. Agreement was measured by Robinson's method (1957).

29. *Beta* = .01. Removal of this variable from the regression equation left multiple correlation at .26, approaching two-tailed significance at the .10 level.

30. See Note 26, discussing the conservative bias in its dichotomization. Also, Furnish (1975) has shown the inverse effect of national headquarters of voluntary associations to be strengthened appreciably when local voluntary associations of a manifestly recreational nature are removed from consideration as city-wide.

31. For example, see Clark (1975) concerning possible effects of Irish Catholic organizational ideology upon municipal scale.

32. The symbolic media of money, power, influence, and commitments are taken from Parsons (1968, 1971a) and here constitute an "accounting scheme" of flows and/or transactions between organizations.

33. That is why we have restricted ourselves to the early phases of public programs throughout this book.

34. Note that none of the remaining variables had a significant effect. Education, as we have already hinted and will pursue as a topic in Chapter Three, may betoken the (extralocal and local) organizational barrenness that accompanied a city's residential status. In support, note that the negative effect of education on antipoverty dollars disappeared once locally complex antipoverty networks were taken into account.

35. No primary data are used in this brief essay, which should be considered a rough sketch of thought and research findings that constitute some details behind the formal theory that interconnects Chapters Two through Five.

36. Coleman (1957) found that "organizational density," mainly among voluntary associations, tended to produce these effects.

Chapter Three

••••••••••••••••••••••
••••••••••••••••••••••••
••••••••••••••••••••••••

CENTRALIZATION, CONFLICT, AND DECISION NETWORKS

••••••••••••••••••••••••
••••••••••••••••••••••••
••••••••••••••••••••••••

*T*he *centralization* of the macro-social unit means that its regulation and coordination are effected by one or a few organizations that are closely tied to one another (whether or not in response to popular sentiment). But one of the main premises on which this book is based is that organizations exist in pluralist states of partial competition and conflict with one another as well as in states of partial cooperation. This means that organizations will resist domination by one or a few of their number—that is, resist centralization. Yet their interdependence, without predictability, as adversaries or in all kinds of exchange means that they require some means of effecting cooperation among them or resolving conflicts concerning specific issues, as Chapter Two has already argued. Large regulating and coordinating organizations with countervailing powers vis-á-vis one another and vis-á-vis private organizations constitute one possible response (that is, their scale and diversification, discussed in Chapter Two). Another possible response is macrosocial *de*centralization.

97

The greater the organizational complexity, the greater the plurality of interests and standards. The greater the plurality of interests and standards, the less the centralization. From these postulates follows the proposition: *The greater the organizational complexity, the less the centralization.* Corollaries of this proposition will be stated in this chapter as they are encountered in the case of metropoli, including ones that describe the structure of the actual decision process under conditions of (at least partial) pluralism.

Centralization, according to dialectical theories—such as those by Marx, Michels, and Dahrendorf already discussed—predict latent dissent against power wielders under conditions of centralization, and so do we here. The greater the centralization, the greater the polarization of interests between the organizations that dominate and the organizationally *barren* (that is, noncomplex) mass. The greater such disparity, the greater the dialectical conflict, once the opportunity arises. From these postulates, it follows that *the greater the centralization, the more likely is dialectical conflict.*

But the same pluralism induced by organizational complexity that opposes centralization also prevents opposition by the mass, because an organized mass has a plural structure of organizations that is unlikely to acquire the consensus and solidarity necessary for united opposition. The greater the organizational complexity, the greater the plurality of interests and standards and the more cross-cutting lines of conflict and accord. The greater this plurality, the less likely is dialectical conflict. The proposition that follows from these postulates is: *The greater the organizational complexity, the less likely is dialectical conflict.* This proposition will also lead to corollaries, as, in the course of the present chapter, we describe dialectical conflict in the large city.

Finally, in this chapter we will suggest that centralized and decentralized structure among a decision-making elite is actually patterned by centralization and decentralization among organizations. No specific proposition is offered in this instance except for the assertion made throughout the book, that macrosocial study, including that of influence, *is* interorganizational study, and evidence is provided from processes of actual decision making in some of our 130 large cities.

Pluralism in Interorganizational Relations

Certain of the contests that occur among organizations, as we already have implied, arise from conditions in which what seems to be a single social system is indeed many quasi-autonomous social systems; ethnic differentiation provides a case in point. In these instances, each social system tends to have its own organizations that promote its own interests and standards, possibly in terms of interaction among its representatives and their counterparts from other social systems (Weber, [1922] 1947, Turk and Lefcowitz, 1962; Pitkin, 1967; Etzioni, 1968, p. 103). Thus, that modern intersystemic differences are mediated through interaction between organizations is clear. However, highly integrated social systems, even ones that appear monolithic, also encompass conflicting interests and standards. Were these to be incorporated within single organizations, either certain of them would disappear entirely, or the organizations themselves might be incapacitated because of indeterminacy or conflict concerning what they should be doing (Litwack and Hylton, 1962). The separation between church and state in contemporary United States society provides a case in point, as does the separation between social rehabilitation and law enforcement. Indeed, overcoordination between agencies—say, in mental health (Black and Kase, 1963)—can mean the nonrealization of one or more specialized interests, even where these fail to be in direct conflict with one another. Budgetary limitations, for example, demand painful decisions.

That organizations tend to enter into conflict with one another at both the national and the local community level is evident from studies of urban renewal controversies, hospital planning, and poverty programs (see, for example, Belknap and Steinle, 1963; Wilson, 1963; Moynihan, 1969, pp. 102–127). But, as has already been said in Chapter Two, organizations may be linked to one another by struggle and at the same time by nonproliferation treaties of the means of mutual destruction.

What this means is that even integration among a pair of organizations is a situation-specific abstraction—as it is in the case of any set of social actors in all but the most undifferentiated of social settings—not a unique and concrete event. The organizational units may exhibit cooperation in certain respects and competition in others, as in the cases of other kinds of social relationships. Moreover, the one instance need not have anything to do with the other. For example, even governments at war with one another have some integrative relations mediated between them, sometimes by other organizations, such as the International Red Cross. This point may also be illustrated at the local level in the problems faced by community consultants, who must make clear to community groups that they have some kinds of problems in common that require cooperative problem solving, even though they may also have other difficulties that are mutually threatening (Moe, 1959). Current concepts having to do with an organization's environment, such as that of "organization set,"[1] can be extended to encompass the multiple relations like these that any one organization may have with another.

Organizations probably surpass individuals in their ability to maintain the dual relationships of conflict and cooperation with one another, because different situations involving the same organizations may involve different specialized representatives (Turk and Lefcowitz, 1962; Freeman, 1968). Thus, interorganizational relations in contemporary, complex society may even be more compartmentalized or segmental than interpersonal relations. Competition is even less likely in the case of organizations than in that of persons to preclude cooperation outside the sphere of competition.

Decentralization of Interorganizational Relations

Nevertheless, the same dualism can account for the observation that interorganizational relations tend to be *horizontal rather than hierarchical,* and to be issue specific rather than to broadly encompass a variety of issues and situations.[2] Thus the claim is not surprising that in the modern urban community, composed of organizations, decision making is for the greater part *decentralized,* as well as confined to participants who are largely specialists (see the studies on urban politics reviewed by Sayre and Polsby, 1965; also Bell, 1973).

The nonhierarchical nature of interorganizational relations and their bases of only partial accord mean that organizations will oppose any attempts to enact or to dominate their relations with one another. Even strong machine-supported heads of city government, for example, generally use their powers to endorse action only after conflict has ended (Sayre and Kaufman, 1960; Banfield, 1961) or to help table unresolved issues (Greer, 1967). And modern societies tend to be republics or unions of republics. Thus, our first proposition about the inverse association between centralization and organizational complexity has been explicated.

Linkage Availability and Decision by Coalition. The nonhierarchical nature of interorganizational relations does not mean that all organizations are alike in the influence that they can exert or that there is no flow of influence at all in the decentralized and situation-specific environment we have described. Nor does the improbability that one organization can fully dominate the others imply that linkage among organizations is not affected by an organization's power, because if power were fully diffused, the macrosocial unit would be incapable of mobilizing itself, be unable to take collective action. That is why we study reasonably *large* organizations.[3] Rather, it is more real to say that the multiorganizational environment affects the *way* in which power is used to provide linkage.

Action at the city level is likely to depend on the number and variety of linkages between power centers[4]—which we have modified to refer to actual or potential relations between large organizations (not, say, gasoline stations, neighborhood stores, or small museums)—available for the formation of *coalitions* within the community.[5] To be sure, the effects of certain interorganizational linkages are lasting.

The organizations that have contributed the most to the availability of linkage in any given issue do so in part on the basis of the permanent coalitions that they had been instrumental in producing or the latent connections that exist as the residues of coalitions that had been formed in the past;[6] they do so also on the basis of their current linkages. At the societal level, decisions allegedly are modified through "countervailing power" or, according to contesting theory, implemented by "military-industrial" coalitions (Mills, 1956; Galbraith, 1958; contrast with Lieberson, 1971).

Thus, power is generated for the macrosocial unit to the extent that organizations seek to effect *political* solutions by causing "winning" coalitions to prevail. This means the mobilization of support among a wide variety of organizations in sometimes temporary, sometimes changing alliances. Under these conditions, an organization's influence would be measured by its capacity to effect winning coalitions in a wide variety of issues. Rather than attempting to *enforce* linkages by imperative, the organization would influence or retain them through bargaining, adjudication, conflict resolution, and participation in alliances. These political processes imply not only that the organization's tangible resources but also that some of the very *interests* it pursues are *negotiable* (more about this later). Under decentralized conditions, power can be challenged by organizational coalitions, and therefore can effectively produce linkages only when the power-wielding organization is part of a coalition itself or uses power to provide some other means of coalition formation or coalition retention.

The more any of the society's or local community's organizations base their action on expectation of fundamental consensus with other organizations concerning either collective need or the extent and manner of its satisfaction, or the more they base their action on the unswerving premise that they are right, the less able they are to attain their objectives through linkage with other organizations. Organizations that pursue absolute values under conditions of organizational complexity lack not only the power to enforce their purposes on other organizations, but also the means with which to bargain for coalitions among them, because whatever is considered nonproblematic or is pursued unswervingly is nonnegotiable. This might be why regulating and coordinating organizations of such a character tend to be fragile and to avoid responsibility for certain decisions.

Centralization and Consensus. The less the organizational complexity, as Chapter Two has shown, the greater the organizational representation of diffuse consensual solidarity. The greater such consensus, the more the legitimation of the regulating and coordinating organization. The more the legitimation of the regulating and coordinating organizations, the more centralized the macrosocial unit can be—and therefore is. From these postulates follows a corollary to the main theorem about low organizational complexity and decentralization: *The greater the organizational representation of solidarity and diffuse consensus, the greater the centralization.* This is *not*, however, to be confused with mass consensus. Furthermore, because consensus is a necessary, thought not sufficient, condition for *social stratification among organizations,* and because pluralism impedes stratification, and because both stratification and centralization are elitist and mutually supportive, the following additional corollary may be stated: *The greater the organizational stratification, the greater the centralization.*

The "Reform" Government Measure of Municipal Centralization. In the United States, certain municipalities have become centralized. Called *reform government,* and nonpartisan in its nature and administered by a paid official, this form of government purportedly represents and has control over all sectors of the community. Although the old commission form of government has also been designated by the adjective *reform,* it appears to have been overshadowed by the city manager form, under which the council acts like a board of corporate directors and which has been described as the most centralized of all (Schnore and Alford, 1963). It has been suggested that reform governments act as though the city were essentially like a business with few conflicts of interest (Schnore and Alford, 1963). One-party government may be similar to reform government in its consequences (Greer, 1962b), but systematic evidence is lacking.

It should follow from our discussion and findings about organizational complexity and the ensuing plurality of interests and standards that where a central organization based on expectations of consensus and absolute values is permitted even a modicum of dominance, other organizations must be weak or be few in number and variety. For this to happen, in other words, an organizationally *barren,* rather than an organizationally complex environment would have to prevail.

It is likely that both reform government and, at least the one-party governments of the Southeast, tend to be monopolistic rather than public oriented, notwithstanding the intent of civic organizations that are said to have impelled their rise (Bollens and Schmandt, 1965). Indeed, it may well be that reform government signifies a monolithically organized sector of the population where other sectors such as ethnic minorities, lower social classes, and residents of "bedroom communities" have no organizations of their own. It is possible, though not documented, that reform government is what some downtown merchants' associations institute wherever they are unopposed.

Where there is reform government, then, one might find a "mass community," which is a product of locality specialization and has become little more than a living place. Only a modicum of its inhabitants' interests are held by such a community—the others are largely fractionated and outwardly oriented. The structure is one of an elite composed of the few whose livelihoods or governmental careers are involved in the community and a large unorganized mass of individuals whose organizational ties tend to be outside the community (Coleman, 1966). Under such conditions of low organizational complexity, centralized governmental organization is possible, according to our own view.

The community literature indicates that power tends to be monopolistically, pyramidally, or monolithically organized to the extent that the community is *autonomous*—that is, independent of outside influences, such as more embracing governments or absentee control of economic enterprises (Gilbert, 1968; Walton, 1968; Warren, 1970). This probably occurs because multiple outside interests, such as those signified by our indicators of external linkage and of organizational complexity, maximize both the pluralism brought about by conflicting organizational goals and inflexibility in local adaptation (Chapter Two). The elements of reform government, which follow, mean centralization by ignoring the partisanship that pluralism produces.

Where there are few organized influences—either internal or external—the "corporate" nature of the city and the presumption of consensus are not only facilitated through the authority of a city manager but are also assured by nonpartisan election of the city council. This aspect of reform government is likely to mean that the noncentralized structures of those organizations called *political parties* are weak and incapable of serving their primary functions of engaging in exchanges of values and interests to the point at which various social cleavages are encapsulated in coalition form under a few simplified issues.[7] Under nonpartisan conditions, such possibly contesting institutional sectors of the community as business or labor are not visibly represented.

The third and final aspect of reform government is the election of council members "at large" rather than from separate districts. This again means the absence of sharp and decentralized representation, this time of the organizations of specific neighborhoods and of the ethnic and socioeconomic categories that populate them.

In sum, reform governments are centralized and based on presumed consensus. According to interorganizational theory, community centralization occurs where organizations are weak and few in number; and the presumption of consensus can exist only where organizations are lacking to express divers interests.

Cities having any two of the following attributes were considered municipally centralized: nonpartisan elections, council elected at-large (not by district), and government by a city manager. Seventy-one cities were centralized in these respects; fifty-nine were not (based on 1962 data found in Nolting and Arnold, 1963). Data were lacking to consider the possible political fragmentation of cities holding partisan elections but having virtually one party (Greer, 1967; Greenstone and Peterson, 1968). Also, certain governmental and electoral forms are determined by state law rather than by community structure and, perhaps for this reason, are sometimes cirvumvented in fact, although not in name.[8] Nonetheless, combining the three features into a four-point index (see Clark, 1971; compare with Lineberry and Fowler, 1967) yielded an estimated Spearman-Brown reliability coefficient of .75 for the 130 cities studied here; the dichotomous version actually used should have even greater reliability. Dichotomization minimized the effects of state law on municipal forms and also allowed for the possibility that decentralization by party or district organization lends strength to mayor *or* to city-manager governments (see Rosenthal and Crain, 1966; Crain and Vanecko, 1968; J. Wilson, 1968; Crain, Katz, and Rosenthal, 1969, p. 182) by aggregating interests and subsuming numerous issues under a few broad ones— as we have noted—so that the administrators, on whose popularity such organizations are dependent (Banfield, 1961, pp. 245–250), may be buffered from the electorate.[9] But even "strong" mayors act more by effecting interorganizational alliances and endorsing interorganizational outcomes than they do by fiat.[10] And certain powerful organizations may only appear to be inactive, whereas their anticipated opposition might actually prevent certain issues from ever arising. In short, this indicator of municipal centralization is a conservative one, and more refined measures are likely to show even higher associations with other variables, in the future, than the associations to be reported.

Municipal Centralization and Organizational Complexity. To recapitulate our first proposition, the more organizationally complex (therefore, the more pluralist) the city, the less the municipal centralization—that is, the less "reformed" its government. Among the 130 cities, economic complexity is inversely but not significantly related to centralization ($r_b = -.15$), but industrialization is—and also in the expected direction ($r_b = -.41$). Expectation is also confirmed in the case of municipal scale and diversification ($r_t = -.36$), which is not only a consequence of and contributor to organizational complexity, as we have seen, but a substitute indicator of municipal decentralization as well.[11] Further confirmation is provided by two of the most general measures of organizational complexity: r_b is $-.26$ in the case of national headquarters of voluntary associations and $-.44$ in that of age of city.

Of the measures of ethnic and other population heterogeneity, the strongest confirmation occurs in the case of the one most clearly organizational: $r_b = -.54$ in the case of pupils in private schools.[12] Expectations are also upheld in the cases of foreign stock ($r_b = -.31$) and the Democratic vote ($r_b = -.16$), but proportion nonwhite did not make a difference ($r_b = .00$).

At first population size did not appear to be correlated with municipal centralization ($r_b = -.01$); but once its high association with number of national headquarters of voluntary associations is taken into account ($r = .71$), its *positive* association with centralization becomes apparent (partial $r = .26$). In other words, *lacking organizations,* the more people there are, the more likely municipal centralization becomes, quite possibly because the unorganized many can more readily be controlled than the unorganized, but less anonymous few.

Municipal Centralization and City-Wide Associations. City-wide associations, we have suggested, occur where organized dissensus fails to exist; and, because "reform" is based on at least the illusion of consensus, one might expect confirmation of the first corollary proposition, which predicted correlation between the extent of such voluntary associations and municipal centralization. Moreover, direct association between civic groups and the "reform movement" has been reported (for example, see Banfield and Wilson, 1963, p. 249). Finally, voluntary civic associations have been conceived by some as political forces (Williams and Adrian, 1959; Rossi, 1961; Greer and Orleans, 1962) that reflect elite attempts to regain power after having been outvoted (Rossi, 1960). Reform government may be seen in a similar light.[13] The expected correlation resulted; the more uncontested and city-wide a city's voluntary associations, the more centralized its government ($r_t = .27$).

Municipal Centralization and Stratification Among Hospitals. According to the second corollary, the more salient *stratification* is among the city's organizations[14] the greater the municipal centralization, because, as we have shown in previous discussion, government reflects the rest of the community's organizational structure. Elitist organizational arrangements in one sector should support those in another, even if both are effects of the absence of organizational complexity.

Hospitals yield excellent data for the salience of organizational stratification. Although privately controlled for the greater part, and constituting only a small fraction of the community's organizational life, health care establishments tend to be considered far more in the public (city) domain than are most of the organizations within other nongovernmental spheres. It is therefore quite likely that hospitals constitute a set of organizations whose elements at least in part reflect or contribute to the basic outline of any dominant stratification system that the city might have. Moreover, the universal commitment to health among modern communities— including those in the United States—suggests at least a modicum of comparability across regional, state, and municipal boundaries. Despite the importance of health issues to the community, and despite high-level and long-term community commitment to hospitals, local concern has rarely been explosive. Therefore, several confounding factors that might have been introduced by considering newer, more transitory, and more volatile multiorganizational phenomena can be avoided by studying stratification systems in terms of these particular health care institutions. Although the criteria for determining hospital prestige may be universal—the degree to which the prestige order is articulated by the community or becomes salient to its actions depends on other sectors within the community and should provide a good, although indirect, indicator of how stratified the city is in general.

Using 1960 operating expenses per patient day as the criterion of a hospital's prestige, T. Turk (1970) provided scores for each of the 130 cities according to the *correlation* (*gamma*) between (1) the prestige of the nationally accredited short-term general hospitals within it and (2) how much money the community allocated (from 1947 to 1968) to each such hospital under the Hill-Burton Act.[15] For example, if a given city had three hospitals, among which the most expensive one received the most Hill-Burton money and the least expensive one the least money, that city has a score of 1.00 and is rated high in the salience of its organizational stratification system. Prestige-based hospital support suggests an elitist community with few organizations to oppose the stratification system and, therefore, may also be expected to affect municipal centralization positively—as it does ($r_b = .21$).

Regression Analysis of "Reform" Government. Considering the foregoing effects simultaneously leads to the results on Table 9. Three separate analyses, however, were conducted first; because high intercorrelations between number of national headquarters of voluntary associations, scale and diversification of municipal government, and age of city precluded their use in the same equation. All three broad indicators of organizational complexity remained inversely associated with municipal centralization ("reform" government). Of the three, the independent effect of headquarters was largest, once population size was taken into account (*beta* = −.33 versus −.20 and −18). The problem of colinearity with respect to the headquarters measure as well as its confounding by population size was solved by an indicator of organizational complexity *relative to* population size (subtracting each city's population rank from its rank according to the number of national headquarters of voluntary associations).[16]

Table 9. Accounting for Municipal Centralization ("Reform" Government) on the Basis of Organizational *Non*complexity, Organizational Stratification, City-Wide Associations, and Demographic Variables Used for Purposes of Control (N = 130 Cities).

Predictor of Municipal Centralization ("Reform" Government)	Estimated Zero-Order Correlation Coefficient, r (association before estimate)	Standardized Partial Regression Coefficient, *beta* (before estimate of r's)
National Headquarters of Voluntary Associations Relative to Population Size	−.33 (−.26)[b]	−.23 (−.19)[b]
Private Schools	−.54 (−.43)[b]	−.41 (−.33)[b]
Education	.39 (.31)[b]	.28 (.22)[b]
Organizational Stratification (Prestige-Based Hospital Support)	.21 (.17)[b]	.22 (.17)[b]
City-Wide Associations	.27 (.17)[b]	.20 (.13)[b]
Multiple Correlation, R (before estimate of r's)	.71 (.56)[b]	
Municipal Scale and Diversification	−.36 (−.21)[b]	−.09 (−.04)[c]
Age of City	−.44 (−.35)[b]	−.07 (−.05)
Economic Complexity	−.15 (−.12)	.01 (.01)
Industrialization	−.41 (−.33)[b]	.03 (.02)
Foreign Stock	−.31 (−.25)[b]	.27 (.19)[a]
Nonwhite	.00 (.00)	.11 (.09)
Democratic Vote	−.16 (−.13)	.14 (.11)
Population Density	−.37 (−.29)[b]	.12 (.08)
Migration	.58 (.46)[b]	.23 (.18)
Poverty	.20 (.16)[a]	.04 (.04)

[a]Significant at the .10 level, based on association before estimates.
[b]Significant at *at least* the .05 level, based on association before estimates.
[c]The variables on the lower half of the table were alternated into the regression equation one at a time. Unless mentioned, their introduction did not alter rank ordering of the *betas* on the top half of the table.

It may be seen from Table 9 that, of the other indicators of organizational complexity, only that of private schools had an independently inverse effect.[17] Age of city and municipal scale and diversification no longer had effects independent of that of headquarters (latter relative to population size).[18] The positive effects of city-wide associations and organizational stratification (prestige-based hospital support) remained much as before.

Introduction of the control variables shows a not fully unexpected positive effect of education on "reform" government.

Several possibilities account for this. Because of a moral commitment to "serve" the public[19] or—as already suggested—because of the increasing power of minorities, reform government appears to be favored by the middle and upper socioeconomic strata (Banfield and Wilson, 1963, pp. 138–186; Schnore and Alford, 1963; W. Hawley, 1974). Yet education is also inversely associated with industrialization ($r = -.46$), nonwhite ($-.33$), and population per square mile ($-.38$). Thus this variable might also signify the organizational barrenness of bedroom suburbs—already alluded to in our discussion of the mass community—or the lack of organizations among lower strata, whose members join voluntary associations at lower rates (see for example, Wright and Hyman, 1958; Williams and Adrian, 1959; Greer and Orleans, 1962; Hyman and Wright, 1971).[20] This latter interpretation follows from our theory of decentralization. The remaining demographic variables failed to have any effect.[21]

The Effects of Region. Examining the effect of relative organizational complexity (and the other effects that stayed significant) independently of region fails to disturb the main results, in spite of highly significant differences in municipal centralization among the five subregions ($p < .001$ by the chi-square test). As in other cases, prediction is least efficient in the industrial region—and the same speculation applies—the pattern remains the same as in other regions.[22] City-wide associations appear to be most closely related to municipal centralization among the western and southwestern cities, but not compellingly so.

Over half of the variation in municipal centralization can be explained, much of it in terms of organizational indicators of complexity, consensus, and stratification. The positive effect of population size on centralization, once the former no longer indicated organizational complexity, was unexpected, but also affirms our idea that centralization occurs in unorganized populations.

Although technical comparison is difficult, our own five predictors within a restricted range of cities appear to account for more of the variation in reform government than did a recent study of all 243 central cities that employed all of the 11 *demographic* variables (plus region) used in other studies of reform government (Dye and MacManus, 1976). Separate predictions were made of the respective elements of the centralization measure we used here.

Table 10. Accounting for Municipal Centralization ("Reform" Government) on the Basis of Organizational Complexity, Other Indicators of Centralization, City-Wide Associations and Demographic Variables Used for Purposes of Control, Independently of the Effects of Region.

Municipal Centralization ("Reform" Government)	All Cities	Cities Located *Outside* of								Cities Located in
		NE	ENC	W	SW	SE	NE & ENC	W & SW	SW & SE	NE or ENC
Percent of Cities Centralized	55	63	60	46	53	50	74	42	47	26
Standardized Partial Regression (*beta*) on:[a]										
National Headquarters of Voluntary Associations Relative to Population Size	−.23	−.28	−.25	−.27	−.21	−.19	−.30	−.24	−.15	−.15
Private Schools	−.41	−.37	−.39	−.46	−.43	−.39	−.25	−.47	−.40	−.34
Education	.28	.27	.31	.12	.31	.30	.29	.16	.33	.23
Prestige-Based Hospital Support	.22	.37	.12	.23	.21	.18	.31	.23	.16	.17
City-Wide Associations	.20	.20	.21	.19	.14	.24	.26	.13	.20	.23
Multiple Correlation, R[a]	.71	.70	.71	.71	.72	.72	.57	.69	.73	.45
Number of Cities	130	101	106	95	113	105	77	78	88	53

[a]*Betas* and R are based on estimated r's.

All of the same variables (or slightly different versions) appear on the tables of the present book, except for rate of population growth and percent in white-collar occupations. Moreover, the rank ordering of variables according to the contribution made by each (possibly also the direction of such contribution) varied markedly when intraregional prediction was attempted in that demographic study. The results, unlike ours, eluded substantive theory.

Organizational Bases of Dialectical Conflict

Even settings that are polarized into active contest between social categories—whether the base is economic, generational, occupational, or ethnic—are most likely to be characterized by conflict among their organizations. Marx and Engels' ([1888] 1959) discussion of the development of class solidarity has been taken as part of Lenin's organizational strategy of revolution (see Selznick, 1952) as we have suggested, in which organizations are deemed to be potential proponents of revolutionary ideologies. The directors of revolutionary organizations might then be prominent members of dissident subsectors of the society. Indeed, the "mass movement" may be little more than a latent interest group (term by Dahrendorf, 1959, pp. 182–189) that is unopposed in the claims it can make on the loyalty of its members.

Although the fact of organizational proponents appears to dampen the heat of controversy prior to referenda by providing numerous cross-cutting allegiances—both within and between organizations (Coleman, 1957, p. 21; Parsons, 1959; Turk, Smith, and Myers, 1966; Clark, 1968a, p. 111)—or mediation with "mass government " (Greer and Orleans, 1962), their absence seems to make polarization and mass protest most likely (Kornhauser, 1959, pp. 99–100). Social movements and revolutions appear to occur where large numbers of individuals experience similar discomfort within some single organizational setting where rapport among individuals is not impeded by conflicting allegiances. Perhaps this accounts for the rapid diffusion of organized student protests of the 1960s and 1970s—against the large-scale educational and other organizational "establishment"—because the student role overshadows all other organizational participation. It may also account for the peasant revolts that have occurred throughout history—because rural areas tend to be organizationally barren. Indeed, domestic class struggles seem to occur more frequently in agrarian or developing nations than they do in the more organizationally complex industrial societies that place conflicting demands on persons within all strata. As protest organization becomes more diversified—that is, organizationally complex—the conflict diminishes (as in the American case of student protest).

An exception, more apparent than real, to this last observation occurs among persons having one societal position that overshadows and influences all other positions held. An example is racially determined minority status in the United States. Here deprivation along racial lines appears to have existed in almost all of society's institutionalized sectors: economic, educational, recreational, and so forth. In such cases, organizational complexity might actually intensify the experiencing of such deprivation and the enhancement of racial rapport. Other investigations of our 130 cities revealed that the *less segregated* nonwhites were, both residentially and occupationally, the more likely was unrest to have occurred, and the greater the external linkage and organizational complexity of a city—here interpreted as the more intense the nonwhite experience—the more probable this mass protest. (Jiobu [1970, 1971] hinted at these ideas, although his terms were different.)

Deductions, in the case of metropoli, from these modifications of classic dialectical conflict theory follow, together with reports of their applicability to our 130 large cities.

Conflict in the Mass Community

The two propositions about dialectical conflict that were stated at the beginning of this chapter have been given substance in American localities. Instances in which associations are not available to mediate between populations and whatever organized sectors of the community there are dramatize the import of organizational forms for contemporary social life. Cases have been cited in which mass communities—composed as they are of an unorganized citizenry and a small, almost isolated governing body—experienced collective uprisings against the government position (Coleman, 1966), which presumably were sparked by splinter organizations that experienced little opposition in their enlistment of "mass" (unorganized) sentiment. Appeals to sentiment, whether by individuals or by organizations, appear to have their greatest effects where such appeals are organizationally unopposed (Turk, 1971a).

Political parties and ward organizations serve to counter extreme appeals by replacing the mass with organization. In the United States, at least, these organizations not only acquire their power from various organized cleavages in an organizationally complex community (Wolfinger and Field, 1968; Turk, 1973b), with which our analysis of "reform" government has shown them to covary, but are also suited, as we have said, to the accommodation of interests under the conditions of bargaining and contest appropriate to a multiorganizational community. They are concerned with the bringing together of whatever set of interests and values will bring about a winning coalition—the one between government and party.

This, as we have noted in our discussion of "reform" government, means that local party and ward organizations emphasize conflict resolution among the groups subsumed under their respective labels through the means that they use to bring together similar interests, encapsulate various social cleavages under a few broad ones, simplify issues through compromise and exchange of support, and otherwise mold issues to a form in which they can be dealt with. Their precinct and ward units, as well as their points of contact for such nongeographically based organizations as business or labor (Rossi and Cutright, 1961) may be conceived as differentiated accommodators to—that is, coalitional linkage producers with—whatever organized interests and values there are within the zone of contact. They may be seen also as bargainers and contestants at the next highest level of organization, where conflicts are resolved, and where they are rivals for the material inducements (for example, patronage, favors, and even money) and value exchanges (for example, campaign "planks") necessary to facilitate such accommodation.

Parties tend to avoid extreme positions, while at the same time paying close attention to the interests of various segments of the community (Banfield, 1961, pp. 235–250, 1965, pp. 12–14). Comparative data suggest greater responsiveness of municipal revenues and municipal expenditures to popular demands—that is, those signified by such factors as class and ethnic composition and residential types—under strong party and ward systems than under weak ones (Lineberry and Fowler, 1967; Turk, 1973b).[23]

Recall that, in addition to aggregating interests, political parties also serve as buffers between the local government and the electorate. The coalitions that they forge as the result of trading in material inducements and the promotion of values enable them to support the actions of any government they might place into power. Nor is the provision of support likely to be costly to the party, for the electoral process makes majority opposition to elected government unlikely, and minority opposition must seek the party's aid if it is to be effective. One might suggest that municipal government's great freedom to initiate action under strongly partisan conditions is not to be taken as centralization but is rather caused by the stable coalition it has formed with the political party. The party itself already reflects an elaborate system of coalitions by way of its aggregation of organized interests. Although our own measure of partisanship-nonpartisanship is gross, this grossness serves to increase predictive error and therefore makes predictive success all the more compelling.

The alternative to party-ward government, it will be recalled, is "reform" government, entailing at-large nonpartisan elections or appointed professional officials such as city managers. Centralized, and presumably based on ideological assumptions of underlying consensus or "correct, nonpolitical solutions" of problems—assumptions sometimes challenged by organized nonelites (Schnore and Alford, 1963)—the tenure of its various members (official persons) whose power rests on appointment or plebiscite rather than on party loyalties and party support) might actually be more fragile, as we have suggested, than that of members of less centralized governments characterized by conflict and compromise. There is an apparent paradox that cities characterized by organized political pluralism can accomplish more than those that appear to have monolithic governments without organized opposition. The absence of strong grass-roots political organization means that certain interests go unexpressed and unrepresented unless and until mobilized in a polarized situation. It also means that reform government can easily be dispossessed as the result of incendiary action by an organized minority and that therefore it will avoid controversial, hence important, issues (Banfield and Wilson, 1963, pp. 165–167).[24] Indeed, the fear of creating organized opposition among an apathetic mass where there has been none may be the reason that "reform" governments exceed other governments in their tendencies to seek ratification of their policies through referenda—which are themselves, be it noted, *organizationally* enabled means of mass action. And, lacking coalition with any political party, such governments tend towards impotence in affecting voting behavior.

What all this means is that the organizationally barren, mass city is likely to be the most volatile of all in a Marxian sense—given some organized means of expressing dissent—because it does not possess the dampening and consensus-promoting mechanisms of cross-cutting internal linkages or the organizational mediation of the community's norms and value orientations (see Postscript to Chapter Two). This is the meat of one of the two main propositions about dialectical conflict stated at the beginning of this chapter, to be applied here to cities. Where there is centralized and rigid hierarchical control in addition, the result may be alienation from the municipal government and receptivity to the appeals of extremist organizations, or so it would appear (Coleman, 1957; Gamson, 1961; Simmel, 1961; Horton and Thompson, 1962; McDill and Ridley, 1962). And this gives substance to the rest of that formal argument.

Under these circumstances, government is powerless. It is without the interest-aggregating and buffering effects of political parties (these themselves strengthened by the partial cleavages produced by organizational complexity). But without large scale and diversification, which also make local linkage available for coalitions, as we assumed to be the case in Chapter Two and shall develop in Chapter Four, local government is equally powerless. This partly post-factum line of reasoning leads to the following postulates. The greater the scale and diversification of the regulating and coordinating organizations or the more centralized the macrosocial unit, the less the availability of internal linkage. The less the availability of internal linkage, the fewer the cross-cutting lines of conflict and alliance. And the fewer such cross-cutting lines, the more likely is dialectical conflict. These postulates produce the following corollary to our main proposition: *The greater the scale and diversification of the regulating and coordinating organizations,* or *the greater the centralization, the more likely is dialectical conflict.*

Recall that scale and diversification of regulating and coordinating organizations can also be considered an indicator of centralization, which provides the fuel for protest according to dialectical theory. Thus the corollary we have just stated could have been deduced, alternatively, from the same postulates as those leading to our first main proposition about dialectical conflict.

Dialectical Conflict about Water Fluoridation. Controversies surrounding fluoridation of city water supplies provide convenient illustrations of the application of our theory (see Coleman, 1957; Gamson, 1961; Simmel, 1961; Horton and Thompson, 1962; McDill and Ridley, 1962). The issue was a new one, without any kind of political history that might have complicated its study; it did not touch on heavily vested interests, as would have been the case with taxes, bond issues, or city and county unification; and water fluoridation apparently was not expensive, required little cooperation among organizations to implement, nor was there any compelling evidence at the time of study that it was other than beneficial to health. Support by the elite and by the medical profession was virtually unanimous (Rosenthal and Crain, 1966).

This volatile issue has been investigated in a sample of cities that only partly overlaps with the 130 cities we consider here (Rosenthal and Crain, 1966; Crain, Katz, and Rosenthal, 1969). It was found that cities with nonpartisan elections for council held relatively many referenda and had lower adoption rates than did other cities. The present 130 cities serve to verify and extend these results.

Whether or not the city had fluoridated its water supply by 1966 estimates a continuum of the absence of one kind of city conflict (U.S. Department of Health, Education and Welfare, 1967).[25] According to our first proposition based on classic dialectical theory, (1) the more municipally centralized the city, the more likely is conflict. According to interorganizational theory, (2) the more organizationally complex the city, the less likely is conflict. Also according to interorganizational theory, a corollary to both preceding propositions, (3) the greater the municipal scale and diversification, the less likely is conflict. These approaches fail to contradict one another; indeed, they overlap, because the inverse association between organizational complexity and centralization has been deduced from interorganizational theory and demonstrated in the prediction of both municipal scale and diversification and of the absence of "reform" government, respectively. The direct effect of organizational complexity proved to be more debatable, however, than its indirect effects through the two municipal measures.

It may be seen from Table 11 that the latter held no surprises: "Reform" government, the least ambiguous indicator of municipal centralization, has both an overall and independently inverse effect on fluoridation of the water supply. The related indicator of prestige-based hospital support has an insignificantly inverse effect. And, insofar as diversification implies decentralization, the positive effect of municipal scale and diversification is also in accord with the dialectical perspective.

Yet, for reasons that produced the corollary, this last finding also fits the view that organizational complexity dampens conflict indirectly through the internal linkage its regulating and coordinating organizations and its party and political organizations make available to produce cross-cutting lines of conflict and coalition that make overall polarization unlikely. Partly supporting this view is the positive effect of the economic measure of organizational complexity on water fluoridation, but this is confined mainly to the east north central and western cities, as Table 12 shows.

The latter finding and the lack of an independent effect by the number of national headquarters of voluntary associations, age of city, and size of city—as well as their lower predictive power when substituted for municipal scale and diversification—are not in accord with either approach. It might be suggested, with some hesitation, that mutually canceling influences occurred. These four variables indicate the community's organizational complexity, to be sure, but also indicate its external linkage; they may not only signify the means that the community has for dampening or avoiding dialectical conflict, but also *the lines along which models of conflict*

Table 11. Accounting for the Absence of Community Conflict (that is, for Fluoridation of the Water Supply) on the Basis of Municipal Centralization ("Reform" Government), Organizational Complexity, and Demographic and Other Variables Used for Purposes of Control ($N = 130$ Cities).

Predictor of Fluoridation	Estimated Zero-Order Correlation Coefficient, r (association before estimate)	Standardized Partial Regression Coefficient, *beta* (before estimate of r's)
"Reform" Government	−.27 (−.17)[b]	−.24 (−.16)[b]
Municipal Scale and Diversification	.29 (.17)[b]	.24 (.13)[a]
Economic Complexity	.28 (.21)[b]	.16 (.16)[b]
Foreign Stock	−.09 (−.07)	−.27 (−.16)[a]
Multiple Correlation, R (before estimate of r's)	.45 (.31)[b]	
Prestige-Based Hospital Support	−.08 (−.06)	−.02 (−.06)[c]
National Headquarters of Voluntary Associations	.22 (.17)[b]	−.12 (.01)
Age of City	.24 (.19)[b]	−.02 (.08)
Population Size	.21 (.16)[b]	.07 (.07)
Industrialization	.20 (.15)[a]	.08 (.11)
Private Schools	.14 (.11)	.14 (.21)
Nonwhite	.18 (.14)	−.06 (.02)
Democratic Vote	.13 (.10)	.17 (.15)
City-Wide Associations	−.01 (−.01)	−.04 (.00)
Population Density	.25 (.20)[b]	.20 (.19)[a]
Migration	−.10 (−.08)	.13 (.01)
Education	−.18 (−.14)	−.14 (−.07)
Poverty	−.02 (.01)	−.12 (−.09)
Per Capita Expenditures for Health and Hospitals	.12 (.09)	−.05 (.02)
Per Capita Expenditures for Education	.26 (.20)[a]	.16 (.14)[a]

[a]Significant at the .10 level, based on association before estimates.
[b]Significant at *at least* the .05 level, based on association before estimates.
[c]The variables on the lower half of the table were alternated into the regression equation one at a time. Unless mentioned, their introduction did not alter rank ordering of the *betas* on the top half of the table. The apparent effect of population density results from colinearity with variables in the equation and is also an artifact of regional differences.

are diffused from one city to the next. It appears, by way of example, that some of the externally most linked cities experienced some of the "hottest summers" during the recent years of ghetto unrest (this is in keeping with conceptualizations that view cities as local sites for national conflicts).

Table 12. Accounting for the Absence of Community Conflict (that is, for Fluoridation of the Water Supply) on the Basis of Municipal Centralization ("Reform" Government), Organizational Complexity, and Demographic Variables Used for Purposes of Control, Independently of the Effects of Region.

Municipal Water Fluoridation	All Cities	Cities Located *Outside* of										Cities Located in	
		NE	ENC	W	SW	SE	ENC & W	W & SW	SW & SE	NE & SE	ENC	ENC	ENC & W
Percent of Cities with Fluoridation	38	41	34	43	40	35	38	46	36	37	58	39
Standardized Partial Regression (*beta*) on:[a]												
"Reform" Government	−.24	−.39	.09	−.23	−.30	−.29	.18	−.28	−.37	−.49	−.87	−.60
Municipal Scale and Diversification	.24	.17	.43	.25	.26	.16	.47	.29	.20	.03	.20	.10
Economic Complexity	.16	.19	.20	.03	.13	.29	.02	−.04	.29	.35	.24	.35
Foreign Stock	−.27	−.09	−.39	−.26	−.33	−.20	−.29	−.33	−.30	.03	−.07	.10
Multiple Correlation, R[a]	.45	.62	.51	.36	.48	.50	.45	.39	.56	.65	.91	.75
Number of Cities	130	101	106	95	113	105	71	78	88	76	24	59

[a]*Betas* and R are based on estimated r's.

The apparently inverse effect of foreign stock will later be shown to be an artifact of region. The positive effect of per capita municipal expenditures for education, introduced along with health and hospital expenditures to indicate child-oriented organizations favorable towards fluoridation, is statistically inseparable from that of municipal scale and diversification. Yet both organizational variables appear to operate, because the effects of neither one fully cancelled the effects of the other when used in the same equation.

What is striking thus far is that only the theoretically most meaningful variables have been found to account for the absence of one kind of community conflict—and these are all organizational variables. Taking region into account specifies these results farther. The spuriously inverse effect of foreign stock just mentioned is attributable to the large foreign populations and the low fluoridation rates of northeastern cities, because Table 12 shows that *beta* is virtually zero for cities outside this region, and further examination showed the same to hold true *within* the region.

Note, however, that each of the other effects on fluoridation is reduced to zero—in the case of "reform" government even reversed—as one or more subregions are removed from consideration. Yet wherever the effect of the one municipal indicator of centralization (or local complexity) is zero, that of the other is not. Moreover, and contrary to the case of foreign stock, each effect is particularly high *within* the subregions whose exclusion makes it drop to zero. Thus, the apparent influence of reform government on mass protest against fluoridation is very high in the east north central cities (see the righthand side of Table 12); that of small municipal scale or nondiversification was found to be large along the East Coast (NE, SE); and lack of economic complexity only made a difference in the Midwest, West, and Southwest (ENC, W, SW).

The regions selected for special consideration in Table 12 differ from those used before, because the possibility of fluoridation was first introduced in the Midwest, and resistance only mounted during the course of the issue's spread (Crain, Katz, and Rosenthal, 1969, p. 30).[26] Correspondingly, the combined predictive power of the three organizational indicators was here found to be highest among the east north central cities and second highest in the western cities. One might well ask, in future studies, whether the factors associated with the early history of a new form of conflict might not differ from those associated with its spread. Our dialectical perspective is most clearly illustrated by the inverse effect of "reform" government (assuming that it most clearly measures centralization) on fluoridation in the east north central cities, where it all began, while the dampening effects of municipal scale and diversification (assuming it to measure the availability of local linkage more clearly) seem to predominate elsewhere.[27] It suffices for the present that organizational indicators, including ones associated with organizational barrenness, even account for an appreciable portion of a phenomenon that rests heavily on "mass" opinion.

Interorganizational Centralization and Decision Making

This is not the place to review the voluminous literature on power and decision making, other than a small portion that points to another implication of an interorganizational view of macrosocial units. In ones like the cities under study, organizations also become the main actors in the allocation and mobilization of power—more specifically, in the decision-making process. Thus, correspondence was expected, and will be demonstrated, between the structure of actual decision making and the organizational characteristics of the city, which have been developed during the discussions of Tables 1 through 10.

In the modern macrosocial setting, power seems to depend on organizational memberships. It is frequently discharged on behalf of and under the mandate of organizations that the power wielder represents (Turk and Lefcowitz, 1962). Three recent case studies of cities make this clear (also see Babchuk, Marsey, and Gordon, 1960; Freeman and others, 1962). First, intensive examination of a variety of local issues faced by the city of Chicago led to the thesis that political influence is the interplay, to large extent, among representatives of economic, political, service, and other organizations (Banfield, 1961). Second, not only was close correspondence found between organizational affiliation and community power position "by reputation" in Syracuse, New York, but it was also found that clusterings among twenty-nine local issues were more sharply defined on the basis of the organizations typically represented in each area of decision making than on the basis of the actual individuals who took part (Freeman, 1968). Third, this thesis has been extended in a study of still another city (unnamed), which showed that the larger the number of organizations in which the individual held high position, the greater was that person's involvement in various local issues and the greater was that person's local influence according to various measures (Perucci and Pilisuk, 1970). Mounting evidence has shown that individuals do not affect the mobilization of power in large cities as much as do the organizations that these persons represent.

It has been suggested that the dominating individuals of the metropolis tend to be elected officials and the managers of large public bureaucracies (Sayre and Kaufman, 1960; Banfield, 1961; Greer, 1962). Also, a comparative analysis of 166 previously published community studies suggested that officials and politicians rather than informal leaders tend to dominate the "power structures" of cities with more than 100,000 inhabitants—some of the communities considered in the present study (Gilbert, 1968). One might expect structural similarity, then, between the exercise of power—community decision making—and the governmental organization through and from which power flows.

That political contest, rather than its obverse, "reform" government, tends to prevail in cities with decentralized power structures has been the conclusion of other comparative studies (Gilbert, 1968; Walton, 1968; Aiken, 1970; Clark, 1971). This criterion is upheld by the reliability coefficient reported earlier that permitted incorporating type of executive into the present reform index, along with partisan and by-district elections, because, as noted, one way in which nonmanager forms of government differ from their city-manager counterparts is in the degree of their decentralization. However, there is a more direct way of verifying nonreform government, and municipal scale and diversification as well, as indicators of decentralization.

Of the 51 cities whose decision patterns were described in 1967 by the National Opinion Research Center (NORC), 36 are also among the present 130 (Clark, 1968b, 1971). Each city had been scored according to the degree of decentralization of its decision making, measured by the number of different persons reported to have been involved in deciding on four actual issues of the kinds that most cities face: mayoral elections, urban renewal, antipoverty programs, and air pollution control. In the case of each issue, knowledgable informants gave names of initiators of the issue, those who supported the action, those who opposed it, who negotiated with whom, and whose views tended to prevail. Reflecting both the number of participants in each issue and the turnover in participants from one issue to the next, the total number of separate persons named was divided by how many of the four issues occurred in the city, to yield that city's decentralization score.[28] Clearly, such a score measures complexity as well.

There is a close relationship between the detailed decentralization of decision-making score and our twin indicators of municipal scale and diversification and the absence of reform government, even though prediction is from 1960 to 1962, respectively, to 1967. All five of the cities with both municipal characteristics had decentralization scores above the median; eleven of the nineteen with only one such characteristic had scores as high; while only two of twelve with neither municipal feature had above average decentralized decision scores. That the two deviant cases also had the two highest rates of population growth may suggest that a widely dispersed decision structure is not only a function of the community's organizational structure, but also of the level of disorganization. The Clark-NORC score did have some explicitly interorganizational foundations, because different incumbents of approximately similar—presumably organizational—statuses such as "labor leader" were counted as a single individual (Clark, 1971). Thus the correlations between the scores and our municipal variables may be partly tautological.

The upper portion of Table 13 mirrors these results, and the lower part shows outcomes, none of them compelling, of attempts made to invalidate them. Note (the lower third column) that each additional indicator either had no effect or had the reverse of the effect that might have been predicted on the basis of the book's discussion to this point, because all have been taken as positive or negative measures (or results) of organizational complexity. Migration, as the footnote to the table indicates, must be treated somewhat

Table 13. Accounting for the Decentralization of Community Decision Making on the Basis of Municipal Centralization ("Reform" Government), Organizational Complexity, and Demographic and Other Variables Used for Purposes of Control (N = 36 Cities).

Predictor of Clark-NORC Decentralization Score in 1967	Estimated Zero-Order Correlation Coefficient, r (association before estimate)	Standardized Partial Regression Coefficient, *beta* (before estimate of r's)
"Reform" Government in 1962	−.53 (−.42)[b]	−.59 (−.45)[b]
Municipal Scale and Diversification in 1960	.37 (.29)[b]	.46 (.33)[b]
Multiple Correlation, R (before estimate of r's)	.70 (.53)[b]	
Prestige-Based Hospital Support	−.29 (−.29)[b]	.04 (−.11)[c]
National Headquarters of Voluntary Associations	.34 (.34)[b]	−.13 (.18)
Economic Complexity	.26 (.26)[a]	.00 (.14)
Age of City	.51 (.51)[b]	−20.48 (.30)[a]
Population Size	.18 (.18)	−.16 (.03)
Industrialization	.27 (.27)[a]	−.46 (−.03)
Private Schools	.53 (.53)[b]	−.33 (.31)[a]
Foreign Stock	.45 (.45)[b]	.08 (.27)[a]
Nonwhite	−.05 (−.05)	−.07 (−.06)
Democratic Vote	.31 (.31)[b]	−.52 (.00)
City-Wide Associations	−.33 (−.26)	.09 (−.08)
Population Density	.43 (.43)[b]	−.33 (.22)
Education	−.48 (−.48)[b]	.35 (−.26)
Migration	−.50 (−.50)[b]	[d] (−.25)

[a]Significant at the .10 level, based on association before estimates.
[b]Significant at *at least* the .05 level, based on association before estimates.
[c]The variables on the lower half of the table were alternated into the regression equation one at a time. Unless mentioned, their introduction did not alter rank ordering of the *betas* on the top half of the table.
[d]It is impossible to separate the effects of migration from those of "reform" government among these 36 cities, for r between the two is estimated to be .93 (.74).

differently; substituting that variable for "reform" government yielded the slightly higher multiple correlation of R = .55. Yet throughout the previous analyses migration has been shown to have no independent effect on the several organizational phenomena predicted—indeed, it has already been shown to be an inverse correlate of several indicators of organizational complexity—although some of its overall (zero-order) correlations are appreciable.

Thus one might suspect that migration, like decentralization of decision making, is an outcome and spongelike indicator of the city's more fundamental organizational composition.

Uncritical reliance on the results of the third column of Table 13 is unwarranted: first, because of unreliability, given only thirty-six cities, in the estimates on which they are based; second, because some of the indicators are highly correlated with the two measures of municipal government.[29] Thus especial attention should be paid to the results of the second, overly conservative analysis that appear in the parentheses of the fourth column. The effect of migration on the decentralization of decision making was insignificant, but about equal to that of each of the two municipal variables. Education, its close correlate and possible indicator of organizationally barren bedroom communities, had an infinitesimally lower effect than the municipal variables. Population density and national head-quarters of voluntary associations had effects that were close to those of municipal scale and diversification but less than those of "reform" government.[30] The effect of foreign stock failed to occur outside of the eight northeastern cities. The ones of private schools and age of city were indistinguishable from the original ones of "reform" government and municipal scale and diversification, and this held as each subregion was excluded from the analysis in turn.[31] The fact, however, that the effects of the various continuous variables, several of them broad and spongelike in addition, failed to surpass those of the two dichotomies favors our organizational interpretation.

Whatever the degree of independent contribution the controls leave to the two municipal variables, it is noteworthy that both private schools and age of city have been taken to be indicators of organizational complexity and therefore also predictive of community decentralization according to our pluralist theory of partial conflict and partial cooperation among organizations. Also to be noted is that "reform" government, the least ambiguous measure of municipal centralization, continued to have a significantly independent effect on the decentralization of decision making as each third indicator was considered, except in the case of migration, for reasons already given.[32]

The usual table of regional details would seem pretentious in the light of unreliabilities in an analysis of thirty-six cases. Yet cities differed by region in the decentralization of decision making ($p < .02$ by the Kruskal-Wallis test). And those in the two regions that stand out in their decentralization—the industrialized northeast and east north central (see Appendix Figure A)—also, it will be recalled, tended to have "nonreformed" governments or ones that were large in scale and diversified. Nevertheless, the two municipal indicators yielded estimated multiple correlation coefficients of .85 with the decentralization of decision within the combined regions and .50 outside them. The structure of actual decision processes within the community does indeed appear capable of prediction on the basis of its more fundamental organizational composition.

Decision Making and Community Conflict. Table 14 shows the effects of the decentralization of decision making on water fluoridation, the measure of the absence of one kind of community conflict, examined together with the respective organizational indicators

Table 14. Accounting for the Absence of Community Conflict (that is, for Fluoridation of the Water Supply) on the Basis of Municipal Centralization ("Reform" Government), Municipal Scale and Diversification, and the Decentralization of Decision Making, Independently of the Effects of Region.

Municipal Water Fluoridation	All Cities	Cities Located *Outside* of				
		NE	ENC	W	SW	SE
Percent of Cities with Fluoridation	31	36	23	30	29	34
Standardized Partial Regression (*beta*) on:[a]						
"Reform" Government	−.41	−.53	−.12	−.36	−.57	−.48
Municipal Scale and Diversification	.25	.37	.27	−.09	.39	.37
Decentralization of Decision Making	.09	.33	.18	−.04	.00	.00
Multiple Correlation *R*[a]	.51	.80	.42	.36	.62	.57
Number of Cities	36	28	30	23	34	29

[a]*Betas* and *R* are based on estimated *r*'s.

of municipal centralization and scale and diversification. Although the zero-order correlation is estimated at .40 ($p < .05$), the independent effect of the decentralization score disappears once the two municipal measures are taken into account (*beta* = .09). It does, however, make a modest contribution among cities outside the northeast (*beta* = .33, $p < .10$). Yet whatever the additional contribution of this other, possibly also organizational, indicator of decentralization to the absence of community conflict, however small, attests further to the utility of the dialectical perspective. Unorganized and unrepresented masses need not be powerless elsewhere, or even hold low socioeconomic status, in order to attend revolutionary appeals by protest organizations, just powerless in the system at hand.

Summing Up

As in Chapter Two and on Figure 2, a *plurality of interests and standards* has been assumed to be an outcome of *organizational complexity:* both complexity that external linkage brings with it and complexity that might be more internal in its origins (whether national church-related private schools are externally linked is not too important a question here). In the case of cities, we took the unexpected effect of population's level of education (not shown on Figure 2) to be an indicator of the absence of such complexity in a more residential and thus less externally linked macrosocial unit; but such a convenient interpretation of this demographic variable might be questioned.

Where a plurality of interests and standards exists, organizations will resist *centralization* (Figure 2). This received support from inverse relationships of "reform" government to our national headquarters proxy for external linkage and to the organizational complexity of multiple educational systems that the private schools measure seemed to show. Quite unexpectedly, once its close association with organizational complexity was taken into account, population size had a *positive* effect on municipal centralization (not shown on Figure 2). The larger the *un*organized membership of the macrosocial unit, the more likely is the unit to be centralized.

Figure 2. Interorganizational Bases of Centralization, Dialectical Conflict, and Decision Structures in the Macrosocial Unit (here, the Metropolis): Summary of Chapter 3.

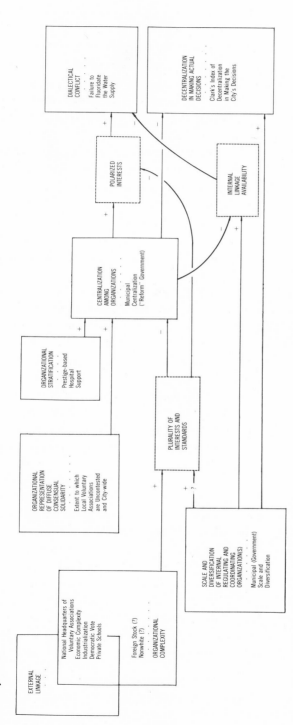

Key. Abstract properties of macrosocial units are in capital letters—in solid boxes if operationalized, in dotted boxes, if not. Lowercase letters are operational definitions of these properties in the special case of the metropolis. Arrows represent direction of causation. Plus and minus signs show direction of association.

Elitism and centralization are assumed to covary and thus to validate one another. Indeed, the more *organizational stratification* (among hospitals) played a role in the allocation of support, the more centralized ("reformist") the macrosocial unit tended to be. This is also in accord with writings that elite-supported interest groups are the ones most favorable to "reform" government. The positive effect of median education on such government could, alternatively, also be seen in such a light.

The positive effect *on centralization* of the *organizational representation of diffuse consensual solidarity* shown on Figure 2 could signify manifest legitimation of centralization, especially in terms of the property's measure by city-wide voluntary associations. The word *manifest* is used advisedly, for elites join voluntary associations in disproportionate numbers; thus legitimation of centralization could be less pervasive in the macrosocial unit than it appears. The point to be made, however, is that legitimation may most forcibly be expressed by uncontested organizations. Again, an elitist characterization of macrosocial centralization has merit.

Given a central elite dominating an organizationally *non-complex* mass, there exist at least three possible bases of *dialectical conflict:* (1) the *polarized interests* between elite and the dominated mass, (2) the *absence* of a *plurality of interests and standards* that would have inhibited polarization, and (3) the *absence* of the *availability of internal linkage* that would have produced the cross-cutting networks of conflict and alliance that also inhibit polarization. The machinery allowing frequent referenda that allegedly accompany the paradoxically fragile "reform" governments provide the organizational means of dialectical conflict.

Whether scale and diversification of the regulating and co-ordinating organizations itself meant *de*centralization of the macrosocial unit or affected plurality of interests and standards cannot be said; hence, the absence of the one arrow on Figure 2 and the question mark in the other. Yet the linkage made available, it is suggested, accounts for the inverse association of municipal scale and diversification with dialectical conflict over fluoridation. (The concept of internal linkage will be discussed in detail in Chapters Four and Five.) It is also suggested that the polarization of interests accounts for the association found between municipal centralization ("reform" government) and dialectical conflict. Somewhat weaker is the possibility that economic (*organizational*) *complexity* had any direct effect; thus the part played by pluralism in inhibiting dialectical conflict is still open to question. That complexity had indirect effects through the municipal structures to which it contributed is clear. It may be that plural interests and standards without the means of interlinking them have little effect. But all three possible correlates of dialectical conflict were strong in the regions having faced their issues early. What began as symbolic conflict might later have turned into something else. After all, the experiences of one macrosocial unit become part of the orientations of the next.

Finally, we find that either decentralization among organizations or large scale but diversification of the regulating and coordinating organizations predict decentralization (or issue-specific diversification) in actual decisions that were made. Chapter Four will show that the effects of the latter, partly person-based measure on macrosocial actions—although measured closer to them in time—will disappear once our two organizational variables are taken into account.

To recapitulate, because organizations tend to pursue conflicting interests and plural standards in certain issue areas but need one another in other areas, they will resist domination by any one or a few of their number. Supporting this, we have found here (or in Chapter Two, respectively) that large scale and diversified or decentralized "nonreform" government is associated with organizational complexity—with the diversity of other nonorganizations (notably ones providing external linkage) within the city. These two municipal variables permitted prediction over time of scores (perhaps surrogate measures of organizational variables) describing decentralization in actual community decisions that were made.

Where organizations fail to abound, power may be wielded by an organized elite over an unorganized mass, thereby creating the conditions of polarized conflict undampened by the crosscutting and issue-specific lines of coalition and conflict existing in organizationally more complex environments. The three indicators of macrosocial decentralization—mainly the two that were manifestly organizational—did indeed have independent effects on the absence of conflict, measured by fluoridation of the municipal water supply. Yet, even in this limiting case, organizations presumably constituted the catalysts of mass protest and provided, through the election machinery, the means of its expression.

Notes

1. The term *organization set* means the organizations constituting the significant environment of any given organization. This idea was suggested by Blau and Scott (1962) and subsequently employed by Evan (1966) and Thompson (1967).

2. Levine and White (1961); Litwak and Hylton (1962); Levine, White, and Paul (1963); and Clark (1965) have viewed these attributes as fundamental to the study of interorganizational relations.

3. Using his own measure of concentration of the labor force into large organizations and reinterpreting Hawley's (1963) ratio of managers, proprietors, and officials to the total labor force (MPO) as lack of such concentration, Lincoln (1976) has utilized our data on 110 of the 130 cities to show positive association between such concentration and the city's ability to mobilize for municipal expenditures, urban renewal, and the War on Poverty. This is not the place to go into the various criticisms and defenses of the MPO ratio. See Straits (1965), Aiken (1970), Williams (1973), Smith (1976), MacGillivray (1973), and Hawley's rejoinders (1965, 1973a).

4. This idea is related to the way in which Aiken (1970) and Aiken and Alford (1970) have discussed community innovations as a function of "interfaces" between power centers.

5. Exceptions are the small producers to which we have referral that require services only available in the metropolis. See Hoover and Vernon (1962, pp. 29–51) and Vernon (1972).

6. Suggested by combining ideas about interfaces with those having to do with interorganizational networks (H. Turk, 1970; Hage and Aiken, 1970, pp. 80–81) and community conflict-formation (Coleman, 1957, 1966; Gamson, 1966).

7. The aggregative effects of party politics have been suggested in slightly different ways by Parsons (1959), Greer (1967), and Lineberry and Fowler (1967) among others. Indeed, Cutwright (1963) views cleavages as sources of strength for political parties, which are themselves aspects of organizational complexity. Also see Almond (1958, 1960) on political interest groups in general.

8. For example, see Banfield and Wilson (1963, p. 151) and Lineberry and Fowler (1967) concerning token nonpartisanship in Chicago and

Boston. This possibility lends a conservative bias to our measure and makes the results all the more compelling.

9. Like Alford and Scoble (1965), Lineberry and Fowler (1967), Alford and Lee (1968), Wolfinger and Field (1968), I also use reform government as a negative measure of the decentralized, interest-aggregating, and buffering effects of neighborhood groups and political parties.

10. The entire contents of the neoclassic political decision studies of New York City, New Haven, and Chicago (Sayre and Kaufman, 1960; Dahl, 1961; Banfield, 1961) can be interpreted in this light.

11. As the bases of our suggestion that decentralization is associated with diversification, see the organizational materials by Thompson (1967, pp. 73–76) and Hage and Aiken (1970, pp. 80–82) and the urban political literature exemplified by Sayre and Kaufman (1960), Banfield (1961), Sayre and Polsby (1965), Greer (1967), Gardiner (1968), and Derthick (1968).

12. This is in accord with Clark's (1971, 1975) discussion of the political activism of Irish Catholics, especially in the East. But here we say that this is so because Catholicism is organizational membership.

13. Consider Williams and Adrian (1959), Banfield and Wilson (1963, pp. 138–186) in conjunction with Schnore and Alford (1963). Also see W. Hawley (1974).

14. For discussions suggesting that even personal prestige and power are *acquired* from organizational affiliations, see Babchuk, Marsey, and Gordon (1960), Freeman and others (1962), Stinchcombe (1965), Freeman (1968), Perrucci and Pilisuk (1970). Thus, a variation on our dominant theme: to study stratification within an urban community is to study stratification among its organizations.

15. See T. Turk (1970) for strong evidence of the validity of this procedure and details of measurement. It has since been determined that r would have been a more sensitive measure than *gamma* and that— unsuitably, for present purposes—children's hospitals had been included. These strong conservative biases makes any predictive power of the indicator all the more compelling, but discouraged any attempts to explore its own causes.

16. First thoughts suggested converting the headquarters measure to a per capita rate. But association headquarters neither employ nor serve many of the local inhabitants; thus such a rate would have very little substantive meaning. Yet we have shown the presence of such organizations to be correlated with the presence of others that are more directly significant locally. Thus our means of taking the number of headquarters relative to city size appeared to provide the most reasonable compromise. Actually the method proved to be conservative, reducing R from .77 to .71. The values before subtraction follow, for readers who may prefer them.

Predictor	r	beta
National Voluntary Association Headquarters	− .26	− .33
Population Size	− .01	.28
Private Schools	− .54	− .40
Education	.39	.37
Organizational Stratification	.21	.22
City-Wide Associations	.27	.21

17. Also found by Alford and Scoble (1965) and anticipated by Cutright's discussion of the effects of organized cleavages within the community on the strength of political parties (cited by Wolfinger and Field, 1968). Substituting foreign stock, whose correlation with private schools is .71, lowers multiple correlation by from .03 to .04. (Also see Note 12.)

18. The lack of effect by municipal scale and diversification might have resulted from colinearity. But resolving the question is not crucial, since small municipal scale and low diversification and "reform government" can be employed together in subsequent analyses.

19. For deep controversy surrounding the "public regarding" concept, see Banfield and Wilson (1963, pp. 234–240), Wilson and Banfield (1964, 1966), Wolfinger and Field (1966, 1968), Lineberry and Fowler (1967).

20. The finding does not necessarily contradict the positive relationship between education and the number of national headquarters of voluntary associations independently of the effects of economic complexity, population size, and age of city (see Table 1 and its discussion).

21. The larger *betas* result from multicolinearity but do not alter the basic equations to any marked degree. Contradicting Alford and Scoble (1965), recent *migration* has no independent effect once its multiple correlation of .83 with private schools (negative) and education (positive) or its − .71 correlation with industrialization are taken into account. Substituting this variable for private schools and education reduces R by as much as .06 to .08. Indeed, even the questionable *beta* of .23 on Table 9 disappears once the southeastern cities are excluded from the analysis.

22. More importantly, the results prove not to be artifacts of Catholics in the Northeast (Clark, 1975) or of western predilections toward "reformism."

23. Parties are likely to provide power that countervails interest groups representing business (Morlock, 1974; W. Hawley, 1974).

24. Greer (1962) observed that in Banfield's (1961) Chicago, the political head will tend to ratify almost any proposal on which principal parties can agree, but is reluctant to force a compromise. Greer notes that half of the public issues studied by Banfield fail to be acted on, possibly for reasons such as these.

25. This measure is conservative in the sense that issues other than

fluoridation could have occurred as bases of disruptive conflict, or that some places have naturally fluoridated water, or that the question of fluoridation had just not achieved sufficiently high priority to have been raised. Yet to the extent that conflict existed or was avoided, such extent lies along a continuum; for its simple presence or absence does not indicate how narrowly fluoridation succeeded or failed.

26. The regions also differed in rates of fluoridation ($p < .05$ by chi-square).

27. Finding fluoridation issues to be good indicators of immediate protest in Canadian cities that held referenda, Hahn (1968) suggested that interest in protest subsided in subsequent referenda held within these same cities. It might be, in the present case, that the east north central cities had had more time to hold additional referenda than did the others. The unusually high rate of fluoridation in that region attests to this. Thus "reform" government might, alternatively, be most instrumental in "keeping the fire hot" over a series of referenda, while the availability of local linkage might have dampening effects and make referenda unnecessary.

28. Clark (1968b, 1971) has provided the details. Note that the thirty-six communities in common exclude my cities over 750,000 and his under 100,000. Thus, lack of comparability, not necessarily theoretical substance, might account for any incompatibilities between the two projects in the conclusions reached.

29. The standard errors of biserial r were found to be from 26 to 32 percent higher than those of the product-moment coefficient in the null case. It is hard to say what effect this would have on higher-order coefficients and on eventual colinearity among them, given the small sample size.

30. None of the variables designated as "significant" met the criterion of tolerated level of colinearity; when substituted for their respective correlates, none produced values of R that exceeded or fell short of the tabled .53 by more than .01. Considering that even a dummy variable based on a median split cannot produce a (point-biserial) value of r greater than .87, one can suggest the superior predictive ability of the two theoretically more meaningful municipal variables.

31. Adding the two additional variables to the regression equation, despite colinearity, increased R from .53 to .60 and produced four insignificantly positive *betas*. Pairing them in all possible ways produced values of R from .53 to .58.

32. The part played by private schools might support what Clark (1971, 1975) and others have observed, that Irish Catholics have historically staffed municipal departments, such as the police, and local political party organization, not to mention their organization into churches, schools, and voluntary associations. This effect, be it noted, is independent of the high concentration of Catholics in the industrial regions. Also see Notes 12 and 17 of this chapter.

Chapter Four

•••••••••••••••••••••••
••••••••••••••••••••••••
•••••••••••••••••••••••••

CAPACITY FOR INTERORGANIZATIONAL RELATIONS

•••••••••••••••••••••••
••••••••••••••••••••••••
•••••••••••••••••••••••

*I*n Chapter Three, we called establishment of decentralized linkage a basic interorganizational process on which concerted action within organizationally complex macrosocial units depends. And Chapter Two suggests that externally provided resources are also sometimes necessary for such macrosocial action. An organization's influence in such a setting has already been defined as its general ability to participate in, newly activate, or reactivate interorganizational relations in response to a wide variety of issues within fluid, uncertain environments. The extent to which certain of the organizations of the macrosocial unit are influential in this sense, and the extent to which others provide the necessary resources, both affect that community's capacity for activating interorganizational relations, as this chapter will show. The extent to which any organization contributes to such capacity depends in part on its interest in doing so. This is sometimes forgotten in discussions of dominance by organizations.

We have already identified the first aspect of this capacity as internal linkage availability, a hypothetical construct employed in the two previous chapters. Although the concept had been developed before those chapters were written, deferring its full explication until now avoids the further complication of an already complex argument. The effect of variability in capacity on interorganizational activation will be shown, in this chapter, to outweigh the effect of variability in "need." The question of need is a knotty one; full discussion of it will be deferred to Chapter Five.

The formal theory to be developed (but modified in the light of data) has as its first part: The greater the scale and diversification of organizations—given their visibility, decentralization, and ability to withstand disruption by inner conflict—the greater will be their political capabilities. The greater the political capabilities of organizations, the greater the availability of internal linkage for the macrosocial unit. The greater the availability of internal linkage for the macrosocial unit, the more likely is interorganizational activation. From these premises, then, it follows that first, *The greater the scale and diversification of organizations—given their visibility, decentralization, and ability to withstand disruption by inner conflict—the more likely is interorganizational activation.* At this point, we can offer the definition that had been tabled: *Regulating and coordinating organizations are ones that exceed others in their political capabilities, that is, in interest in forming or mediating coalitions, in resources available for coercion or exchange, in orientations toward contest and bargaining, in negotiable interests and standards, in multiple contact points, in use made of them by other organizations, and in adaptability to uncertainty.* Given regulations and coordination by coalition formation in the organizationally complex macrosocial unit, any more terse definition would involve gross oversimplification.

The organizational representation of diffuse consensual solidarity, it will be shown (even in the case of the new networks briefly described in Chapter One), also contributes to the availability of internal linkage. The second part of our formal theory begins with the proposition: The greater the organizational representation of diffuse consensual solidarity in the macrosocial unit—given visibility—the more will externally shared interests and standards be evoked. The more externally shared interests and standards are evoked, the greater the capacity to mediate coalitions.

The greater the capacity to mediate coalitions, the greater the availability of internal linkage for the macrosocial unit. The greater the availability of internal linkage for the macrosocial unit, the more likely (as stated before) is interorganizational activation. From this second set of premises, it follows that, second, *The greater the organizational representation of diffuse consensual solidarity in the macrosocial unit—given visibility—the more likely is interorganizational activation.*

Where *de*centralization among organizations might have affected the availability of internal linkage to dampen dialectical conflict—along with scale and diversification of internal regulating and coordinating organizations—organizational representation of diffuse consensual solidarity might, on the one hand, have had a similar effect. On the other hand, it appeared to support the very centralization believed to cause conflict. The cases of interorganizational activation considered here had not, at the time of study, been characterized by pronounced controversy. Thus, the political capabilities of some organizations and the mediating capabilities of others in terms of external interests and standards should have had more to do with making internal linkage available for interorganizational activation that did centralization, which varies directly with the one and inversely with the other.

External linkage provides not only a second route by which externally shared interests and standards are mediated, but also a route for other kinds of externally provided resources (as in the case of federal antipoverty funds). The greater each of these three correlates of the macrosocial unit's capacity for interorganizational relations—organizational scale and diversification (as already qualified), organizational representation of diffuse consensual solidarity, and external linkage—the more likely activation in the metropolis of various kinds of interorganizational relations was expected to be. The theory we have just outlined will first be spelled out in this chapter and then applied to our 130 central cities. Exceptions to its universality will be noted as they are encountered.

Correlates of the Capacity for Interorganizational Relations

To define influence in the interorganizational setting is not to define its sources. An organization is influential—in the meaning of its ability to affect interorganizational relations, that is, to produce linkage—to the extent that it is interested in being influential as well as visible, large in scale, and diversified (provided it can cope with its internal conflicts), or to the extent that it is visible, uncontested, and diffuse in its goals. These several organizational characteristics will be discussed in detail and specified in turn, their indicators given in the case of the 130 United States cities, and the empirical association between these indicators and various kinds of specific formal relations among organizations examined. The first task is addressed in this section, the remaining ones in the sections to follow. The parts played by external linkage both in transmitting conflict and in providing money and shared interests and standards have already been discussed in Chapters Two and Three.

Organizational Scale. A major basis of such influence is organizational scale, which determines the resources—both human and material—by use of which an organization may coerce, bargain, or otherwise effect political solutions. Also, the greater its scale, the more visible is an organization likely to be, because the very existence of any organization means that it is a visible and recognized entity that other organizations can utilize as a tool or a weapon (Maniha and Perrow, 1965). The more prominent an organization is, the greater is this effect likely to be. It should follow that organizational scale is not only an indicator of the command over resources that would have been required had an organization influenced linkages on its own initiative in the past, or that is required if the organization is doing so in the present. Scale also indicates the likelihood that a given organization will be sought out by other organizations in *their* attempts to activate interorganizational relations.

Organizational Diversification. However, the issue-specific nature of participation at the macrosocial level, variability in the power arrangements from one issue to the next, and the variety of political problems requiring solution will very probably help to account for some of the immobilization that has been observed in communities with rigid organizations (Coleman, 1966). Thus, scale reflects the linkage available over time, provided only that it does not impede an organization's ability to adapt itself to uncertain surroundings in general and to influence a variety of interorganizational relations in particular.

Diversification in an organization's activities is associated with differentiation, which in turn affects the organization's ability to adapt to uncertain environments, its rate of innovation, and its participation in joint programs—that is, forming linkages—with other organizations. Innovativeness and joint participation, it has also been suggested, mutually affect one another.[1] Combining of general organizational theory with studies of municipal government[2] also suggests that diversification *within* an organization is associated with its decentralization; and, although this is only hinted, decentralization may also be associated with interorganizational linkage—although not very importantly, as we have already assumed.

Moreover, given large scale, the direct effect of the diversification of an organization's activities is on the number of contact points provided; and this, in turn, affects the number and variety of linkages the organization is likely to effect or attract (inferred and taken in part from Thompson, 1967, pp. 46–48; Hage and Aiken, 1970, pp. 80–81), because each area of activity tends to have its own cluster of interested organizations (Thompson, 1967) among which it may have resources, power, and visibility. Nonetheless, the simultaneous occurrence of decentralization and diversification implies that the more diversified an organization, the more autonomous its components are likely to become, especially where boundary-spanning components are important to it (deduced from Thompson, 1967, pp. 74–79)—and these are indeed important under the urban conditions of action by interorganizational relations.

The limiting case of autonomy is the fragmentation of a large organization or its decomposition into smaller specialized organizations, each of which participates in one or two issues, at most, and each of which is likely to compete with the others. The midpoint between centralization and fragmentation that is necessary to any large organization in acquiring multiple linkage is likely to be achieved through the provision of means of resolving internal conflict among organizational components (empirically supported by Lawrence and Lorsch, 1967a, 1967b). Therefore, on these means depends the association between an organization's diversification and the multiplicity of linkage it can effect. The predominant mechanism of conflict resolution within a diversified organization is likely to be political and to involve coalition forming (deduced from Thompson, 1967, pp. 125–143). Therefore, one might also expect that the more diversified an organization, the more capable would it be of generalizing its means of internal mediation to the kinds of external mediating of linkages required by the organizational complexity of the macrosocial unit that is characterized by shifting and cross-cutting lines of conflict and alliance.

Diffuseness of Organizational Goals. The diffuseness of an organization's manifest goals is associated with its ability to adapt to a changing environment (works cited by Wilson, 1966a). Goal diffuseness may be illustrated by that kind of nonspecificity that enables competing business organizations to join the same Chamber of Commerce under the umbrella of general references to "civic betterment" and "the public good," and of stated intentions to bring various community elements together.

Such goals may contribute either to the resolution of intra- organizational conflict, because the more numerous the interests and values, the more abstract must be the means of their reconciliation; or to political capabilities, because interests and values that are only loosely tied to main goals can more readily be used for negotiation. If an organization with diffuse goals were also to exhibit a tendency toward conflict avoidance, however, it would be capable of selecting from among a wide variety of interests and standards, but inclined to advance only the relatively noncontroversial. Under these conditions, an organization with diffuse goals is likely to provide solidary linkage among other organizations, at least in part, because—externally cloned as it is from organizations elsewhere—such diffuseness enables it to adopt and proclaim the interests and standards of the external context, which are least likely to arouse organized controversy or are most likely to reduce controversy to contest between a few broad positions.

Link-Producing Organizations in United States Cities

The part played by external linkage in providing money, standards, interests, and other resources to American cities has already been discussed in Chapter Two. What follows applies to the internal determinants of the availability of linkage.

Organizational scale, diversification, and diffuseness of goals

are here considered to be correlates of the ability to affect interorganizational relations in multiorganizational settings of all kinds.
However, the concrete types of local organizations that vary in
these respects may differ from one society to the next. Once the
specific organizations that make internal linkage available are
named, generalizing to other societies, in which concrete organizations with entirely different names may possess the requisite characteristics, must be attempted with caution. Yet the research literature and other scholarly writings produced mainly within and about
the United States may be combined to suggest pathways—perhaps
even contrasting ones—to research elsewhere.

In the United States, individual businesses and similar special
interest groups within the city are either so externally linked to be
disinterested in major local influence or comparatively too small in
scale, too little diversified, too little visible, or too specific and controversial in their locally relevant goals to play major parts in affecting interorganizational relations, either politically or through the
production of solidary linkage. Nor can "business" be considered
as some form of superorganization within the community that has
these capabilities. The individual components are too numerous
and too independent of one another to permit coordination without
prohibitive loss of time, and their respective interests are too di-
vergent to allow for the resolution of conflict (Banfield, 1961, pp.
294–391)[3]—with the exception of benevolent activities, to be discussed later—or to render them visible as a single entity. Business
might provide the only values that are shared among the organizations in certain cities, as in the case of the mass community already
discussed in the previous chapter, but these may be the very ones
that are contested by, say, organized labor in other cities (Form and
Miller, 1960; Schnore and Alford, 1963). Business might also constitute a latent veto that prevents certain issues from ever arising
(such as ones having to do with environmental pollution or taxing
business enterprises), but data are lacking for us to consider this
here. Therefore, the ability of such voluntary business associations
as Chambers of Commerce to provide linkage around common
local values by avoiding controversy in this pursuit may be assessed
in each city, but should not be taken for granted. Local newspaper
organizations, on the other hand, might enjoy the scale, diversifica-

tion, visibility, and decentralization required to produce linkage, or the diffuse and noncontroversial content, given their visibility, that linkage might also require. However, at present we lack the information to assess their effects.

Municipal governments and those local voluntary associations (including certain business associations) whose city-wide significance, visibility, and noncontroversial activities have been established each have major linkage-producing capacities. Even the least compelling examples within each type are either sufficiently large in scale, diversified, visible, decentralized, and capable of resolving internal conflict, or sufficiently visible, noncontroversial, and diffuse in their respective goals to seek their effects on the local linkage made available among a city's organizations with respect to any given community problem.

Partial Conflict and the Scale and Diversification of Municipal Government. City government can provide linkage among organizations under the conditions of partial conflict that characterize the multiorganizational city. Locally dependent as it is, it has vested interests in exerting influence. Government-sponsored action systems were found to be overwhelmingly associated with dissensus— that is, political—situations (Warren and Hyman, 1968; also, see the literature cited by W. Hawley, 1974). The agencies of diversified local government may or may not be deliberately constituted to serve as community decision organizations (Warren, 1967a, 1967b). Yet, where their scale is large, they can control enormous resources, human, technological, and material, that enable them to bargain and play a part in power struggles (this may be inferred from a combination of main points made by Sayre and Kaufman, 1960; Banfield, 1961, esp. pp. 266–267; Greer, 1967). Their capabilities of autonomous action within their respective spheres, which is the measure of government's decentralization, vary positively with their scale (Gardiner, 1968; Derthick, 1968). To the extent that these agencies are differentiated from one another, they form coalitions amongst themselves and with private organizations, acting as core organizations regarding certain issues and as satellites concerning others (Sayre and Kaufman, 1960, pp. 709–713).[4] Themselves differentiated, the agencies of municipal government exist in states of partial conflict both internally and with one another to such an extent that their respective goals are even more diffuse and the interests available for bargaining more numerous than those of businesses, than one might expect on the basis of government's general role as a mobilizer of community power. But problems of coordination and potential for conflict are not so great (as they are in the business sector) that the governmental sector is incapable of acting as a "whole," amorphous though that whole may be. Indeed, resolving internal conflict may be the principal activity of its top executive body, which also mediates conflict with and among nongovernmental organizations (Sayre and Kaufman, 1960; Morris and Rein, 1968). That large-scale and diversified government tends to operate under conflict conditions may reduce any solidarity-producing effects it may have as a generalized source of national standards; yet certain resources of municipal agencies, like those of expertise (Banfield, 1961, pp. 330–331), can be employed to generate legitimating symbols for one course of action or another. And because government is at the very center of a community's affairs and represents some of them at the national level (Greenstone and Peterson, 1968), it may also come to symbolize some of the community's main national interests and standards (see Shils, 1962; Turk, 1971a), or at least to advance them in seeking winning coalitions. That large-scale and diversified government can command multiple and varied points of contact, and that as a possible resource it is highly visible to other organizations is evident, from the extensive treatment it is given by the press—perhaps because the contentious situations in which it tends to play a part are newsworthy. Chapter Three has documented empirically its association with decentralized decision processes. According to the general theory we have outlined, then, the linkage-producing capabilities of large-scale and diversified municipal governments exceed those of their smaller or less diversified counterparts in the multiorganizational city, which is characterized by cross-cutting lines of partial conflict and partial accord.

Diffuse Consensual Solidarity and City-Wide Voluntary Associations. A suggestion that national values are implemented over the twin routes of nationally oriented organizations and local organizations with diffuse goals, called *city-wide associations,* was provided to me by a collaborative investigation of organizational responses to the assassination of President John F. Kennedy conducted early in 1965.[5] Eighteen matched pairs of organizations were studied— two supermarkets, two department stores, two auto rental agencies, and so on. The main distinguishing characteristic within each pair was whether the enterprise was a branch of a national firm or mainly under local ownership and control. However, even locally owned enterprises are "cloned" from others like them elsewhere; witness the similarity of establishments listed in the classified telephone directories of different cities. The data did not support the hypothesis that the national firms would be more likely than their local counterparts to symbolize national values by such official acts as closing their doors, giving time off during the funeral, or issuing official statements of mourning. Why this was so is hinted by what an executive said in answer to an unscheduled question by one interviewer about why his organization took the action that it did. He said that he just called the Chamber of Commerce to find out "what the others were doing about it." This suggests that at least some of the diffuse goals pursued by the city-wide associations discussed in Chapter Two are societal in their content.

In spite of their failure to participate in controversy and in spite of the likelihood that emphasis on consensus precludes their internal differentiation, city-wide associations can nonetheless affect interorganizational relations. They can initiate and pursue noncontroversial civic projects and play mediating roles in disputes by introducing *un*disputed value inputs for partisans to employ as legitimating forces.[6] Locally dependent, they are also interested in exerting this type of influence.

The extent to which a city's voluntary associations are uncontested and city-wide might, it will be recalled, just mean disproportionate consensus among members of the higher strata to whom they are available and who themselves may constitute the elite representatives of other organizations.[7] If this is so, city-wide associations are a means of mitigating strong interorganizational contest by means of overlapping and cross-cutting memberships. They are also a means, then, of articulating shared values, which we have claimed are often national, and applying them to the resolution of conflicts that would otherwise divide the other organizations that the members represent.

By reasons of their elite membership bodies—often those of a mobile, national, externally oriented elite—and of the diversity of organizations they represent, city-wide associations may also be expected to offer numerous points of contact to other organizations and to constitute highly visible means for the latter to utilize, however loose, amorphous, and undifferentiated the solidarity linkage that they provide might be (also, see Hawley, 1950, pp. 221–222, for a discussion of "categoric groupings" of organizations).

Capacity for Interorganizational Relations in the Metropolis

To recapitulate, in macrostructures like the modern metropolis the capacity for interorganizational activation is determined by factors that arise out of the special characteristics of multiorganizational settings. Because the partial conflict and partial cooperation that characterizes interorganizational relations results in the decentralized, rapidly changing, and cross-cutting alliances, disputes, and "mixes" of interests and standards that constitute a "fluid community," certain macrosocial characteristics have been considered particularly significant in the production of internal linkage for deciding on and effecting new interorganizational programs or reactiviting old ones. Although general in their most abstract form, these characteristics are embodied in municipal governments and certain quasi-local voluntary associations, once large American cities become the objects of study.

Prediction of Specific Interorganizational Relations. The worth of describing large-scale modern macrosocial units as relations among formal organizations can be established most clearly by predicting either new interorganizational relations or the reactivation of existing ones on the basis of linkage-producing organizations, like the two just discussed, that constitute fundamental characteristics of the setting. The more linkage that can be provided the greater is the capacity of a macrounit *either* to support *or* to resist new interorganizational activities and arrangements.[8] Linkage could provide the resources, predictability, and coordination that are necessary for new interorganizational networks to occur, or for new activities by those networks that already exist. It could just as readily provide the basis of a united front against interorganizational activation. Even where such activation occurs, it may constitute a token response to dissatisfaction with the status quo that is really designed to preserve it. Our theory and data pertaining to polarization in the mass community suggest that linkage-producing organizations contribute heavily to the formation of "winning" coalitions, for example, that can resist the realization of minority positions—be these local or extralocal in their origins—as in the case of fluoridation protest. Such coalitions can equally serve to retain the unorganized status of, say, the poverty stricken, or to coopt them.

In brief, the "higher" a city is characterized in terms of the municipal and associational properties just discussed, the more will it constitute a multiorganizational complex that can form networks to cope with what are nationally defined as urban problems. Added to this is the expectation that, given these two "controls" for the fragmenting effects of extralocal linkage, the more externally linked the city, the more resources will there be available for such networks.

Whether in the self-interested search for winning coalitions or in the establishment of the priorities of shared "public" values, the greater the influence on coalitions of each of the two kinds of American organizations having linkage properties, the more likely are the most dominant national interests and standards to prevail, quite apart from whether the external linkage transmitting these standards are particularly robust or free of conflict. These standards are probably themselves the reflections of partial conflict and cooperation among national organizations and between the organizations of different cities. They can either serve to legitimate existing power arrangements or serve to promote new ones.

It is therefore to be expected that formal relations (the activation of interorganizational networks) in any broad class of local organizations will occur more frequently (1) *the greater the municipal scale and diversification* or (2) *the greater the extent to which local voluntary associations are uncontested and city-wide.* Because "reform" government is related negatively to the first of these two sources of local linkage and positively to the second,[9] no specific formulation of that characteristic's influence on the production of new formal relations can be attempted.

To be added is a third hypothesis in the light of our discussion of the resource-providing *versus* solidarity-inhibiting effects of external linkage in Chapter Two. *For equal levels of internal linkage, the same formal relations will occur more frequently, (3) the larger the number of national headquarters of voluntary associations (and related indicators of external linkage), or the greater the more directly measurable externally provided resources.*

In the following two sections, the linkage-producing organizations (municipal government and city-wide associations in the case of the United States), as well as measures of external resources, will be used, first, to predict two new kinds of interorganizational network—the one mainly public and in the broad area of welfare, the other mainly private and in the area of health. The first of these could either represent efforts at effecting sweeping social change, or token efforts preventing it, depending on the opinion of the observer. The second could represent attempts either to realize national values of cost reduction, or to effect monopoly by maximizing predictability among a set of organizations by means of formal relations between them. Such ambiguities of purpose are irrelevant to this portion of our theory.

Formal Welfare Relations: War on Poverty Networks

That part of the poverty program called the Neighborhood Youth Corps (NYC) permitted controlled inquiry into the occurrence of complex antipoverty networks. Local organizations or local federations that federal agencies funded to sponsor such projects undertook to provide training, work experience, counseling, and placement for disadvantaged youth and young adults. In certain cases, this meant that the local sponsor had to seek still other organizations as loci of work or training. The American values of self-help, education, and the rights of youth, which these projects symbolized, probably made this component of the War on Poverty even less vulnerable to open public resistance than the rest of the program was in its early years.

More important, however, was the occurrence of simple and complex variants among the interorganizational networks of NYC sponsors and their granting agencies. In the networks that interest us here, the projects involved the regional offices of both the U.S. Department of Labor, which funded all NYC projects, and the U.S. Office of Economic Opportunity, which funded the newly established community organizations called *Community Action agencies*. A Community Action agency was an umbrella organization designed to coordinate local antipoverty activities (at the time of study), and its governing body consisted of major functionaries from the community's other organizations (for example, the mayor or the mayor's representative, the school superintendent or a member of the superintendent's staff, labor union officials, officials of the Catholic archdiocese, and representatives of various civic groups and associations of businesspersons). Sponsorship by a Community Action agency of one or more NYC projects within a given city meant a complex interorganizational network composed not only of these organizations, but also of linkage to other organizations that provided the work-training sites.

By way of contrast, the elementary alternative was sponsorship of NYC projects by one or more autonomous or semiautonomous organizations having far less broadly based structures than those of the federative Community Action agencies. Requiring funding by only one federal agency (the U.S. Department of Labor), and most often already in existence before the War on Poverty, this less complex form of sponsorship included such organizations as church groups, school systems, nonprofit welfare agencies, municipal departments, and labor unions.

Between 1964 and June 6, 1966, 29 of our 130 cities could be classified as high along a continuum of network complexity (at least one NYC project sponsored by a Community Action agency). Forty-three others had elementary (less complex) networks (NYC projects, none of which were sponsored by Community Action agencies). The remaining 58 cities were low along the continuum of network complexity—no NYC projects of any kind (data from U.S. Office of Economic Opportunity, 1966, files of the U.S. Department of Labor). The unique opportunity affords itself to control the effects of the program's content by comparing analyses of the complex and elementary variants as though they constituted separate continuua.

Considering the complex antipoverty networks first provides unambiguous support for the first two parts of the hypothesis. Both measures of the general availability of internal linkage for all manner of specific new interorganizational relations show substantial overall association with the complexity of these special networks: $r_t = .60$ in the case of municipal scale and diversification and .38 in that of how contested and city-wide are the city's voluntary associations. And the supported predictions were made over time!

The third through sixth columns of Table 15 show these effects to remain strong independently of one another and of other effects that did make or might have made a difference. Unlike the case of the flow of poverty dollars (see Chapter Two), the poverty rate (percent of families with less than $3,000 annual income in 1959, it will be recalled) did contribute to the prediction of network complexity. Introduced for purposes of control, as were the remaining indicators of organizational complexity and their respective correlates,[10] industrialization also proved to have an effect, possibly because industrial training sites were most easily adapted to the program or because the Department of Labor favored such sites. The measure of federal poverty dollars discussed in Chapter Two was added to the regression analysis (a conservative step); it may be seen from the two columns on the far right that, despite that measure's appreciable association with municipal diversification and scale, the outcome is virtually unaltered. This is particularly striking, since poverty dollars do not only represent flow of resources to the city that made NYC programs possible, but are also redundant as the *result* of the viable, complex NYC networks they have been claimed to be (at the end of Chapter Two).

The apparent inverse effect of migration on network complexity may be discounted in the light of that indicator's multiple correlation (R) of .75 with the other predictors in the regression equation. As with the complexity of antipoverty networks, *non*-migration appears to be a direct or indirect *outcome* of organizational

Table 15. Prediction over Time of Complex Antipoverty Networks on the Basis of Internal Linkage, Externally Provided Resources and "Need," and on the Basis of Indicators of Organizational Complexity, Specialized Organization, Centralization, and Demographic Variables Used for Purposes of Control ($N = 130$ Cities).

Predictor of NYC Programs Sponsored by Community Action Agencies during 1964–1966	Estimated Zero-Order Correlation Coefficient, r (association before estimate)	Standardized Partial Regression Coefficient, *beta* (before estimate of r's)	
Municipal Scale and Diversification in 1960	.60 (.36)[b]	.51 (.30)[b]	.36 (.21)[b]
City-Wide Associations in 1960	.38 (.19)[b]	.32 (.17)[b]	.30 (.15)[b]
Poverty in 1959	.23 (.17)[b]	.33 (.25)[b]	.28 (.21)[b]
Industrialization in 1958	.31 (.23)[b]	.25 (.23)[b]	.22 (.18)[b]
Federal Poverty Dollars, 1964–1966	.61 (.44)[b]	— —	.36 (.31)[b]
Multiple Correlation, R (before estimate of r's)		.76 (.48)[b]	.83 (56)[b]
Economic Complexity	.34 (.24)[b]		−.02 (.01)[c]
National Headquarters of Voluntary Associations	.25 (.18)[b]		−.14 (−.02)
Age of City	.54 (.39)[b]		.13 (.14)
Population Size	.16 (.12)		−.15 (−.05)
Private Schools	.26 (.19)[b]		.03 (.04)
Foreign Stock	.19 (.14)		.10 (.07)
Nonwhite	.36 (.26)[b]		.11 (.10)
Democratic Vote	.37 (.27)[b]		.06 (.07)
Per Capita Welfare Expenditures	.48 (.34)[b]		.09 (.11)
Per Capita Education Expenditures	.45 (.33)[b]		.11 (.11)
Population Density	.38 (.27)[b]		.10 (.08)
Migration	−.52 (−.37)[b]		−.31 (−.24)[b]
Education	−.54 (−.39)[b]		−.26 (−.18)
"Reform" Government	−.26 (−.14)		−.14 (−.05)
Prestige-Based Hospital Support	−.01 (−.01)		−.06 (−.05)
Decentralization of Decision Making ($n = 36$)	.29 (.20)		−.04 (−.01)

[a]Significant at the .10 level, based on association before estimates.
[b]Significant at *at least* the .05 level, based on association before estimates.
[c]The variables on the lower half of the table were alternated into the regression equation one at a time. Unless mentioned, their introduction did not alter rank ordering of the *betas* on the top half of the table.

complexity of a more fundamental kind, rather than a cause of either. Expenditure measures of possibly related prior activity by municipal organizations in education and welfare had no direct effect.

In parentheses, to the left of the main results shown in Table 16 are the correlates of the elementary ("other") antipoverty networks used for purposes of control. Aside from the obviously positive effect of poverty dollars, the forecasters of complex antipoverty networks are seen to be negative or missing in the case of elementary NYC networks. Undue emphasis must not be placed on the negative signs attached to the main two coefficients, for the complex and elementary dichotomies were constructed so that one is partly the negative of the other. This method, however, allowed the effect of local linkage on network complexity to be assessed independently of the network's content or its funding level. Its execution led to unambiguous results. Complex networks proved to be functions of municipal diversification and scale, of how uncontested and community-wide are the city's voluntary associations, poverty, industrialization, and of the flow of material resources. The last of these, as we have just noted, depended in turn on the city's more general extralocal linkages.

Table 16 shows these effects to be strongest outside of the industrial regions, within which the cities have already been shown to be more specialized than elsewhere and therefore less capable of yielding generalizations. Nonetheless, the only effects to disappear are those of "need," measured by the poverty rate, and of industrialization. The idea that need does not determine community action unless the capacity for such action is also present will be discussed in Chapter Five. The fact that the effect of industrialization, one that is very likely specific to this federal program, disappears in several instances is theoretically trivial. The important findings are the respective effects of the availability of local linkage and externally provided resources on the formation of specialized interorganizational relations, once the effect of each on the other is held constant. Although the assumed causal direction between externally provided resources and interorganizational networks has been shifted, recall the independent influence of external linkage on these resources, analyzed in Chapter Two.

Table 16. Prediction over Time of Elementary (Control Condition) and of Complex Antipoverty Networks on the Basis of Municipal Scale and Diversification, City-Wide Associations, Poverty, Federal Poverty Funding, and Industrialization, Independently of the Effects of Region.

	All Cities		Cities Located *Outside* of								Cities Located in
Community Action Agency (CAA)-Sponsored (Other) NYC Programs during 1964–1966	Not CAA-Sponsored	CAA-Sponsored	NE	ENC	W	SW	SE	NE & ENC	W & SW	SW & SE	NE or ENC
Percent of Cities with at Least One CAA-Sponsored (Other) NYC Program		22 (33)	16 (36)	23 (32)	28 (32)	25 (32)	20 (35)	14 (34)	33 (29)	23 (34)	34 (32)
Standard Partial Regression (*beta*) on:[a]											
Municipal Scale and Diversification, 1960	(−.37)	.36	.27	.49	.32	.30	.32	.30	.24	.23	.17
City-Wide Associations, 1960	(−.21)	.30	.59	.23	.37	.29	.23	.77	.39	.19	.32
Poverty, 1959	(.03)	.28	.42	.30	.11	.27	.22	.54	.09	.19	.07
Industrialization, 1958	(.09)	.22	.34	.15	.09	.18	.28	.21	.01	.24	−.03
Federal Poverty Dollars, 1964–1966	(.28)	.36	.36	.26	.40	.38	.38	.20	.44	.40	.43
Multiple Correlation R[a]		.83	1.03	.85	.78	.79	.79	1.20	.72	.73	.62
Number of Cities		130	101	106	95	113	105	77	78	88	53

[a]*Betas* and R are based on estimated r's. Since R is more than 1.00 in several cases, it is clear that r's have been overestimated by the biserial and tetrachoric approximations. However, a return to the respective underestimated correlation matrix in order to rewrite each equation did not appreciably alter any of the above ten patternings of *betas*.

Formal Health Relations: Hospital Councils

The foregoing case represents fairly unambiguous deductions from our theory. Both major sources of local linkage, identified in 1960, forecast the occurrence of complex antipoverty networks some three to five years later. That the city's external linkages with federal funding agencies assisted in such prediction is also as anticipated. The preponderance of outcomes that favor the interorganizational framework of describing modern urban communities may also be shown within an entirely different content area—one tending toward the private sector—namely, the delivery of health care. Given the generality of our approach, the results may be expected to be similar. We should find it possible to predict formal relations among a city's hospitals on the basis of the same two sources of linkage. Here, hospital councils constitute the formal relations to be predicted. Hospitals are mainly professional organizations. The practicing professions are organized about such compelling societal standards and interests as life, salvation, and justice—and these values are likely to filter into their organizational loci. This also means that their activities are especially subject to outside influence. Such influence also occurs because of the "cosmopolitan" nature of professions and of the associations that professions form, which not only cut across various organizational boundaries but also across the boundaries of cities.

The Hospital Survey and Construction Act of 1946 (Public Law 79-725, commonly known as the Hill-Burton Law), mentioned in the discussion of prestige-based hospital support, provided for coordination in the establishment and improvement of hospital and health facilities at a state-wide level (Abbe and Baney, 1958). Moreover, national funds have become available for area-wide health planning (Weil, 1969, pp. 7–8, 165–166), and local hospital councils are believed to contribute to this objective, however public oriented or self-serving the actual reason for their formation may be.

The occurrence of hospital councils can be expected to be closely related to the kinds of municipal government and voluntary associations located within the city, because health services are of widespread concern in any community, however fragmented its overall structure. Thus, what has been said about organizational governing boards in general should apply to hospitals in particular. Hospitals are governed by boards composed of the leaders of prestigious and powerful organizations—often outside the health arena—or other kinds of highly regarded members of the community (implied, for example, in Blankenship and Elling, 1962; Morris, 1963a, 1963b; Elling and Lee, 1966). Several possibilities stem from this formulation. First, as representatives of broader social entities (for example, common religious bodies or entire cities), these boards may be seen as mediators between the expediential needs of hospitals, on the one hand, and their realization of the social values of the larger body on the other; they may also be seen as guardians of the hospital's purse strings. Therefore, the more local interorganizational linkage available within a community, the more unified should be the boards of its various hospitals and the more likely should coordination among hospitals be. Moreover, the assumption that centralization is an inevitable trend in community health should lead to the prediction of formal relations among hospitals wherever the community is not unduly fragmented.

A case in which nonintegration among the boards of various hospitals (very likely because of cleavages in the community) prevented merger has already been cited (Blankenship and Elling, 1962). Also, the extent to which the community's inhabitants are organized into different ethnic, class, or religious groups may make interhospital coordination impossible. Moreover, a community that is not autonomous, we have already suggested, is more likely to be fragmented than one that is; and according to our theory, overall fragmentation in the community should be associated with fragmentation within its more specialized sectors. An intensive study of the effect of absence of political autonomy, called *political fragmentation,* on fragmentation among mental health services was conducted in 6 of the 130 cities (Connery, Backstrom, Friedman, Marden, Meekison, Deener, Kroll, McCleskey, and Morgan, 1968). As expected, such fragmentation also proved to be perfectly associated with nonoccurrence of our own city-wide associations. Contrary to expectation, fragmentation failed to be inversely associated with our measure of municipal diversification and scale, possibly because the latter variable is both associated with city-wide associations and with the fragmenting property of pluralism (see Chapter Two).

Hospital Councils and Other Formal Relations.[11] Of the 130 cities, 46 had hospital councils in 1969, 34 of these councils being formed after 1960. The fact that the presence or absence of a hospital council reflects an underlying continuum of cooperation among hospitals is witnessed by a multiple correlation coefficient (R/R_{max}) of .67 with the prevalence of twelve kinds of activities that summarized the results of a telephone survey of four health leaders in each of the 127 cities that had at least one hospital.[12] Furthermore, grouping these activities on the basis of factor analysis yielded what we called "extrahospital relations," "economies of scale," and "health service delivery."[13] The finding that the first of these factors yielded the highest correlation with the presence or absence of hospital councils ($r_b = .50$ compared to .36 for the second factor and .21 for the third) is consonant with the idea that hospital councils are of interest to, and therefore likely to be affected by, community organizations other than the participating hospitals themselves.

Predictors of Hospital Councils. The results confirm prediction much as they did in the case of antipoverty networks. The overall correlations between the general availability of local linkage with the extent of formal relations among health delivery organizations, measured by the presence of a hospital council, are $r_t = .58$ in the case of municipal scale and diversification and .20 in that of the extent to which the city's voluntary associations are uncontested and community-wide. Moreover, such relationship remains strong when the effects of the two local linkage indicators are considered independently of one another and of the other variables that were introduced for purposes of control.

The need for formal relations among hospitals first appeared to be measurable simply in terms of the number of hospitals in the city. Interorganizational relations are needed to the extent that organizations are aware of their interdependence with other organizations (Form and Miller, 1960, p. 6; Litwak and Hylton, 1962; Emery and Trist, 1965), and results in attempts at coordination (Levine and White, 1961; Litwak and Hylton, 1962; Levine, White, and Paul, 1963). The sheer number of organizations of a given type, here hospitals, can create interdependencies among them, as noted in Chapter Two, that generate mutual need to regulate competition, to institutionalize conflict, and to develop other means of action in the common, complex environment to whose generation they have contributed (Emery and Trist, 1965; Terreberry, 1968).[14] Their large number can also result in outside pressures for them to establish formal interorganizational relations. Other organizations, such as municipal agencies and voluntary associations, may experience the need to exert such pressure, if only to represent the public interest or for the convenience of not having to deal with large numbers of organizations singly. This may be seen in Table 17. Yet the somewhat tenuous evidence suggests that the number of hospitals failed to affect the presence or absence of hospital councils, once population size and the number of national headquarters of voluntary associations were taken into account.[15]

Anticipating the effects of region causes a departure from customary procedure. The factor of municipal expenditures for health and hospitals was retained in the equation as a measure of experience with the organizational regulation of hospitals (although its inverse effect had not been expected) despite lack of significance; because there are well-recognized historical differences among regions in their relative reliance on public versus private hospitals, and the effect might indeed prove to be pronounced within certain parts of the country.

Conduct of a similar analysis after eliminating the twelve cities that had hospital councils formed before mid-1961 yielded virtually identical results (Turk, 1973a), and underscores our ability to predict new interorganizational networks over time. This second analysis also served to suggest the nature of the contribution made by the national headquarters of voluntary associations to the formation of hospital councils, because this effect was no more pronounced after mid-1961 than before, despite the greatly increased national emphasis on the coordination of health services. Thus, contrary to expectation, national headquarters may not have signified the mediation of national standards, but, rather, the presence of organizationally provided transportation and temporary quarters that make possible the flow of clienteles to metropolitan medical centers.[16] The larger population required by divers organizations of the metropolis might also increase the number of potential local clients. Hence, headquarters and population size might both indicate the size of the patient pool. This might signify lack of com-

Table 17. Prediction over Time of Formal Relations in Health Service Delivery on the Basis of Internal Linkage and "Need," and on the Basis of Indicators of Organizational Complexity, Specialized Organization, Centralization, and Demographic Variables Used for Purposes of Control ($N = 130$ Cities).

Predictor of Hospital Council, Generally Formed during 1961–1969	Estimated Zero-Order Correlation Coefficient, r (association before estimate)		Standardized Partial Regression Coefficient, *beta* (before estimate of r's)
Municipal Scale and Diversification in 1960	.58 (.37)[b]		.34 (.16)[b]
City-Wide Associations in 1960	.20 (.12)[a]		.26 (.15)[b]
Per Capita Health and Hospitals Expenditures in 1960	.19 (.14)[a]		−.21 (−.08)
National Headquarters of Voluntary Associations in 1960	.69 (.53)[b]		.55 (.49)[b]
Multiple Correlation, R (before estimate of r's)		.77 (.53)[b]	
Number of Hospitals	.63 (.49)[b]		.18 (.16)[a, c]
Population Size	.67 (.52)[b]		.41 (.30)[b]
Age of City	.53 (.41)[b]		−.01 (.04)
Economic Complexity	.37 (.29)[b]		−.06 (−.04)
Industrialization	.11 (.09)		−.07 (−.02)
Private Schools	.21 (.17)[a]		−.06 (−.01)
Foreign Stock	−.01 (−.01)		−.24 (−.13)
Nonwhite	.23 (.18)[b]		.11 (.08)
Democratic Vote	−.01 (−.01)		−.17 (−.11)
Population Density	.18 (.14)		−.17 (−.10)
Migration	−.17 (−.13)		.08 (.03)
Education	−.04 (−.03)		.03 (.01)
"Reform" Government	−.14 (−.08)		−.08 (−.02)
Prestige-Based Hospital Support	.07 (.05)		.03 (.02)
Decentralization of Decision Making ($n = 36$)	.32 (.15)		−.00 (−.02)

[a]Significant at the .10 level, based on association before estimates.
[b]Significant at *at least* the .05 level, based on association before estimates.
[c]The variables on the lower half of the table were alternated into the regression equation one at a time. Unless mentioned, their introduction did not alter rank ordering of the *betas* on the top half of the table.

petition and therefore remove an impediment to meeting universal need to cooperate for mutual benefit. Given such a possibility, both headquarters and population are indirect predictors of meeting needs and might validly be used as substitutes for number of hospitals, with which they correlate strongly. The headquarters index made the greatest contribution to the presence of hospital councils and was selected somewhat arbitrarily as the one to be used in the regional analysis. Subsequent use of number of hospitals as the measure of need in Chapter Five need not concern us unduly, even though diminished numbers of cases and high intercorrelations prevented control on the basis of the other two indicators.

Table 18 shows hospital councils to occur as frequently in the one region as in the next ($p > .20$ by chi-square), and—except for the expected variation in the effect of municipal health expenditures—the effects reported on Table 17 remain. Except for the greater effect of need for interorganizational relations and for the external flow of clients rather than money, the results parallel those of the less privately arranged antipoverty case and, together with it, provide strong support for hypotheses deduced from our interorganizational theory.

Coexistence of the Two Kinds of Formal Relations Among Organizations

Changes in the local delivery systems of health and welfare services have been considered nationally for more than twenty-five years. Such changes—already mentioned to be in the direction of the coordination of services—may be in a direction of more information exchange, increased service, the joint provision of various services, or the effecting of economies in delivery. The societal organizations that define such change, namely foundations, national (sometimes international) federations of local health and welfare agencies, branches of the federal government, and national professional associations, also tend to provide the relevant interorganizational models. Whether they differ much or little on the breadth of the service sector involved, or whether the appropriate interorganizational model entailed loose federation for airing conflicts or central coordination for their elimination, these national organizations in the period studied still advanced standards that pointed to interorganizational activation (such interests in interagency cooperation and coordination are mentioned by Miller, 1953; Schottland, 1963; Warren, 1967a; Morris and Rein, 1968; Weil, 1969, pp. 7–8, 165–166).

Nationally defined levels of interorganizational activation in

Table 18. Prediction over Time of Formal Relations in Health Service Delivery on the Basis of Municipal Scale and Diversification, City-Wide Associations, Municipal Expenditures for Health and Hospitals, and the Number of National Headquarters of Voluntary Associations, Independently of the Effects of Region.

	All Cities	Cities Located *Outside* of								Cities Located in
		NE	ENC	W	SW	SE	NE & ENC	W & SW	SW & SE	NE or ENC
Percent of Cities with a Hospital Council	35	37	31	34	37	34	32	37	38	38
Standardized Partial Regression (*beta*) on:[a]										
Municipal Scale and Diversification, 1960	.34	.33	.65	.25	.28	.37	.64	.17	.31	.19
City-Wide Associations, 1960	.26	.16	.33	.30	.24	.24	.11	.27	.21	.22
Per Capita Health and Hospitals Expenditures, 1960	−.21	−.07	−.35	−.24	−.19	−.32	−.17	−.24	−.35	−.50
National Headquarters of Voluntary Associations, 1960	.55	.50	.28	.66	.57	.65	.19	.71	.71	.98
Multiple Correlation, R[a]	.77	.75	.79	.82	.74	.81	.75	.79	.79	.94
Number of Cities	130	101	106	95	113	105	77	78	88	53

[a]*Betas* and R are based on estimated r's.

the delivery of health and welfare service, as we have suggested, are not necessarily implemented at the initiative of the affected organizations. Municipal government, voluntary associations (both local and external) may have much more to do with this. To the extent that competition and conflict characterize relations among health and welfare agencies, the strivings of organizations for autonomy might outweigh their inclination to cooperate with one another, even for purposes of securing outside funding (Levine and White, 1961; Litwak and Hylton, 1962; Levine, White, and Paul, 1963; Black and Kase, 1963; Schottland, 1963; Banfield, 1961, pp. 15–56; Marris and Rein, 1969, pp. 151–163). Interorganizational activation among them, whatever it be, may be attributable to the actions of such outside organizations as municipal government and city-wide associations, which are sometimes not themselves directly involved in the provision of health and welfare services.

These observations, coupled with the theoretical expectations stated at the beginning of this chapter, account for modest association, ($r_t = .35$, $p < .05$), among the 130 cities between the occurrence of hospital councils and the occurrence of complex antipoverty networks. But they account even more for the *absence* of such coexistence once the scale and diversification of municipal government as well as the incidence of city-wide associations are taken into account (partial $r_t = -.08$)! *There is no evidence of any causal connection between the two kinds of specific networks.*

A Second Generation: The Model Cities Program

The metropolitan characteristics of organizational scale and diversification (given mechanisms of conflict resolution), visibility, decentralization (given scale and conflict resolution), means of internal conflict resolution, and diffuse goals as well as conflict avoidance (given visibility) have purportedly been embodied by municipal governments, city-wide associations, or both of these. Even in the United States, however, other organizations could also have these characteristics. The following case illustrates this principle by showing that the effects of certain umbrella organizations, presumably established where municipal government or city-wide voluntary associations made sufficient linkage available, may have provided the linkage needed by even newer umbrella organizations. This was unexpected, but does not invalidate our general theory.

The Comprehensive City Demonstration Programs, enacted in 1966 (Public Law 89-754) and commonly known as the Model Cities legislation, had as their stated purpose "to provide financial and technical assistance to enable cities of all sizes to plan, develop, and carry out locally prepared and scheduled comprehensive city demonstration programs containing new and imaginative proposals to rebuild or revitalize large slum and blighted areas." The legislation specifically stated that "financial assistance will be provided if . . . there exist administrative machinery through which coordination of all related planning activities of local agencies can be achieved, and evidence that necessary cooperation of agencies in related local planning can be obtained." Whether a city was one of the chosen forty-two in the first wave of Model Cities (*Los Angeles Times,* November 17, 1967), was, it seemed, a planned event requiring much coordination (Glazer, 1970).[17] Devised to coordinate various services at the neighborhood level, the Model Cities program required widespread organizational participation in the initial application for funds by such entities as city planning agencies, Community Action agencies, boards of education, Urban Renewal agencies, and health and welfare councils. The local government was required to designate City Demonstration agencies in these applications for the purpose of coordinating the activities of the other agencies serving the model neighborhood. The official reasons given at the federal level for approving or rejecting applications had to do both with need and the city's apparent capacity to carry out its plans (*Los Angeles Times,* November 17, 1967).

Although the legislation required that applications for assistance be approved by the local governing body of the city and was otherwise especially oriented to the institutions of local government (Moynihan, 1969, p. 185), neither the scale and diversification of municipal government nor the occurrence of community-wide associations, it is suggested by Table 19, seemed to have anything to do with the selections made among the 130 large cities. But this might be statistically artifactual. Or, alternatively, we have seen federal antipoverty funding to be associated with the establishment

Table 19. Prediction over Time of "Model City" Status on the Basis of Internal and External Linkage as well as Externally Provided Resources, "Need," and Specific Organizational and Demographic Variables Used for Purposes of Control (N = 130 Cities).

Predictor of Inclusion In First Wave of Model Cities in 1967	Estimated Zero-Order Correlation Coefficient, r (association before estimate)	Standardized Partial Regression Coefficient, $beta$ (before estimate of r's)
National Headquarters of Voluntary Associations, 1960	.63 (.49)[b]	.47 (.36)[b]
Urban Renewal as of 1960	.52 (.40)[b]	.23 (.18)[b]
Per Capita Poverty Dollars, 1964–1966	.56 (.40)[b]	.23 (.17)[b]
Democratic Vote, 1960	.43 (.33)[b]	.20 (.15)[b]
Multiple Correlation, R (before estimate of r's)	.79 (.60)[b]	
Municipal Scale and Diversification	.48 (.29)[b]	−.19 (−.05)[c]
City-Wide Associations	−.14 (−.09)	−.14 (−.08)
Economic Complexity	.34 (.26)[b]	−.07 (−.04)
Industrialization	.12 (.09)	−.10 (−.08)
Age of City	.52 (.40)[b]	−.23 (−.18)
Population Size	.54 (.41)[b]	.17 (.13)
Private Schools	.25 (.19)[b]	−.18 (−.14)[a]
Foreign Stock	.28 (.22)[b]	−.03 (−.03)
Nonwhite	.19 (.14)	.01 (.01)
Population Density	.46 (.36)[b]	.07 (.05)
Migration	−.22 (−.17)[a]	.19 (.15)[a]
Education	−.14 (−.11)	.11 (.08)
Poverty	.08 (.06)	.09 (.07)
Prestige-Based Hospital Support	.14 (.11)	.12 (.10)
"Reform" Government	−.22 (−.13)	.08 (.05)
Decentralization of Decision Making (n = 36)	.30 (.28)[b]	−.14 (−.11)
Per Capita Welfare Expenditures	.43 (.33)[b]	.07 (.05)

[a]Significant at the .10 level, based on association before estimates.
[b]Significant at *at least* the .05 level, based on association before estimates.
[c]The variables on the lower half of the table were alternated into the regression equation one at a time. Unless mentioned, their introduction did not alter rank ordering of the *betas* on the top half of the table.

of complex antipoverty networks and affected in part by municipal scale and diversification. Such funding may be taken to indicate Community Action agencies and other antipoverty federations not directly measured that were established in 1966 or earlier and affected Model City status in 1967. A similar argument can be made for the urban renewal status of the city in 1960.[18] At that time, cities ranged from inactive through planning to the execution and subsequent completion phases in urban renewal. A viable urban renewal program required the existence of an interorganizationally composed Urban Renewal agency; and it may be the existence of such an agency within the city that, like its antipoverty counterparts, provided the linkage necessary for the preparation of a successful Model Cities application.

Clearly, both antipoverty funding and urban renewal activity also reflect external linkage between the city's organizations and federal agencies (both urban renewal and Model Cities funding are dispensed by the U.S. Department of Housing and Urban Development). The pronounced effect of the number of national headquarters of voluntary associations on the city's selection also appears to indicate the importance of external linkage. Thus the third part of our hypothesis (about externally provided resources) has direct support.

Although an explicit objective stated in the Model Cities legislation was to "reduce dependence on welfare payments," per capita municipal expenditures for public welfare were not associated with selection as a Model City (also, see Glazer, 1970, concerning the alleviation of municipal expenditure for neighborhood improvement). Moreover, poverty also failed to make a difference.

At the time the awards were made, there were charges and denials that political considerations entered into the selection of cities (*New York Times,* November 17, 1967; *Business Week,* November 25, 1967). Yet, among these 130 large cities, the relationship with relative size of the county's 1960 Democratic vote for President was low compared to the other organizational predictors. Indeed, region-by-region examination revealed that whatever relationship there is occurs within the southeastern region (*beta* = .65 compared to *betas* ranging from negative to less than .06).

The apparent effects of private schools and migration disappeared, and therefore presumably were artifactual, once they were separately sought within and outside the industrialized north-eastern and east north central cities. Regional differences failed to materialize in Model City awards ($.20 > p > .10$ by chi-square). In accord with previous difficulties in characterizing the industrialized regions, urban renewal failed to affect the Model City status of northeastern and east north central cities (Table 20). The industrial cities of that region proved to be the ones most likely to be Model Cities.

Noteworthy (Table 20), however, are the independent and pervasive effects of the two measures of external resources no matter which set of regions was considered. To the extent that both are correlated with municipal scale and diversification, they might have obscured the effect of that indicator of the availability of internal linkage. That the Model Cities program emphasized coordination among public agencies might account for the lack of any effect of the extent to which the city's voluntary associations were uncontested and community-wide in their impact. Alternatively, that variable's complex interrelations with the other indicators might have obscured any such effect.

There is no reason here to reject our initial formulations, and some reason to accept them in modified form, but the main verdict in the case of Model Cities has to be "not proven" for the first two parts of the hypothesis (the third was upheld). Yet the municipal and local voluntary association indicators *did* make a difference, as will be shown in the next chapter, in specifying the *association* between the "need" for status as a Model City and becoming one— this despite the failure of need to have an effect in the foregoing analysis.

Formal Relations Based on Consensus

The process of urban planning involves many of the considerations that have concerned us from Chapter Two on: the various effects of external and internal linkage on pluralism, consensus, solidarity, and the availability of resources for interorganizational activation.

Relations Between External and Internal Linkage in Planning. The need to specify the conditions of positive or negative association

Table 20. Prediction over Time of "Model City" Status on the Basis of National Headquarters of Voluntary Associations, Urban Renewal Status, and Poverty Dollars, Independently of the Effects of Region.

Inclusion in First Wave of Model Cities in 1967	All Cities	Cities Located *Outside* of								Cities Located in
		NE	ENC	W	SW	SE	NE & ENC	W & SW	SW & SE	NE or ENC
Percent of Cities in First Wave	32	28	34	32	35	32	29	36	36	38
Standardized Partial Regression (beta) on:[a]										
National Headquarters of Voluntary Associations, 1960	.47	.39	.50	.50	.47	.45	.42	.49	.47	.59
Urban Renewal, 1960	.23	.34	.20	.16	.17	.32	.32	.07	.24	.03
Per Capita Poverty Dollars, 1964–1966	.23	.17	.21	.34	.23	.19	.17	.36	.19	.43
Democratic Vote, 1960	.20	.18	.24	.23	.22	.11	.24	.25	.12	.13
Multiple Correlation, R[a]	.79	.74	.81	.86	.77	.78	.75	.86	.75	.87
Number of Cities	130	101	106	95	113	105	77	78	88	53

[a]Betas and R are based on estimated r's.

between external and local linkage can be seen in the instance of federal versus local planning. On the one hand, the rapidity with which social planning is developing at the federal level may impede coordination of social planning at the local level, for more than one hundred separate federal programs in some way have impinged on the local community, each having its own local interorganizational points of contact (Schottland, 1963). On the other hand, a number of federal programs require local planning as a condition for their implementation in the local community (Schottland, 1963); this suggests, as did our discussion of federal poverty funding in Chapter Two, that external organizations (in this case, federal agencies) do not always have a fragmenting effect on the local community, but can directly provide incentives and demands for local organization. To carry the point farther, to the extent that national programs become comprehensive and require planning at the local community level, linkage among local organizations should be enhanced. Although outside agency support may be made available for organizations that band together and may be withheld from those that do not, these bands are likely to reflect the special-interest planning of such organizations outside the local community as the Ford Foundation, the national health agencies, the Federal Urban Renewal program, the President's Committee on Juvenile Delinquency and Youth Crime, and the Hill-Burton Hospital Construction Program, to mention but a few. At the local level, federations are created that may reflect these special external interests, such as Community Progress, Inc., redevelopment authorities, and broadened school systems or health departments that assume responsibilities for community-wide planning along the axes of special interests (Morris and Rein, 1963). Yet the very existence of such large-scale and differentiated organizations or organizations of organizations should provide the generalized linkage our theory considers instrumental in local coalition formation. Moreover, the ensuing proliferation of organizations should serve to increase the community's organizational complexity, which we have assumed to be instrumental in making contextual values salient to any action at the level of community. Finally, *models* for local linkage may be transmitted via external routes.

Not only federal agencies but also national voluntary associations are significant for internal linkage in these respects. The number of national headquarters in a city, as suggested, may mean that the city has available to it the resources, incentives, models, and organizational complexity necessary for internal linkage. On the other hand, external linkage may mean external and conflicting control over locally based organizations, which therefore cannot establish linkage with one another and thereby constitute a fragmented community. These questions merit further attention in the subsection that follows:

Planning by Health and Welfare Councils. During its initial stages at least, health planning depends on the behavior of organizations, both of those that are actively involved in the provision of health care, and of others, such as government, churches, and certain industries, that have material or ideological investment in the process. The general idea of health, as we have observed, tended to be noncontroversial within the city at the time of study, while at the same time it is considered to be in the public domain.

Health and welfare councils have constituted traditional, federated means of coordination among agencies and, to lesser extent, of interagency planning (see, for example, Miller, 1953, p. 174; Warren, 1966). Although some specialists depict these voluntary networks as incapable of operating or planning amid a welter of special interests, multiple jurisdictions, and support by or responsibility to a myriad of state and national agencies (Miller, 1953; Sower, Holland, Tiedke, and Freeman, 1957; Schottland, 1963), others—although aware of such potentially fragmenting influences on community health and welfare planning—suggest that the voluntary council has been able to screen out major sources of conflict divisiveness by bringing together only those organizations, and their representatives, that have a largely common foundation of interest and association (Morris and Rein, 1968). By excluding potential contestants, they appear to present neutral fields within which controversy can be aired and conflict avoided, and they take action in the name of the total city only where overwhelming consensus has been achieved (Morris and Rein, 1968).

At the national level, the various local councils interact with one another through such organizations as the United Community Funds and Councils of America, Inc. National standards in the field of health, in turn, have placed increasing emphasis on joint comprehensive planning by local groups and organizations concerned with health services. The 1965 Amendment (Public Law 89-239) to the aforementioned hospital construction legislation broadened its goals to include coordination of health activities of all kinds for research and the improvement of health manpower. The Comprehensive Health Planning and Public Health Services Amendments of 1966 (Public Law 89-749) provided for the establishment of state health planning councils composed of state as well as for local agencies and groups that either provide or consume health services. This growing national emphasis on local health planning was expected to have had an impact on the planning activities of city health and welfare councils.

On study, bibliographies that listed health and welfare council reports prepared in 43 of the 130 cities during the years 1961 to 1969 (United Community Funds and Councils of America, 1961–1969, annually) turned out to deal with broad questions concerning the community's delivery of health services. Such broad reports, requiring interagency cooperation as they did, measure the degree to which the city activated an interorganizational network in accordance with national emphases on coordinated planning, especially since more than half of these reports were produced after the comprehensive planning legislature of 1966. The correlates of this form of interorganizational activation appear in Table 21.

As expected, the presence of city-wide associations partly accounted for the activation of these consensus-based networks. The contribution made by national headquarters may be expected in the light of national emphases on planning. But the finding that municipal scale and diversification had no measurable effect, contrary to expectation, may be because, as it has been suggested, government-sponsored action systems tend to occur under situations of *dis*sensus (Warren and Hyman, 1968).

That prestige-based hospital support proved to be inversely related to the preparation of these broad planning reports, coupled with the part played by national headquarters, suggests that councils either fail to exist or are inactive in mass communities. The effect of Republican voting patterns suggests the absence of minority organizations; this might contribute to the ease of establishing an apparent consensual basis for health and welfare councils.

Table 21. Prediction over Time of Health and Welfare Council's Health Planning Reports on the Basis of Internal Linkage and "Need," and on the Basis of Indicators of External Linkage, Specialized Organization, Centralization, and Demographic Variables Used for Purposes of Control (N = 130 Cities).

Predictor of Broad Health Planning Report during 1961–1969	Estimated Zero-Order Correlation Coefficient, r (association before estimate)	Standardized Partial Regression Coefficient, beta (before estimate of r's)
City-Wide Associations, 1960	.22 (.13)[a]	.28 (.16)[b]
National Headquarters of Voluntary Associations, 1960	.46 (.35)[b]	.53 (.40)[b]
Prestige-Based Hospital Support, 1960	−.21 (−.16)[a]	−.28 (−.21)[b]
Democratic Vote, 1960	−.14 (−.11)	−.25 (−.19)[b]
Multiple Correlation, R (before estimate of r's)	.63 (.47)[b]	
Municipal Scale and Diversification	.30 (.17)[b]	.04 (.03)[c]
"Reform" Government	−.19 (−.11)	−.13 (−.05)
Economic Complexity	.33 (.26)[b]	.07 (.06)
Age of City	.37 (.28)[b]	.20 (.17)
Population Size	.38 (.29)[b]	.08 (.07)
Industrialization	.11 (.09)	.05 (.03)
Private Schools	.05 (.04)	.03 (.02)
Foreign Stock	.05 (.03)	.14 (.08)
Nonwhite	.05 (.04)	−.05 (−.03)
Population Density	.06 (.04)	−.03 (−.04)
Migration	−.16 (−.12)	−.17 (−.13)
Education	.08 (.06)	.03 (.02)
Poverty	−.15 (−.12)	−.08 (−.05)
Decentralization of Decision Making (n = 36)	.17 (.13)	−.04 (.00)
Per Capita Health and Hospitals Expenditures	.21 (.16)[a]	.11 (.10)
Per Capita Welfare Expenditures	.11 (.08)	−.01 (.01)
Crude Death Rate	.17 (.03)	.08 (.07)

[a]Significant at the .10 level, based on association before estimates.
[b]Significant at *at least* the .05 level, based on association before estimates.
[c]The variables on the lower half of the table were alternated into the regression equation one at a time. Unless mentioned, their introduction did not alter rank ordering of the *betas* on the top half of the table.

Clearly, the organizational characteristics of the city outweigh selected apparent population counterparts in predicting the interorganizational process of health planning. They appear to describe a type of city that surpasses others in the degree of diffuse consensual solidarity among organizations it is able to maintain.

Need for this form of activation could be assumed to follow the demands on health care implied by the city's death rate. Although the crude death rate for 1960 measures a variety of factors (simultaneously including the relative number of very young and very old persons in the population, socioeconomic deprivation, and the quality of health care), it does indicate need for health planning for all of these reasons. Either before or after the fact, death, whatever its cause, generally involves or has the potential for involving health service. Per capita municipal health expenditures are taken to reflect the inclination to reduce community costs in 1960 and constitute the second indicator of need. (Both the death and the health expenditure indicators were constructed on the basis of data from U.S. Bureau of the Census, 1962a.) The allocation of funds and other resources is a major concern of health and welfare councils (for example, see Morris and Rein, 1968) and may therefore be immediately relevant to their planning activities. Yet, as tends to have been the case throughout, neither indicator of need had a measurable impact on interorganizational activation. Again, the city's capacity for linkage appears to have overshadowed its needs, as an influence on formal relations between organizations.

Analysis by region fails to qualify these findings. There were no differences in the rates at which cities in the various regions produced these reports ($p > .50$ by chi-square). And note from Table 22 that the results on Table 21 remain throughout, although the effect of how uncontested and city-wide were the local voluntary associations was greatest among northeastern cities.

Formal Relations Based on Low Commitment: The Community Chest

Mention was made earlier of an exception to the assumption that in the large city businesses are too numerous and too independent of one another to constitute a collective source of linkage

Table 22. Prediction over Time of Health and Welfare Council's Health Planning Reports on the Basis of City-Wide Associations, National Headquarters of Voluntary Associations, the Absence of Prestige-Based Hospital Support, and Republican Voting, Independently of the Effects of Region.

Broad Health Planning Report During 1961–1969	All Cities	Cities Located Outside of								Cities Located in
		NE	ENC	W	SW	SE	NE & ENC	W & SW	SW & SE	NE or ENC
Percent of Cities with at Least One Such Report	33	33	32	31	35	35	31	32	38	36
Standardized Partial Regression (*beta*) on:[a]										
City-Wide Associations, 1960	.28	.12	.49	.26	.47	.23	.55	.56	.41	.51
National Headquarters of Voluntary Associations, 1960	.53	.59	.44	.61	.37	.51	.29	.39	.33	.35
Prestige-Based Hospital Support, 1960	-.28	-.28	-.17	-.31	-.34	-.29	-.17	-.39	-.35	-.40
Democratic Vote, 1960	-.25	-.25	-.27	-.29	-.23	-.22	-.28	-.29	-.20	-.26
Multiple Correlation, R[a]	.63	.67	.55	.66	.62	.61	.68	.65	.58	.61
Number of Cities	130	101	106	95	113	105	77	78	88	53

[a]*Betas* and R are based on estimated r's.

at any large cost in time, resources, or other impediments to the attainment of their respective main goals (Banfield, 1961, pp. 291– 294).[19] Recall, from the discussion of city-wide associations, that corporate officials are generally believed to participate, super- ficially at least, in noncontroversial civic affairs. And the typical campaign of the Community Chest, "United Fund," "United Way," and so on has been low in cost and noncontroversial. It is an inter- organizational product, one that constitutes a source of resources for those supportive organizations thought necessary to the con- tinued viability of economic, governmental, and other kinds of organizations. It is one in which all manner of the community's principal organizations can participate. Linked as it is to the com- munity council, which we have noted tends to support consensus within the community and to exclude dissensus, the fund campaign can be a "safe" place for even the executives of absentee-controlled organizations to participate without unwanted involvement in local controversy and without investing too many of their organizations' resources.

The Community Chest organization is a federation of the representational variety (Form and Miller, 1960, pp. 306–308) and is under the principal control of business organizations with participation by unions, professional groups, and welfare organiza- tions. Studies of Indianapolis, Pittsburgh (Form and Miller, 1960, pp. 310, 327–329, citing a study of Indianapolis by Seeley, Junker, Jones, Jenkins, Haugh, and Miller, 1957, pp. 92–305, and one of Pittsburgh, *Fortune,* April 1957), and Chicago (Banfield and Wilson, 1963, p. 248) suggest the major roles played by large corporations in the conduct and support of such campaigns. Of the funds, 40 to 60 percent are contributed by business firms and foundations in Indianapolis, with the remainder coming from private individuals and employees. In my experience, employees are frequently so- licited from within the administrative hierarchy of work organiza- tions; thus the campaign may also be conceived of as a direct linking of administrative structures to one another. The corporations take turns assigning their executives to the central fund-raising com- mittee. Being on such a committee is a way of meeting "civic respon- sibility" and of carrying on "good public relations" (Banfield and Wilson, 1963) without excessive commitment.

Insofar as this form of fund-raising competes with other

sources of welfare (philanthropic industries, government agencies, union plans, and specialized "drives"), its dollar acquisition may be expected to suffer. Thus, where the total output is high, one may assume a city that is high in the linkage-producing characteristics already discussed; where it is low, one may assume a fragmented city or one with only a few large organizations.

For these reasons, it is not surprising to find (see Table 23) that the community's industrialization, measured by dollar manufacturing output, is associated with the per capita number of Community Chest dollars raised in 1966 (United Community Funds and Councils of America, 1966). That the amount raised was found to be inversely associated with the number of manufacturing establishments in further analysis,[20] however, means that large-scale industrialization, which indicates unions and large corporations, contributes to the amount raised, while small-scale, presumably locally managed industry does not. Nor is it surprising that one of the same two major local sources of linkage as before, the occurrence of city-wide associations, also contributes to output in these campaigns. Diversification among export establishments also has a positive effect on the dollar amount, presumably because it, too, indicates the presence of large-scale organizations to be linked with the industrial organizations.

The external effects signified by national headquarters of voluntary associations may have been unnecessary in the light of the ubiquity of these community campaigns, or may have been obscured by the effects of their economic and industrial correlates. And the unanticipated lack of effect of municipal scale and diversification may indicate the essentially private and noncontroversial nature of these campaigns.

Table 24 shows these effects to be relatively independent of region, although the highest revenues were raised in the northeastern and east north central cities (probability of differences between regions, $< .001$ by the Kruskal-Wallis test). Perhaps because of the high levels of industrialization and economic complexity in those cities, effects were lowered by considering this region.

Need for Community Chest funds would have been difficult to assess, first, because of the diversity of kinds of services supported (hardly all of them intended for the poor), and, second,

Table 23. Prediction over Time of Community Chest ("United Fund," "United Way," and so on) Revenue on the Basis of Internal Linkage, Organizational Complexity and Demographic Variables Used for Purposes of Control (N = 130 Cities).

Predictor of Per Capita Community Chest Revenue in 1966	Estimated Zero-Order Correlation Coefficient, r (association before estimate)	Standardized Partial Regression Coefficient, *beta* (before estimate of r's)
City-Wide Associations in 1960	.10 (.08)	.15 (.12)[a]
Economic Complexity in 1963	.31 (.31)[b]	.22 (.22)[b]
Industrialization in 1958	.47 (.47)[b]	.43 (.43)[b]
Multiple Correlation, R (before estimate of r's)	.54 (.53)[b]	
Municipal Scale and Diversification	.29 (.22)[b]	.03 (.03)[c]
"Reform" Government	−.28 (−.23)[b]	−.15 (−.09)
National Headquarters of Voluntary Associations	.25 (.25)[b]	.10 (.10)
Age of City	.37 (.37)[b]	−.00 (−.00)
Population Size	.07 (.07)	.08 (.08)
Private Schools	.29 (.04)	−.11 (−.11)
Foreign Stock	.04 (.04)	−.07 (−.07)
Nonwhite	−.03 (−.03)	−.07 (−.07)
Democratic Vote	.04 (.04)	−.02 (−.02)
Population Density	.17 (.17)[a]	−.13 (−.14)
Migration	−.39 (−.39)[b]	−.06 (−.06)
Education	−.13 (−.13)	.12 (.12)
Poverty	−.13 (−.13)	−.04 (−.03)
Decentralization of Decision Making (n = 36)	.41 (.41)[b]	.19 (.21)

[a]Significant at the .10 level, based on association before estimates.
[b]Significant at *at least* the .05 level, based on association before estimates.
[c]The variables on the lower half of the table were alternated into the regression equation one at a time. Unless mentioned, their introduction did not alter rank ordering of the *betas* on the top half of the table.

because the largest donations may be impelled by organizational goals that are promotional rather than exclusively humanitarian. Therefore, no attempt at measurement was made. Note, however, that Community Chest revenues were almost one third accounted for by measures of capacity, most of which (perhaps all) were organizational in their nature.[21] Impressive here is how important a bit of money or of energy expended by each of a large number of

Table 24. Prediction over Time of Community Chest ("United Fund," "United Way," and so on) Revenue on the Basis of City-Wide Associations, Economic Complexity, and Industrialization, Independently of the Effects of Region.

Per Capita Community Chest Revenue in 1966	All Cities	Cities Located Outside of									Cities Located in
		NE	ENC	W	SW	SE	NE & ENC	W & SW	SW & SE	NE or ENC
Mean Rank of City[a]	65.5	67.5	72.0	61.7	63.5	62.5	77.2	58.0	59.4	48.6
Standardized Partial Regression (beta) on:[b]										
City-Wide Associations, 1960	.15	.13	.22	.16	.14	.15	.22	.14	.13	.12
Economic Complexity, 1963	.22	.24	.34	.17	.19	.23	.40	.13	.20	.10
Industrialization, 1958	.43	.51	.26	.44	.47	.42	.18	.47	.45	.24
Multiple Correlation, R[b]	.54	.61	.52	.51	.54	.51	.56	.50	.51	.27
Number of Cities	130	101	106	95	113	105	77	78	88	53

[a]Rank among all 130 cities, 1 representing the largest per capita Community Chest revenue and 130 the smallest.
[b]*Betas* and *R* are based on estimated *r*'s.

organizations is once they are linked to one another, and how unimportant is the aggregate socioeconomic status (measured by
poverty and median years of education) of the individual persons
inhabiting the community.

Linkage Availability, Person-Based Meaures, and Parts Played by Specific Sectors

Note that the organizational predictors of the activation of
formal relations failed to be affected by the demographic rates
and other person-based measures. This section reviews the pertinent analyses. It also shows that, with one exception, the various
kinds of specific formal relations fail to affect one another directly
and fail to be affected by specialized organizations.

Demographic Predictors and "Need." Tables 15 to 24 make a
strong case for the importance of the preexisting organizational
and interorganizational characteristics of cities in predicting new
and specific interorganizational outcomes, such prediction failing
to have been confounded by the demographic predictors selected
for inclusion as controls. In the case of antipoverty networks, the
poverty rate is the only one of five predictors that is demographic,
and had only modest overall and independent effect, which was
geographically restricted.[22] Here, poverty signified the size of the
relevant clientele, to which our model assigns a place.

In the case of hospital councils, all of the predictors, except
possibly the correlates of national headquarters of voluntary associations, were organizational. Even in the event of the possible
exception, the size of the relevant clientele might again have been
measured. This very likely served to reduce competition among
organizations, thereby inclining them to cooperate. In neither the
antipoverty nor the health delivery case did population characteristics have any conceivable direct effect other than indicating
"need."

In the case of Model Cities, only voting patterns showed a
modest effect that might not have been organizational, and this
proved to be limited to only one of five geographic regions.

Again, in the case of health planning, only one apparently
demographic variable had an effect—the lowest effect—and even
this one might actually have signified interorganizational con-

sensus. Finally, the Community Chest results had no measured correlate whatsoever that failed to be organizational.

It is noteworthy that only in the case of antipoverty networks did our initial measures of "need" have a demonstrable effect. Capacity for interorganizational relations appears to outweigh the need for them. But, as the next chapter will show, capacity can create the *conditions* under which need does have the expected effect.

Turning to other demographic predictors that we have employed for more general purposes of control, selection was predicated on their having figured widely in research projects related to those in this book. However, many such studies were frankly exploratory, without firm rationales. Had we been provided with population variables not suffering from this limitation, who knows what the results might have been? At least alternative models could have been specified.

Decentralization of Decision Making. It is noteworthy that the Clark-NORC measure of the decentralization of decision making failed to have an independent effect on the five kinds of interorganizational activation, once its associations with organizational complexity in general and municipal structures in particular were taken into account, even though the organizational predictors were the more removed from the predicted events in time. Tables 15, 17, 19, 21, and 23 show the standardized partial regression coefficient (*beta*) for the decentralization of decision making to be insignificant in every case. But it should be recalled that Clark's indicator had a heavy organizational component and therefore might have been partly redundant with our own municipal scale and diversification indicator. Also note that only thirty-six of his cities coincided with ours.

The Nature of the Organizational Predictors. When antipoverty networks were considered together with hospital councils, they were found not to effect one another directly, but rather to be common products of our two most general indicators of the availability of local linkage. The fact that, of all five outcomes, antipoverty programs alone affected Model City status was determined by the very federal rules involved. Turning to the health and welfare planning reports, one finds no independent association with the other four kinds of interorganizational activation.[23] Nor were there any direct effects on Community Chest revenues.[24] With the exception of Model City status, the community's more fundamental organizational properties explained any apparent relationship between one specific kind of interorganizational activation and another.

Moreover, the community's prior activity within specific specialized sectors only partly affected new interorganizational events in these sectors. Municipal activity in education and welfare had no demonstrable effects on networks for training disadvantaged youth. Municipal health activity failed to aid in the establishment of hospital councils, even appeared to serve as their substitute within the northeastern cities. Local welfare expenditures showed no association with Model City status, even though these were assumed to measure "need." Nor did these municipal variables affect health planning or Community Chest campaigns. The organizational composition of the total city—its local and extralocal linkages in general—appeared to have more to do with specific interorganizational activation than did the prior characteristics of the sector in which such activation occurred.

Summing Up

Figure 3 recapitulates the theory and findings of this chapter. The four macrosocial properties assumed to affect the activation of specific interorganizational networks appear in the center. The (municipal) *scale and diversification of internal regulating and coordinating organizations* provides the *political capacity* to link organizations to one another, while *organizational representation of diffuse consensual solidarity* (by city-wide voluntary associations) provides the *rationales*. External linkage and, more directly, *externally (organizationally) provided resources* constitute the wherewithal, as in one or possibly two cases did the *magnitude and complexity of internal (organizational) resources*.

The first three of these properties accounted for newly established interorganizational networks, sometimes municipal in part, in federally sponsored antipoverty programs as well as for councils of mainly private hospitals. The existence of networks such as the

Figure 3. The (Re-) Activation of Specific Relations between Organizations within the Macrosocial Unit (here, the Metropolis): Summary of Chapter Four.

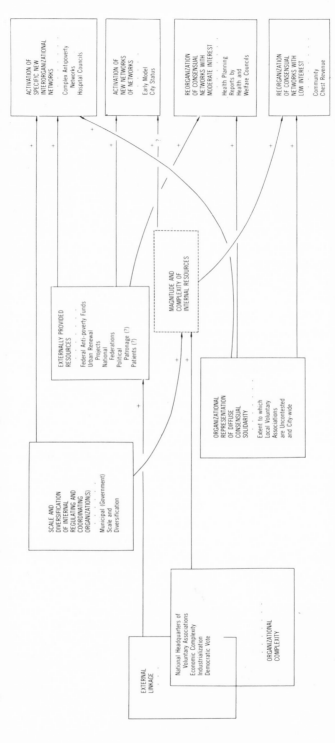

Key. Abstract properties of macrosocial units are in capital letters—in solid boxes if operationalized, in dotted boxes, if not. Lowercase letters are operational definitions of these properties in the special case of the metropolis. Arrows represent direction of causation. Plus and minus signs show direction of association.

former were required in order to fund networks of networks under federal Model City auspices (hence, the arrow with the question mark from the internal resources construct).

The second property measured by city-wide associations, consensus based and consensus forming as these seem to be, appears to contribute to the activation of consensus-seeking and conflict-avoiding networks such as health and welfare councils; municipal diversification and scale, apparently oriented to dissensus situations as macrosocial regulating and coordinating organizations are assumed to be, failed to have an effect in this instance. For similar reasons, the solidary form of linkage-producing organization very likely affects Community Chest campaigns, in which linkage has to be established with a large number of organizations.

Community Chest campaigns also provide an example of the noncontroversial case in which organizational complexity, in this case, of business and industry, *directly* provides sources of and internal resources for local linkage and provides administrative structures for the interorganizational production of macrosocial outputs.

In many instances, the "need" for interorganizational activation failed to affect its occurrence, wherever need could be measured, and all demographic variables had low or nonexistent effects. Moreover, the general organization of the macrosocial unit seemed to have much more to do with the activation of specific interorganizational relations than did other such specific relations (with the exception of Model City status) or than did the prior characteristics of the specialty sector within which each one is classified. General linkage-producing organizations appear to hold the key. Sector-specific studies (say, of health and welfare organizations), it would seem, must perforce be incomplete. And there is little evidence in support of the popular belief that "networks beget networks," unless the incentive to do so is external.

Notes

1. This propositional inventory rests upon organizational research reported by Lawrence and Lorsch (1967a, 1967b), Aiken and Hage (1968), Hage and Aiken (1970, pp. 33–38, 80–82), Hage and Dewar (1971).

2. See the organizational materials by Thompson (1967, pp. 73–76) and Hage and Aiken (1970, pp. 80–82) and the urban political literature

exemplified by Sayre and Kaufman (1960), Banfield (1961), and Sayre and Polsby (1965).

3. Also see Duncan and Schnore's (1959) critique of Hawley's (1950, pp. 221–222) assertion that sustenance-providing units have the greatest effect on the functioning of other units in the metropolis.

4. This important study of New York City provided the impetus for our measure of municipal diversification and scale. It actually measures how like New York is each city's government.

5. Unreported research project by Herman Turk, Alan Booth, and others, available from Alan Booth, Department of Sociology, University of Nebraska, Lincoln, NEB 68508.

6. Banfield (1961, pp. 269–270) described such a case but evidently failed to attach as much importance to it as our comparative findings to be described seem to justify.

7. One may make this tentative generalization on the basis of case reports by Williams and Adrian (1959), Rossi (1961), Rossi and Cutright (1961), Perrucci and Pilisuk (1970).

8. Suggested by Stinchcombe's discussion of the effects of "richness" within a social setting in either providing facilities conducive to the establishment of organizations or constituting means of restricting their encroachment (1965).

9. See Turk (1973b, chap. 3). "Reform" cities may display characteristics similar to ones with city-wide associations, but—unlike the latter—they do so at the expense of the capacity for coalition that the aggregating and buffering effects of local political parties or political districts that also might affect the capacity for coalition.

10. All of the analyses reported in this chapter, including this one, seek to invalidate our predictions through the introduction of each indicator as control that might even remotely be expected to affect the results. Doing so, even in the absence of clearly formulated alternative hypotheses, is conservative, but prudent in the light of the newness of our theory and of the manner of its implementation.

11. Stephen McConnell is coauthor of this subsection.

12. Joint fund raising, nurse affiliation, patient use studies, personpower surveys, seminars and training programs, accounting systems, group purchasing, wage and salary surveys, emergency communications, specialized medical facilities, patient referral, and laboratory facilities.

13. The first five kinds of activities of the previous note are arranged in the order of their respective correlations with the first factor, the next five in the order of correlation with the second, and the last two in the order of correlation with the third—in each case starting with the highest correlations and ending with kinds of activities correlated with more than one of the three factors. Only this early analysis used R/R max.

14. Litwak and Hylton (1962) suggest a curvilinear relationship between number of organizations and formal coordination among them,

because as number surpasses a certain threshold, coordination becomes unfeasible. However, the critical number is not likely to be reached in this study of hospital councils; thus, any relationship between number or organizations and formal relations among them may be assumed not to change in direction.

15. The possibility cannot be discounted that this outcome resulted from multicolinearity among these three independent variables (r's range from .71 to .82). Yet population size and national headquarters, taken singly, each removed the effect of number of hospitals on hospital councils, while inclusion of the latter failed to disturb the effect of each of the other two variables.

16. See Philbrick (1957) for a discussion of spatial propinquity among competitors, in order to create centers that increase their aggregate clienteles.

17. Subsequent waves of Model Cities were selected after considerable national controversy. Extraneous and situation specific factors undoubtedly entered in, and we would hesitate to use them for our predictions.

18. Note from the tables in the Appendix that several alternative equations are quite possible in the light of the substantial correlations that all of the local and extralocal indicators of linkage have with model city status, and their relatively uniform correlations with one another, and the possible "suppression" of the effects of community-wide associations. But note also that the equation believed to be most descriptive of the data (by stepwise regression) fails to contradict the spirit of the deductions of our theory, although it contradicts the letter by substituting new possible indicators of local linkage—that is, of Community Action and Urban Renewal agencies—for older ones. Yet the statistical relationships are such that Model City status, Urban Renewal stage, and poverty funding (*or* complex antipoverty networks) could also have been common outcomes of our more basic measures of local linkage, had there been less measurement error.

19. This assumption is qualified by our untestable proviso, however, that the threat of such linkage might well prevent certain possibilities from ever arising.

20. Inclusion of this variable provided an estimated *beta* of $-.36$ and raised the respective *betas* for industrialization, economic complexity, and city-wide associations to .58, .40, and .18. This increased multiple correlation (R) to .60.

21. A disclaimer of possible contamination of the indicator of city-wide associations by Community Chest campaigns and other kinds of interorganizational activation is in order. None of the city-wide associations referred to are hospital associations or health and welfare councils; nor do the latter two duplicate one another in any way. The health and welfare councils are not themselves fund-raising entities, having the re-

sponsibility for administration and planning, rather than for support; thus prediction of broad council reports in the field of health is uncontaminated by predicting the outcome of Community Chest drives. Certain of the city-wide associations named (not many of them) were in fact Community Chest organizations. But this does not signify redundancy; for among the cities only certain of these fund-raising associations were named as city-wide in their impact, and the mere naming of such an organization does not signify the success of its campaign.

22. The rank order of predictors according to variance uniquely explained is the same as the rank ordering of *betas* on all twenty-four tables discussed so far.

23. The partial correlation coefficients were insignificant in every case and ranged from −.17 (sic!) to .10, irrespective of whether or not zero-order r's were estimated.

24. Again the partial correlation coefficients were insignificant and ranged from −.11 to .07, irrespective of manner of computation.

Chapter Five

••••••••••••••••••••
••••••••••••••••••••••
••••••••••••••••••••••••

"NEED" FOR INTERORGANIZATIONAL RELATIONS

••••••••••••••••••••••
••••••••••••••••••••••
••••••••••••••••••••••

With some exceptions, the manifest "need" for new interorganizational relations or for the reactivation of old ones (see Chapter Four) failed to account for their occurrence, magnitude, or outputs. Our theory attributes this to the overriding importance of the sheer amount of external linkage (measured here by the number of headquarters of national voluntary associations and related variables) or of the availability of internal linkage that depends on certain key organizational properties (measured here by municipal scale and diversification and by city-wide associations) that are required for any activation of interorganizational relations according to nationally transmitted prototypes—irrespective of how great or small the need might be. *Capacity* accounted for interorganizational activation, largely apart from any other cause. There was probably no city among our 130 that could not claim at least some need for interorganizational activation, but not all of them were capable of filling that need. (Although it was not part of our inquiry, even the wealthy city of Beverly Hills, California, it is instructive to note, applied for antipoverty funds.)

Without capacity, need has no effect. Therefore capacity and need are not additive—they are multiplicative.

In order to understand the part played by manifest need in establishing new organizational networks or in reactivating old ones, it is necessary to understand *the process by which need is translated into prevailing* demand *and how, in turn, such demand is translated into interorganizational* supply. Both prevailing demand and mode of supply, we shall argue, are patterned by external standards.[1]

Extension of the interorganizational version of pluralism in this chapter will suggest that—as was the case for sheer capacity for interorganizational activation—this coming together of need, prevailing demand, and supply is a consequence of organizational scale and diversification (given decentralization, visibility, and the means of resolving inner conflicts), diffuseness of organizational goals (given visibility and lack of contest), and the operation of external (here national) interests and standards. The following formal theory codifies this process.

The greater the scale and diversification of internal regulating and coordinating organizations or the greater the organizational representation of diffuse consensual solidarity, the greater the availability of internal linkage. The greater the availability of internal linkage, the more salient are externally shared standards in determining not only the *form* of interorganizational activation, but also the level at which some variable state of macrosocial units requires action. Demand alone, however, cannot affect interorganizational relations unless there is also capacity for them. Yet the greater the availability of internal linkage, as Chapter Four has shown, the greater also is the *capacity* for interorganizational relations. Therefore, the greater the availability of internal linkage *and* the higher the relevant state level ("needs") of the macrosocial unit, the more likely is the activation of specific interorganizational networks. From this series of postulates comes the single proposition of this chapter: *The greater the diversification and scale of internal regulating and coordinating organizations* or *the greater the organizational representation of diffuse consensual solidarity, the more will demand-relevant states of the macrosocial unit (externally defined internal "needs") affect the activation of interorganizational relations.*

There would be *no way* that the operational versions of this proposition could be confirmed if there were no national standards both with respect to what constitutes need for interorganizational relations or what constitutes their supply. This restriction is often overlooked when need is employed as a factor in comparative urban research. Also, let it be understood that we make no assumptions about the purposes of these standards: whether they exist as rationalizations to placate at minimal cost and preserve the status quo, or whether they are meliorative, possibly revolutionary, in their intent, as opposed to advancing vested interests. Our macrotheory fits the idea of national or international "social system" as well as it does "political economy." The issue between these two popular perspectives is not one having to do with local *as opposed to* national or multinational interests, but one having to do with how concordant these interests are and of how they are advanced in social structures. It is not necessary to take sides. We observe the fact of a "winning coalition" without having to go into whether it won by acclamation, through repression, or by revolution.

Thus the scale and diversification of municipal government and the extent to which the city's voluntary associations are uncontested and city-wide will continue to constitute important variables in the case of cities in the United States—*this time* to specify the conditions *under which nationally defined levels of local need affect nationally defined modes of local interorganizational supply.*

External Standards and Internal Needs

At any given point in time, the macrosocial unit is characterized by the relative prevalence of various contesting interests and standards among which selections are made through coalition and contest.[2] It is a plural setting, in which competing demands are initiated, transmitted, evaluated, confronted, and decided on by the unit's organizations or by coalitions of its organizations (Banfield, 1961; Sayre and Polsby, 1965; Sayre and Kaufman, 1960). Inaction may result. However, where decisions are implemented, the process is still very often the unanticipated one of blind contest and/or accord. Here the interplay is among divers organizations or coalitions among them that value (or are made to value) the decision to meet a certain demand and that possess the necessary resources to do so (see Stinchcombe, 1968, pp. 188–198, for a lucid interpretation of Banfield's 1961 case materials, along related lines).

More specifically, even such general interests as the provision of health care or public safety is subject to contest and bargaining, because the degree of realization of all of them cannot be maximized at once (Warren, 1967b, 1970).[3] This means that at each point in the society's or the local community's life there is a "satisficing" mix of degrees to which divers interests are maximized. The mix is likely to be unstable, because even the value commitments of organizations are, under certain conditions, considered negotiable (Parsons, 1971a; Simpson, 1971), and the less satisfying a bargain the more likely will be the search for a new one. It follows that even the most altruistic of organizations not only find their "public-serving" interests in the macrosocial unit in conflict with the exclusively self-serving interests of other organizations, but that they also find them in conflict with other public-serving interests (Banfield, 1961, pp. 15–56, 315).[4] Under these conditions, the interorganizational coalitions that result from conflict and bargaining determine the nature of needs for whose satisfaction the local community or society will commit its resources.

This exposition sketches the process by which certain interests are translated into demand for action by the macrosocial unit. Interorganizational linkages have further importance in determining how demand is to be satisfied and also in constituting its means of satisfaction. The use of any broad interorganizational network (often itself a coalition) in such satisfaction is likely to prevent its use for other purposes. Moreover, it may come to be in competition with other networks, constituted either for the same or for different purposes (suggested by reading Morris and Rein, 1968). Therefore, the objective of satisfying any demand at the level of local community or society does not automatically determine the interorganizational *means* of its satisfaction. Further, the interests that organizations have in maintaining themselves at an optimum level within their environment can also affect the networks that they form with one another.[5] This has two implications. First, if the formation of a new interorganizational network or the reactivation of one that has lain dormant were exclusively under the control of its participant organizations, certain demands whose satisfaction may be defined by other organizations as "in the general interest" might go unmet. Or, second, the nature and level of whatever interorganizational activity the participant actors and other partisans might demand could come to be questioned by some of the remaining organizations as "corruption," "self-serving opportunism," "monopoly," or "manufactured demand." In such confrontation of the interests of potential network participants with the values of other organizations, certain interorganizational arrangements can be eliminated by selecting only certain organizational purposes as acceptable bases of demand. Furthermore, such confrontation may operate to regulate interorganizational output in preventing what might ultimately be derogated as "oversupply." In sum, not only demand, but also the decision process connected with its satisfaction, as well as the mode of satisfaction, are outcomes of the interplay among the multiple interests and standards advanced by the community's various organizations.

The demand that a given organization might generate under these conditions (including demand that it be the supplier) or any manner of demand satisfaction that it envisages—no matter how disinterested its own participation—is subject to challenge by other organizations. Thus, internal linkage is a prerequisite for the ascendancy of any demand.

As suggested in the earlier chapters, the major process of establishing linkage in the community is by way of forming coalitions on the bases of compromise, sanction, and bargain. Through these processes, support for various interests and standards may be exchanged or combined in such a manner that ensuing proposals do not meet the opposition that often causes them to be tabled (see Greer's 1967 interpretation, to this effect, of Banfield's 1961 case studies).

Internal Linkage Availability and the Effects of "Need"

In order to affect supply, any "need" for interorganizational activation must be translated into demand by a "winning" coalition that overrides the demands advanced by other organizations or by other coalitions of organizations. Whether or not a winning coalition can be formed in the macrosocial unit depends on the availability of internal linkage. Not only can we expect that such linkage should affect the fact of interorganizational activation where capacity exists, but we can expect that it should also determine the nature of such activation; for different coalitions might demand that different networks (perhaps the coalitions themselves) be activated. Where a single demand fails to predominate, as in the case of equally strong coalitions that oppose one another (whether external in their origins or internal), interorganizational activation is less likely than otherwise; where the capacity for interorganizational activation is lacking, however, activation is impossible. *That any social event is the joint effect of incentive and opportunity is pertinent to all levels of analysis, from the intrapersonal to the intersocietal.*

To say that one demand is dominant, even where it is external in its origins and uncontested, is not to identify the need that prompted its expression. For example, an organized minority may be concerned with the need to mitigate a certain social problem. Aware of this need, and fearing loss of power as a result, a majority coalition might experience a need to provide some token or symbolic response and activate an interorganizational network to that end. Such activation might prevent activation of other networks more directly responsive to minority needs, networks that may, however, threaten existing power arrangements among organizations. This example, where needs that oppose one another can lead to apparently similar demands for interorganizational activation, is only one among several that could have been mentioned. The conflict may even be generated extralocally, to be played out locally; both national accord with respect to certain questions, we have claimed, and national disputes with respect to others may flow along external routes. Whether the somewhat cynical view of interorganizational activation implied by our present example is taken or whether the equally unsupported, more benign one is adopted, viewing such activation as a "best guess" of how to meet a consensually defined need effectively, is irrelevant to our theory.

In short, whether the interests and standards proclaimed in support of the decisions of winning coalitions are rationalizations in a broader political economy ("opiates for the masses"), or whether they are deeply felt and widely shared convictions that guide interorganizational activation does not have to concern us in terms of our theory, other than to reaffirm that the standards and interests that are most widely proclaimed (external, in the main) are the ones about which a "winning" coalition forms. A winning coalition among organizations, like one of its producers, the organizational representation of diffuse consensual solidarity, does not necessarily imply consensus beyond that of, say, an organized elite, but only signifies the lack of organization among the dissenters. Yet the idea that organizations exist in states of partial conflict with one another, both externally and internally, would suggest that externally advanced interests and interorganizational standards for their implementation are the external results of bargaining, contest, and invocation of even more abstract interests, which Durkheim saw as outcomes of complexity within the broader social environment. Whatever the prevailing demand or whatever the nature of the need on which it is based, its dominance in an organizationally complex, macrosocial unit depends on the availability of linkage for the political and consensual aspects of coalition formation.

Linkage by Organizational Scale and Diversification. The resources associated with organizational scale, as noted, facilitate both sanction and bargain, provided the organization can adapt itself to a constantly changing environment. Diversification within an organization means that it has a multiplicity of resources that it has applied or can apply in this manner, but also that it can participate in what might be an even more fundamental means of effecting adjustments between supply and demand. Concerting the latter two processes might involve the exchange of support by each organization in matters it considers minor with other organizations that need support, in return for support in matters it considers major.[6] The more diversified an organization, the more numerous the specific issues it will span and the larger the stock of support it has on hand to make available for exchange. Moreover, the idea that an organization's diversification is associated with its meeting issues politically, as we have argued it is, means that its various interests are negotiable rather than absolute.

Linkage Through Organizational Representation of Diffuse Consensus. Provided that they are visible, neutral organizations that represent solidarity and advance diffuse common interests, at least within a broad interest block—although not themselves reactants in the process of coalition forming—can nonetheless have a catalytic effect on the probability of action by the macrosocial unit, through the linkage that they mediate. The diffuse purposes of such organizations and their failure to threaten the realization of interests by other organizations enable them to be used as legitimators. Organizational contestants may be said to form the imaginary coalitions with such neutral organizations that are implied by claims of membership in a common interest block ("The press supports us in this view" or "We are as one with the Church in defending this principle"), and rival positions might draw closer together as a result. Neutrality also enables organizations to provide linkage more directly, by the overt assumption of mediating and conciliatory roles. Or they can constitute assemblies for the contesting organizations, in particular, and play the roles of disseminating and reinforcing agents of the interests that organizations share, in general.

Once such organizations enter the arena, other organizations may use the common standards that are articulated as negotiating devices to shift the balance of power, or they may adopt them as central symbols around which more discrete interests and standards can cluster. The linkage made available by neutral organizations serves to mediate coalitions in terms of standards around which consensus on issues can focus. By promoting uncontested outcomes, such linkage has positive effects in general on the linkage formed among other organizations.

Here, as well as elsewhere, one might expect a "division of labor" among organizations, for organizations that are active contestants as regards specific interests and standards are not as likely as others to play mediating roles in terms of common interests.[7] However, this is not to say that the existence of the one kind of organizational precludes the existence of the other. Nor is it to deny that the more numerous and varied the linkage offered by any organization, the more likely it is to promote the standards of the macrosocial unit as a whole. It is only to say that organizations that avoid contest are the most credible in the promotion of such standards. Common standards may be promoted by linkage of any kind, for various reasons already mentioned. Or such standards may be because numerous contacts bring increased awareness of the usefulness of standards in the formation of viable coalitions. They may also be mediated because multiple commitments increase the need to emphasize eternally rooted, common standards, to avoid the loss of linkage in one given area on the basis of that which is formed in the next.

Thus, in the United States, one might expect the influence of any apparently widely recognized need for interorganizational activation on its occurrence, whether token or not, to be greater where municipal government is diversified and large in scale, or where city-wide associations exist, than where these local linkage-producing features are absent.

Further, such need-based activation depends on the operation of uniform national criteria among cities—sometimes nationally *competing* criteria—that stipulate the level of need that should result in interorganizational activation. Like other external standards, these "guides" are most likely to prevail where considerable internal linkage results in the mediation of external matters.

Such guides are attested to in that many daily affairs of cities are conducted by national or international organizations or by respective branches, chapters, diocese or synods, consulates, district offices, campuses, and affiliates. National conglomerates constitute examples; so do chains, monopolistic athletic leagues, newspaper wire services and broadcast networks, postal services, and national federations of municipal agencies (such as mayors' conferences) and local organizations (such as members of the U.S. Chamber of Commerce) of all kinds. Further, the social technology, interests, and other kinds of information that flow through these national organizations or from the organizations of one city to those of the next can serve to pattern strictly local organizations according to national prototypes. National professional associations and organizations that implement mass communication also exemplify ones instrumental in these respects. Yet the nationally patterned affairs of local organizations are not only those of accord (as, we shall see, is the case with federal influence on the local coordination among health and welfare organizations), but also ones of conflict, as in the case of local instances of industry-wide disputes between corporations and labor unions.

All this has prompted some to suggest that the internal structures and dynamics of United States cities parallel one another (Schnore and Alford, 1963; Warren, Rose, and Bergunder, 1974; and possibly Castells, 1974). But the assumptions made and problems investigated in the present work permit us to bypass such questions, much as we avoided the ambiguities inherent in distinguishing between hierarchy and specialization among cities and distinguishing among regions or between region and nation in discussing a city's impact (see Chapter Two). We do not ask *whether* each city is like the others—just *how much* like the others each one is.

Hypotheses Based on Urban Linkage Production

The larger the scale of municipal government and the more differentiated it is, by way of review, the more numerous its interests and the greater its visibility and decentralization. The more likely, therefore, are its components to provide a flexible set of points around which (or in response to which) winning interorganizational coalitions either exist or can be formed, or can acquire some legitimation on the basis of national standards—however benign, coercive, meliorative, or manipulative these standards may be. The more city-wide and uncontested the city's voluntary associations—therefore also the more diffuse their goals, the greater their avoidance of conflict, and the greater their visibility— the more can the solidary linkage they provide serve to support consensus on externally acquired interests and standards that are shared by other organizations, to legitimate coalitions, and to suppress conflict. In terms of this chapter's argument, then, *we might hypothesize the* covariation *between generally recognized need for formal relations in any broad set of local organizations and the occurrence of such activation to be greater (1) the more diversified the municipal government and the larger its scale, or (2) the less contested and the more city-wide the voluntary associations.*

Nationally Defined Need in Health and Welfare

Nationally defined levels of need for interorganizational activation in the delivery of health and welfare service are not necessarily transmitted as demands by the affected organizations. Organizations such as the producers of extralocal and local linkage already discussed may have much more to do with transmission. To the extent that competition and conflict characterize relations among health and welfare agencies, (see, for example, Levine and White, 1961; Litwak and Hylton, 1962; Levine, White, and Paul, 1963; Schottland, 1963; Black and Kase, 1963), the strivings of agencies for autonomy might outweigh their inclinations to cooperate, even for purposes of securing outside funding (Banfield, 1961, pp. 15–16; Marris and Rein, 1969, pp. 151–163). Interorganizational activation among them, whatever it be, may be attributable to the actions of other local organizations. It proves possible, then, to extend the analysis of antipoverty funding begun in Chapter Two and some of the analyses of interorganizational activation begun in Chapter Four to compare the effects of need under conditions of high and low availability of internal linkage.

Need for Antipoverty Funds

Rough guidelines set by federal agencies established funding levels on the basis of the size of deprived populations served by local organizations whose applications had been approved (personal communication with informed federal officials). This meant that the need for these funds was established in terms of national criteria and could be measured by the actual poverty rate (proportion of families with less than $3,000 annual income in 1959). The process of translating need into demand in the process of applying and negotiating for funds may have involved simple petition by organizations that represent deprived populations or the perception of a ready clientele by federal or local agencies. Competing demands may have been made by agencies seeking to preserve their autonomy or by organizations that were ideologically opposed to "welfare economies" or ones that feared political changes for which portions of the War on Poverty were intended (for example, see Greenstone and Peterson, 1968). It may also be, according to some social philosophers, that the guidelines purporting to estimate need actually assessed the potential for protest and change. Under this argument, federal and local agencies preempted the field of welfare, especially where need was great, before revolutionary organizations could do so. Whatever the "real" reason—and all kinds probably went into the winning coalition that made the poverty program into a law—we can expect that the extent to which the indicators of need accounted for funding should be higher among cities with relatively large-scale and diversified governments than among other cities and higher among cities having at least one city-wide association than among cities without any. The poverty rate proved to be correlated with per capita number of poverty dollars among the 37 cities with large-scale and diversified governments ($r = .47$) and uncorrelated ($r = -.03$) in the remaining cities. The effect of city-wide associations on the correlation between need and funding proved to be insignificant and the reverse of that expected ($r = .00$ where there were city-wide associations and .13 where there were none).[8] But both indicators of local linkage had the expected effect where not just antipoverty funding but also antipoverty networks were at issue. Indeed, specifying the flow of poverty funds might have been ill advised in the light of their partial dependence on such networks. (This portion of the research had been completed before the relevant analyses of Chapter Two were conducted.)

Need for Activation of Antipoverty Networks

The same poverty measure may be used to estimate the need for formal relations among organizations that participated in local antipoverty activities, and for the same reasons as in the case of level of antipoverty funding. Here, the availability of linkage is also assessed by the occurrence of large-scale and diversified municipal government or of city-wide associations. Among cities having large-scale and diversified municipal government, the poverty rate measured in 1959 to 1960 yielded a correlation of $r_b = .72$ with the establishment in 1964 to 1966 of Neighborhood Youth Corps projects sponsored by Community Action agencies, but a correlation of only .03 in the remaining cities. Such correlation was .42 among cities with city-wide associations and $-.22$ among those without. Both findings show once again that the capacity for interorganizational activation must exist in order for need to have a demonstrable effect.

Need for a Model City Program

The second generation of interorganizational networks implied by Model City programs very likely generated a second set of needs, including the survival needs of organizations established by earlier programs. Nonetheless, the poverty rate yielded a correlation of $r_b = .24$ with Model City status among cities with relatively large-scale and diversified governments and only .07 among the other cities. Because the reduction of municipal welfare expenditures was a professed aim of the Model Cities program, welfare expenditures might have been expected to influence Model Cities awards under conditions of high local linkage and not under those of low linkage. This was the case; the association (r_b) between need for interorganizational activation and its supply was an appreciable .50 where municipal scale and diversification were great, and only .18 where not. The finding that the general availability of local linkage did not have a direct effect on the secondary networks (Table 19) did not preclude its role in translating need into demand in terms of external standards. Perhaps because of the official aim of involving local governments in the Model Cities program, the presence or absence of city-wide associations had less effect (although in the expected direction) on the extent to which need for Model City status determined its supply—yielding coefficients r_b of .15 and .04, respectively, in the case of poverty and ones of .48 and .40 in that of welfare costs.

Need for Hospital Councils

The need for formal relations among organizations (in this case among hospitals), as we have observed, does not necessarily generate such relations, however, even if capacity for them exists. Need must be translated into demand through interorganizational communication, perhaps especially in the present case, and must compete with other demands such as demands for free enterprise or for decentralization of the services provided by the community. The more diversified the municipal government and the larger its scale, or the less contested and the more city-wide the associations, the more likely are these competing demands to be communicated and evaluated by all interested organizations in the city. And where national trends exist to advocate increased cooperation, as is the case in the delivery of health services, the need for cooperation posed by the number of hospitals is likely to be translated into demand that it be met by a hospital council. Here we consider only the thirty-four cities with councils formed after mid-1961 and the eighty-four with none, so that prediction could be prospective.

The degree to which hospital councils could be predicted on the basis of the number of hospitals in the city was $r_b = .60$ for cities with large-scale and diversified municipal governments, and .44 for those without. Such correlation was .68 for cities with city-wide associations and, again, .44 for those without. Again, need made more difference for cities relatively high in the availability of local linkage than for cities in which linkage was low. The possibly confounding effects of number of national headquarters of voluntary associations and of population size, however, detract from the persuasiveness of this particular conclusion.

Need for Health Planning by Local Councils

It will be recalled that both the city's death rate and its municipal health expenditures were taken as indicators of need for broad-based evaluation of and planning for health services. It will also be recalled, from Table 21, that the consensus-forming linkage provided by city-wide associations affected the preparation of the appropriate evaluations and plans by consensus-based health and welfare councils. And, further, the activation of these councils was not affected by dissensus-oriented municipal government. Perhaps for this reason, city-wide associations seem to have more to do with the association between need and its fulfillment here than did municipal scale and diversification. Prediction of these broad council reports was $r_b = .34$ in the case of deaths for cities having at least one city-wide association and not affected by deaths at all ($r_b = -.08$) for cities with none. The corresponding predictions in the case of health costs follow a similar pattern ($r_b = .29$ versus .08). Prediction based on the first of these need measures was $r_b = .25$ where municipal government was large and diverse and only .05 where it was not. Predictive differences were not quite as pronounced in the case of health costs, the coefficients being .24 versus .11.

Summing Up: Capacity and Need for Interorganizational Activation—An Overview

Taken in the aggregate as shown on Table 25, these results make a compelling case for viewing the modern macrosocial unit as an organizationally complex arena in which "needs" are expressed as various kinds of demand that compete with one another until a demand can be found around which the winning coalition organizes or until a stalemate is reached.[9] Figure 4 represents the theory proposed to account for the importance of *internal linkage availability* for concerting capacity and demand in the activation of specific interorganizational networks. The sheer capacity for interorganizational relations depends directly on the availability of local linkage for any major coalition within the macrosocial unit, which is affected, in turn, either through the political capabilities of the *large-scale and diversified organizations* that have within them the means of conflict resolution or through the solidarity and consensus mediating consequences of *visible organizations with diffuse noncontroversial purposes*. This is shown by the second highest horizontal arrow on Figure 4, which summarizes a major portion of the argument of Chapter Four.

But the *mode* of interorganizational activation, like also many of the macrosocial unit's internally oriented organizations, is likely to be patterned by *external standards*. And the greater the internal linkage availability the more likely is such patterning, for the more likely is the "winning coalition" to form around these standards. The top arrow indicates this effect on the capacity for interorganizational relations. Turning to the lower portion of the figure, it is true that certain cities have more of a given "problem" than do others, but *which variable state of the macrosocial unit* determines a

Table 25. Prediction over Time of the Activation or Reactivation of Interorganizational Relations on the Basis of Demand, Given Varying Degrees of the Two Indicators of Internal Linkage Availability.

Indicator of Demand	Interorganizational (Re-) Activation Supplied	Relative Scale and Diversification of Municipal Government, 1960				Extent to Which Local Voluntary Associations are Uncontested and City-Wide, 1960			
		Great		Small		Great		Small	
		Estimated r (association before estimate)		Estimated r (association before estimate)		Estimated r (association before estimate)		Estimated r (association before estimate)	
Poverty 1959	Complex Antipoverty Network, 1964–1966	.72	(.57)	.03	(.02)	.42	(.32)	−.22	(−.14)
Poverty 1959	Model City Award, 1967	.24	(.19)	.07	(.05)	.15	(.11)	.04	(.03)
Per Capita Municipal Welfare Expenditures, 1960	Model City Award, 1967	.50	(.40)	.18	(.13)	.48	(.36)	.40	(.31)
Number of Hospitals, 1960	Hospital Council, 1961–1969	.60	(.47)	.44	(.32)	.68	(.54)	.44	(.33)
Death Rate, 1959	Health and Welfare Council Health Report, 1960–1969	.25	(.20)	.05	(.04)	.34	(.27)	−.08	(−.06)
Per Capita Municipal Health Expenditures, 1960	Health and Welfare Council Health Report, 1960–1969	.24	(.19)	.11	(.08)	.29	(.23)	.08	(.06)
NUMBER OF CITIES (N)[a]		37		93		76		54	

[a] The four N's (left to right) were reduced to 31, 87, 69, 49 in the sixth analysis above to allow prediction over time by removing cities with hospital associations that were established before 1961.

Figure 4. The Processing of Internal Demands by External Standards in the (Re-) Activation of Specific Relations between Organizations in the Macrosocial Unit (here, the Metropolis): Summary of Chapter Five.

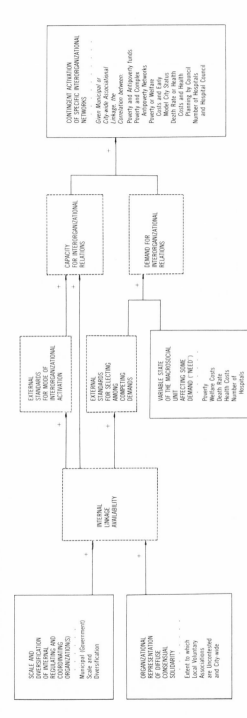

Key. Abstract properties of macrosocial units are in capital letters—in solid boxes if operationalized, in dotted boxes, if not. Lowercase letters are operational definitions of these properties in the special case of the metropolis. Arrows represent direction of causation. Plus and minus signs show direction of association. Single arrows from two boxes represent joint (multiplicative) effects—that is, specified or contingent association.

problem and *how much* of a problem demands solution is again affected by the external standards around which a coalition forms and that are employed to select from among competing demands. Any demand for interorganizational activation goes through this process. Thus, the macrosocial unit's internal availability of linkage means that external standards will be applied to both the demand that is to be met and to the interorganizational means of meeting it.

Given the capacity and the demand for specific interorganizational networks, they will occur. If either capacity or demand is fully lacking, the networks will not be formed. Each of our 130 metropoli could generate some demand of the kinds listed, but not all had the requisite internal linkage availability to meet it. Moreover, ones that had the availability could form networks on the basis of minimal need. Hence, one might suppose, the results of Chapter Four hold, namely that capacity outweighed demand. The results of Chapter Five may, then, be summarized as follows: Given the capacity for interorganizational relations, their occurrence will be associated with the externally defined level of the state of the macrosocial unit that affects demand (see bottom center of Figure 4); given the absence of such capacity, this will not be the case.

That demand can only determine supply when there is linkage has general implications for market phenomena. What sometimes fails to be recognized in studying markets—using the term *market* in its most comprehensive sense, which includes but goes beyond the mere provision of economic goods and services—is that in order for supply to bear any relation to demand there must exist the necessary set of linkages called a *marketplace* through which wants and dispositions to provide can be articulated with one another, even if for no other reason than that they have become known to their respective holders. Today, organizations are required to generate any large-scale marketplace, which after all provides the means by which "needs"—often uncritically accepted as universal "givens"—may be articulated and transmitted as competing demands. Similarly, the mere existence of facilities—here claimed to be mainly interorganizational—cannot affect anything unless there are linkages through which availability of these facilities is translated into supply. One has only to take the obvious example of the nonexistent stock market on days when stock exchanges or brokerage firms close their doors.

Moreover, in order to compare markets with one another as is done here in large United States cities, it was necessary to investigate comparative needs and comparative supplies. For this to be done, common standards have to be available from one market to the next on the bases of which need may be decided and the appropriate supply generated. A "common currency" is necessary. Otherwise, what may be considered, say, *high* health expenditures to be met by coordinated health planning in one city may be considered either *low* or unimportant or procurable by different means in another city. In the present instance, the common standards were those of a more inclusive external context, the nation. This is not to say that these were the sole standards; only that they proved to be dominant, once linkage enabled most of the relevant organizations to enter the arena of competing demands. It also bears repetition that any given demand for interorganizational activation may be based directly on some "obvious" need or else on a derived need to avoid the first need's satisfaction save in a token way. Our discussions fall short of stating which one is the case in any given instance; the scope of our theory makes such statements unnecessary.

In sum, the availability of linkage not only affects the macrosocial unit's capacity for interorganizational activation (see Chapter Four); it also affects the coordination of such activation with levels of "need" as these are defined externally. That any social event is the joint effect of incentive and capacity is pertinent to all levels of analysis, from the intrapersonal to the intersocietal.

Another very abstract aspect of this analysis, not specific to interorganizational relations (one that prompted it but has generally been misunderstood) is how the outlines of the theory may be deduced from the concept of "system." Very likely tautological, the term *system* means both "interconnectedness of parts" and "covariation among properties," whatever else it has come to mean (falsely) in a value-laden sense. Here we define *interconnectedness* as internal linkage availability (that generates the marketplace) and *covariation* as between demand for specific interorganizational activation and consequent supply. But even radical conflict theory can be viewed in system terms: There, interconnectedness might be repression, exploitation, and class solidarity; and the covariation is between the deprivation-based demand for revolution and its consequent supply.

Notes

1. An integral part of the overall development, this chapter summarizes and provides excerpts from Turk (1973b), which may be consulted for detail about the portions of the model it contributed and for more finely controlled analyses conducted in its light.

2. This is a reasonable inference from other writings and not only from those that explicitly recognize the interorganizational level. See, for example, such varied sources as Form (1954), Long (1958), Banfield (1961), Dahl (1961), Williams, Herman, Liebman, and Dye (1965), Sayre and Polsby (1965), Smith (1968), Warren (1971, p. 148).

3. Ecologists Duncan and Schnore (1959) recognize that "power struggles" occur where the realization of certain interests adversely affect the realization of others.

4. For controversy surrounding the "public regarding" concept see Banfield and Wilson (1963, pp. 234–240), Wilson and Banfield (1964, 1966), Wolfinger and Field (1966, 1968), Lineberry and Fowler (1967).

5. Here we may juxtapose the literature on goal displacement (Michels, [1915] 1958; Thompson and McEwen, 1958; Parsons, 1960; Etzioni, 1964, pp. 10–12, 27–28, 84–85; Thompson, 1967, pp. 79–81, 128–131; Cyert and McCrimmon, 1968) with that on "domain consensus" among organizations and their cohesion through "variant values" (Levine and White, 1961; Levine, White, and Paul, 1963; conclusion to Turk, 1963) to suggest that organizations with complementary, rather than identical goals are most likely to interact with one another. Although these considerations do not preclude voluntary interorganizational cooperation in terms of the values of some broader system, they do tend to make such cooperation problematical.

6. For an individual-based approximation of this exchange model, see Coleman (1964). For its counterpart at the macrosocial (national) level, see Lieberson (1971). Whether or not only certain sets of interested organizations participate in any given coalition with tacit acquiescence by others that abstain need not concern us.

7. This observation is in accord with the more general ones previously stated that separation among organizations is a device through which contradictory requirements may be fulfilled by society and that overcoordination or consolidation among organizations can lead to the loss of certain community outputs.

8. This might have resulted from the part played by national head-quarters of voluntary associations in specifying this correlation (see H. Turk, 1970) and the latter variable's negative relationship to city-wide associations (see Chapter Two).

9. The overall results are elusive of conventional tests of statistical significance. For approximate tests and more detailed analyses that show the results to hold independently of the introduction of other variables for purposes of control, see Turk (1973b).

Chapter Six

•••••••••••••••••••••
•••••••••••••••••••••••
•••••••••••••••••••••••

MULTIORGANIZATIONAL
SETTINGS
REEXAMINED

•••••••••••••••••••••
•••••••••••••••••••••
•••••••••••••••••••••

*T*he interorganizational frame-
work has the potential of merging social differentiation with elitist,
pluralist, and dialectical perspectives in macrosocial inquiry (and
is basically not at variance with the political or human ecological
branches of social organization)—at least among the 130 metropoli
among which selected hypotheses were tested.

The Interorganizational View

The major conclusion to be drawn is this: Definition of broad
settings, the macrosocial units, in terms of their multi- and interorganizational characteristics has proven fruitful. Within the restriction of what was measured and what was not, these characteristics were capable of accounting for one another (even over time,
it appears) to an appreciable degree, and mainly without the intrusion of nonorganizational factors. The empirical utility of an
interorganizational level for the analysis of such macrosocial units—
here they were cities, but could as well have been societies, multi-

social communities, or even nonterritorial complexes—has been supported by the contribution that organizational variables made, unconfounded by selected demographic characteristics, in accounting for other organizational characteristics of the city, or for effecting the linkage in interorganizational networks that the city activated (see Chapters Two and Four). This tended to hold even where individual persons rather than organizations constituted the beneficiaries of organizational and multiorganizational action, as in the cases of education, health, and welfare (see Chapter Four). It could also be seen in the greater efficiency achieved in predicting both the absence of community conflict and the community's interorganizational "outputs" on the basis of organization-based rather than person-based measures of the community's organizational complexity and its consequent decentralization (see Chapters Three and Four).

Even widespread needs within the population or prevalent opinion (although these themselves are very likely organizational in their origins) require organizational mechanisms for their expression as protest or for their satisfaction. This, we have shown, has major implications for dialectical conflict theory in general (see Chapter Three). Needs also require organized means of their translation into demands that compete with other demands (including those that seek to establish a given source of organizational or interorganizational satisfaction), which are often themselves generated interorganizationally (see Chapter Five). This idea speaks directly to an extension of pluralist thought. The literature cited and the United States urban data presented about the hints of greater influence of religiously organized subpopulations or ones with foreign backgrounds (presumably richer in organizations) than of nonwhite minorities on metropolitan life (see Chapters Two to Four); about the greater responsiveness to "need" and other interests of subpopulations where municipal governments are large in scale and complex than where they are simpler or less powerful (see Chapter Five); and about the roles played by certain voluntary associations in establishing the relevance of even such platitudinous standards as preservation of life and abolition of deprivation (also see Chapter Five)—all serve to support such generalization.

Dynamics of the Macrosocial Unit: The Case of the Metropolis

Although one can only speculate as to the detailed processes involved, the present synthesis of ecological, economic, political, organizational, sociocultural, and general macrosociological literature, as well as the present comparative analyses of the largest American cities, are congruent with the following model of modern macrosocial life.

Organizations. It is impossible for large numbers of people made increasingly heterogeneous but decreasingly self-sufficient by modern technologies and other social forces to be related to one another except by formal means. Organizations constitute such means.

Clustering of Organizations. Once organizations exist, other dependent organizations or ones depended on—sometimes serving entirely different parts of the environment—tend to cluster into *macrosocial units* as part of a broader set of interorganizational interdependencies, simultaneously establishing thereby the external linkage and organizational complexity of these large units. Empirically inseparable in part, the indicators of these two properties were expected to covary because of interdependence among organizations—and indeed tended to do so. The premise that interdependence both enables and necessitates large-scale and diversified organizational regulation and coordination led to the successful prediction of large-scale and diversified municipal government on the basis of nongovernmental indicators of a city's organizational complexity.

Theories of "mass" society suggested the directly inverse relationship found between the macrosocial unit's (here, the city's) external linkages and organizational complexity, on the one hand, and organizational representation of diffuse consensual solidarity (the extent to which local voluntary associations were uncontested and city-wide) on the other. But, unexpectedly, this same complexity, operating through municipal diversification and scale, also affected such solidarity *in a positive direction*. Alternatively, the interdependence between macrosocial unit and its external context can lead to externally provided resources that might depend on the existence of specific interorganizational networks, which have, in turn, been enabled by the aforementioned characteristics of the regulatory and coordinating organizations and of organizations representing diffuse consensual solidarity, respectively.

Decentralization and Conflict. Yet, because organizations tend to pursue conflicting interests and plural values in certain issue areas but need one another in others, they will resist domination by one or a few of their number, but still form the networks and coalitions for specific macrosocial action that underlie decentralized decision making. Supporting this assumption, we find that in our own cities large-scale but diversified—as is decentralized ("nonreform")—municipal government (see Chapters Two and Three) is associated with organizational complexity, namely the number and diversity of other large organizations (notably ones with external links). These two municipal variables also enable longitudinal prediction of a more direct, possibly person-based measure of decentralization in the actual decisions that are made (see Chapter Three) and explain that measure's effects on various urban innovations (see Chapter Four).

It follows that municipal centralization occurs where organizations fail to abound. So does centralization's potential consequent, polarization. In such organizationally barren, "mass" macrosocial units, power may be wielded by an organized elite over an unorganized mass, thereby creating the internal conditions of polarized (dialectical) conflict, undampened by the cross-cutting and issue-specific lines of coalition and conflict existing in organizationally more complex and more interlinked units (see Chapter Three).

Capacity for Interorganizational Relations. Organizations with certain attributes exceed others in their capabilities to provide linkage for networks, coalitions, or solidarities regarding a wide variety of issues. Both the interorganizational links that tie the macrosocial unit to its broader sociocultural environment, external linkage (here to organizations outside the city), and those that connect its internal elements to one another, internal linkage, provide latent or active structures that may be used or modified for new purposes, provide points of articulation, or, at the very least, serve as models for new interorganizational networks. Prior external linkages can convey the materials and messages necessary for interorganizational flows among the systems of the external context (including

ones of conflict), while internal linkage can select from among
these divers flows in order to provide the means or models for the
establishment of elaborate interorganizational networks. Whether
these networks or external flows are conflicts, solidarities, revolutionary, or counterrevolutionary is irrelevant to our theory (see
Chapter Four).

External linkage. The possibility may not be discarded (although direct evidence is lacking) that external linkage affects
the transmission of internal conflicts such as ones about fluoridation of municipal water supplies (see Chapter Three) as readily as
it transmits the collective endeavors, whether meliorative in intent
or token in nature, such as those of the War on Poverty or the Model
City programs (see Chapters Two and Four). While external linkage provides certain resources for the activation of internal interorganizational networks, as in the latter cases, or indirectly by facilitating municipal diversification and scale, conditions are suggested where they also cause the internal pluralism associated with
complexity that works against the availability of internal linkage—
here the occurrence of city-wide associations—that is required by
such networks (see Chapter Two). The extent to which internal
linkage requires external resources appears to determine which
of these two effects prevails. In certain instances, it was also suggested, internal linkage was *prerequisite* to the external provision
of resources, as in the cases of complex local antipoverty networks
required for certain antipoverty funds (see Chapter Two) and the
preexisting structures required for the provision of Model City
funds (see Chapter Four). But any simple use of sheer amount of
external linkage as a measure of input of specific external interests and standards (for example, as an indicator of the dominance
of the interests about which coalitions form, or the standards by
which levels of local need are defined) is impossible. Specific external links carry specific standards and interests, which may conflict with those of other links; this is not as true, as the cases of early
antipoverty and early Model City funding suggest, where the provision of material resources rather than standards is in question.
Internally dominant standards and interests, although external in
origin, become dominant as they are filtered through internal
linkage.

Availability of internal linkage. The scale and diversification of an organization affect its political ability to link organizations together into networks and coalitions, provided it can resolve its internal conflicts. The extent to which these or other organizations produce consensus and solidarities because of their diffuse goals and avoidance of conflict, coupled with visibility, also affects formation of these networks and coalitions. In the United States, the first of these sets of organizational characteristics is exemplified by large-scale and diversified municipal government, which set has also been considered to be an indicator of decentralization. The idea of organizations with plural interests and values suggests that small governments that are limited in scope are either weak or exist in organizationally barren communities; neither is conducive to collective community action based on linkage into interorganizational networks. The second set of characteristics is embodied in the extent to which organizations represent diffuse consensual solidarity—in the case of the United States, in how uncontested and city-wide are the city's voluntary associations. One or both of these two indicators of the availability of internal linkage or ones of the availability of external resources (most broadly measured in the United States by the proxy of national headquarters of voluntary associations, but also by specific externally produced resources) predict the activation of interorganizational networks and of the coalitions that concert these networks with "need."

Interorganizational Activation. Our operational referents of interorganizational activation have been called "innovation," "policy outputs," and "power mobilization" (for example, see respectively, Aiken and Alford, 1970; Clark, 1973; Lincoln, 1976). Closer examination shows several published applications of these labels to be manifestations or products of interorganizational relations.

The same two indicators of the availability of internal linkage associated with the formation of federally sponsored local antipoverty networks in the United States also affect the activation of quite different organizational networks—namely, the formation of councils among hospitals. Again, quite independently of whether federations such as hospital councils are self-serving, altruistic, or responsive to external interests, the same broad, preexisting sources of linkage account for their formation (see Chapter Four).

The term *linkage availability* is a comprehensive one that refers (1) to the politically forged permanent as well as transitory coalitions and (2) to the macrounit-wide solidarities and abstract consensus that mediate coalitions. Both appear to be necessary for interorganizational network activation in organizationally complex macrosocial units, characterized as these are by partial conflict and partial accord over different issues.

Yet, of the two, only the solidarity-producing mechanisms appear important where the networks formed carefully screen out organizations that may be contentious, as in the case of activities by health and welfare councils. But even here there are hints that the success of such screening depends on the atypical absence of multiorganizational heterogeneity and on noncontroversiality of interorganizational purpose (see Chapter Four).

The role of noncontroversiality was also supported by the ability of large-scale organizations of all kinds, even economic enterprises that may be expected to be in competition with one another, to cooperate in local Community Chest campaigns (see Chapter Four). Although partial conflict or idiosyncratic purposes mostly tend to prevent widespread voluntary cooperation among organizations, such cooperation is potent wherever it happens *not* to be prevented.

In this context, it is necessary to entertain the notion that what appears to be pluralism and partial conflict might actually be mere squabbling among organizational sibs that constitute the power elite.[1] That certain *issues* might never arise—once proven (we lack the data to attempt this here)[2]—would attest to such universal, conspirational, and permanent coalitions. Yet, were organizations to arise among the nonelite under such a possibility, it is very likely that their power to alter the social structure would rest on their respective capacities for linkage, with one another or (very likely, and) for linkage with certain organizations of the elite.

The Effect of "Need" for Interorganizational Activation. Finally, the joint effect of *incentive and opportunity* that may be observed within all kinds of social action systems—from personality to international community—has been highlighted by our comparative findings concerning the relative parts played by internal *capacity and need* in activating interorganizational relations: in the case of the metropolis, for the flow of antipoverty funds to the city, for antipoverty networks, for hospital councils, for Model City programs, for broad health and welfare council reports, respectively, on the one hand, and the subsequent supply of these forms of interorganizational activation, on the other (see Chapter Five). A compelling claim has been made that most social phenomena are thus multiplicative in their effects (Dodd and Christopher, 1966). This is not the place to affirm or to modify such a general claim. It is sufficient to observe that comparative discussions of interorganizational relations (and comparative macroanalyses of all kinds) should go more deeply into the *joint* operation of different factors, a task that has only begun in the present book.

Here we found that, in the United States at least, where there were clear national standards of need on the level of city and of the means to its fulfillment and where material resources could be externally provided, the availability of linkage in the metropolis not only made interorganizational activation possible (or not very costly and therefore more likely) but *also affected the degree of association between the nationally defined level of need for such activation and its actual supply*. This finding underlies much general social science and merits wider test. It simply implies that social actors (here, organizations) must be connected to one another if they are not only to define, but also to respond to situations collectively (whether by conflict or by accord), especially where the responses are themselves the establishment of new connections among these actors. This underscores, for example, that the marketlike concerting of supply and demand depends both on broader contextual standards of "taste" or "utility" and on the communication of "needs" in terms of these standards as well as disposition to supply. Viewing linkage as necessary but not sufficient for responsiveness to needs that are defined in coalitions as demands (taken in conjunction with crudity of indicators used to document this) helps to account for the absence of very high association between local capacity *or* local need for interorganizational activation (the latter also defined according to the standards of the more inclusive social context) and the subsequent supply of activation. Just because events are needed by some *or* just because they can transpire among social actors does not mean that they will. In the case of interorganizational relations at least, capacity appears to overshadow need. But where both exist, as several of our cases have suggested, the likelihood of the anticipated interorganizational response, even interorganizational change, is high.

Another way of looking at this is in terms of *how much of a system exists—be it one of conflict or of cooperation,* because here "system" only has implied (1) *interconnectedness* of parts in a setting, and (2) *covariation* among the setting's properties. The *availability of internal linkage* measured the first and *correlation* between the demand for interorganizational activation with its subsequent supply, the second. For supply and demand processes to occur, there must first be linkage available for that set of connections called a *marketplace*—so obvious a specification, once mentioned, that it is often overlooked or is considered fixed. Actually, our 130 macrosocial units varied in both respects, thereby permitting empirical tests of the effect of interconnectedness (the marketplace) on covariation between macrosocial properties (between the market processes of demand and supply). How oligopolistic any market is, is a question for future study.

Alternative Models

Using the special case of cities, we have conceived of macrosocial units as constellations of organizations. This means that action at the macrosocial level occurs primarily as the result of coalition formation among organizations. Communities differ in the general availability of linkage for such coalitions, for the transmission of relevant information about values and needs, and for interorganizational responses to value-based demands. Where there are several conflicting values and interests, linkage alone may be insufficient to assure a winning coalition, and stalemate or chaos may result; but where linkage is missing, large coalitions, whether they are supreme or contested by equally large coalitions, are impossible. In a way, the interorganizational approach points to the absurdity of distinguishing between "consensus models," "conflict models," "equilibrium models," "change models," and so on. It suggests that all so-called models are actually abstractions that refer to the geometry of the linkages formed among organizations within macrosocial units and by the corresponding contest, concert, modification, and other forms of interplay among the various interests and standards advanced by these organizations either individually or in concert with other organizations.

The reader is invited to evaluate these models in terms of the relationship that each has to the foundations of our theory. The partial conflict among organizations and their facilitating interdependence means the operation of contest and bargaining in the emergence of outcomes as well as the assimilation or emergence and retention of overarching interests and standards that make certain outcomes more probable than others—that provide "information" rather than "energy" in a cybernetic sense. Industrialized nations and multipurpose cities appear to behave in this way.

We might also propose, but with greater hesitation, that where organizations are few or where cross-cutting lines of interorganizational conflict and dependence do not occur, macrosocial action might just not take place. Instead, it may be the outcome of total dialectical conflict between separate interorganizational coalitions involving equally absolute but mutually incompatible values, or whatever organizational fabric exists may break down. Emerging nations and bedroom (mass) cities seem to fit one or the other of these latter possibilities.

In all cases, where certain interests and standards fail to dominate or where they fall short of being principal counterforces, it is difficult to conceive of predictable social process. Still, the ensuing turbulence may cease and predictability return, once chance or some other factor has produced a new mix of interests and ensuingly prevailing standards.

The Case of the United States. Our findings in the United States fail to support several seductively simple assertions. The first of these is the monistic and neodialectical one that macrosocial units are simply components of a broader Leviathan that they serve and that dominates them. *The broader context is very important,* but in a more subtle way. It provides, first, the material *resources* without which the macrosocial unit cannot survive. This is true for the British Isles or international oil production in the world economy, as well as for New York City or possible military-industrial complexes in a national economy. Yet these same resources must be *translated* into regulation and coordination of the macrosocial unit; they do not themselves constitute control.

In the American metropolis, we have seen the effect of external linkage to be indirect. It provides for the needed flow of external resources, to be sure; but without *diversified and large-scale* local organizations having the *interest in* and *political capability of* enabling coalitions, or without these and other local organizations that *represent solidarity and consensus and mediate coalitions* at some abstract level, the city cannot produce the interorganizational networks required for its mobilization into concerted action.

Another version of the hierarchical view that also fails to be supported is one of some variable natural affinity or hierarchical arrangement between the *regulators and coordinators* of the broader external context and their counterparts within the macrosocial unit. In our case, there is little evidence of any *direct* effect between the *scale and diversification of municipal government* and the amount of federal support the city received. The popular notion that big and complex local governments have more federal "clout" or "grantsmanship" than others is just not supported. Organizations in the private sector can have these capabilities as well. One hears as much about federal support of industry as one does about federal support of municipalities. In the case of antipoverty programs and Model Cities awards, local government was instrumental in linking the interorganizational networks that secured federal resources, but did not covary directly with such procurement. With hospital councils (these were also federally funded to some degree), municipal health expenditures—an indicator of local governmental health activity—were actually inversely correlated with interorganizational activation in certain regions. Despite this, municipal scale and diversification did have a positive effect on council formation—but only by making linkage available locally, it seems. These findings are instructive in a second way; like other organizations, local and federal agencies might actually compete and be in conflict with one another as readily as they might be in accord. "General revenue sharing" seems to represent a victory for the former; and categorical federal grants to private organizations, a victory for the latter. In the cases of health planning, which also was federally sponsored in part, municipal government had no demonstrable effect whatsoever. There is no evidence of any naturally variable affinity between federal and local government, taken either as wholes or in terms of their component counterparts. We cannot say that no such affinity exists, only that the "bigness" of local government and federal action did not appear to covary and that in isolated cases the two might even confront one another in the struggle for local control. Organizations that are in full accord with one another tend to merge.

Nevertheless, external linkage provided the organizational complexity that created demand for and enabled large-scale and diversified coordinating and regulating organizations—in our case, municipal government—having this character. And, in the specific case of federal funding, external linkage enabled the Community Action and Urban Renewal agencies. Both local government and the latter agencies were instrumental, in turn, in generating the local linkage required for further federal funding. Clearly, the city's structure cannot be understood apart from the national scene, but simple models of economic dominance by national organizations or a hierarchy of federal and local governments (we did not consider intervening ones such as state, district, or county) do not fit our data. Neither did all cities respond similarly to federal programs, nor were they similarly treated in those respects; and the type of city government had no demonstrable effect on the availability of the federal resources considered here.

Clearly, however, there could have been struggles at the national level that determined the kind and magnitude of resources, both federal and private organizational, available to organizations within cities or to the networks that the city's organizations formed. Interorganizational theories of pluralism, countervailing power, and horizontal rather than hierarchical relations would lead us to expect such struggles, although data were lacking. The organizational complexity of the macrosocial unit's context should have the same consequents there as it does within the unit.

Where interests and standards are concerned, however, there is no more evidence of the macrosocial unit's independence from its external context than there is of its economic independence. Cities, for example, do not invent their police departments, schools, YMCA's, Black Panthers, political ward organizations, merchants' associations, Community Chests, health and welfare councils, hospital councils, criminal gangs, urban renewal agencies, or antipoverty networks. And nations do not model their foreign offices, armies, and industries independently of other nations. All these are modeled by national, sometimes international standards and in terms of interests that are also defined by such divers standards. (We also have had some small hint that even the scripts for internal conflicts are externally produced.) Because of this, we have suggested (and the data have failed to contradict) that the more internally linked the organizations are with respect to any given issue, the more likely are these external standards both to prevail and to allow the activation or nonactivation of interorganizational networks in their light. In any externally oriented macrosocial unit, these external standards may be the only ones likely to provide the prevailing internal linkage or the "winning" internal coalition. This can be said irrespective of whether the standards are democratic, repressive, or Machiavellian in their operation.

In the three respective cases of resources, regulation and coordination, and standards, we seem to have a two-step process. Macrosocial units vary in the need and ability to dance; when they dance, it is an intricate dance, but one to an externally produced tune. Material resources, control, and standards come from outside organizations, but they are implemented through or granted in response to the internal relations among organizations that these externalities facilitate but do not determine.

This raises another question. The potencies of different organizations in these internal processes depend on how interested each one is in participating and whether each has the political or the standard and interest-mediating capacities to make linkage available for coalitions or for other kinds of interorganizational networks. *To divide the macrosocial unit into interest sectors, however, is to oversimplify.* To understand, say, health care or welfare in a city, it is insufficient to study these sectors in isolation. Each issue has its own set of interested organizations, to be sure, but interest is not enough. We suspect this on the basis of the lack of measurable effect of sector-specific municipal organizations—estimated by health, welfare, and educational expenditures—on interorganizational relations in these areas; we have seen the far greater effects of externally provided resources, scale and diversification of internal regulating and coordinating organizations, and the internal organizational representation of diffuse consensual solidarity.

Never mind that these internal properties are externally cloned. *Even the very idea of organization is external in its origins.* And is it really so contrary to classic theory that extensively administered (not centralized) and manifestly solidary social units are more likely than others to act in concert, especially where they have external support? Do not organization and consensual solidarity of the branch as well as directives or support from the home office all have something to do with the actions of that branch? In asking this, we make no assumptions about how repressive or benign the entire process is.

Another popular assumption is that networks beget networks much as bureaucracy begets bureaucracy, as though there were some grand conspiracy afoot to stagnate all of social life. Countering this, one must not forget that each bureaucracy's expansion is likely to be in competition with that of another, and interorganizational networks are not even as stable as are organizations. Witness that only in the case of Model Cities—where specific networks were demanded—did we find any direct association between the activation of one of the kinds of networks that we studied and the activation of any other; that is, such general factors as externally or internally provided resources, and internal regulating and coordinating organizations or organizations that represented consensual solidarity affected the different networks and accounted for any coexistence that could be observed among them. Organizations may need external resources in order to survive, but whether they compete or cooperate with one another in obtaining them and whether the networks supported by one resource are the same ones supported by another is a question likely to elicit as many negative as positive replies. In terms of our admittedly limited inquiry, there is no more evidence that specific interorganizational networks affect one another than that the occurrence of any such network can be determined through exclusive attention to the specific organizations that comprise it. The broader institutions of the macrosocial unit and of its external context are the key to understanding.

In sum, one cannot understand the macrosocial unit without

taking into account the participation of its organizations in much broader, external, and organizationally complex networks, but, in the United States, it would be a mistake to oversimplify any such participation or what goes on inside the unit as a result. A more complex two-step variant has been proposed.

Outside the United States. But what of the cases in which the macrosocial unit is externally dominated to far greater degree than in the United States? One should still be loathe to abandon it as an appropriate object of study until several possibilities have been ruled out, preferably through comparative inquiry. Clearly, the more centralized the broader setting, the more pertinent is that part of our theory that has to do with external standards. But it is also hard to believe that organizations—even "branches"—can exist in, say, a city without taking one another into account and without having the capability of collective outputs—even if these outputs are simply requests made by the city of the more powerful entities to which it is subject.

Certain matters of today, such as regional planning, pollution control, and the allocation of locally obtained revenues still seem to be territorially bound and, at the very least, capture the interest of local organizations. If this surmise should be wrong, the very least that cross-national inquiry can establish are the concrete limits of interorganizational structure and process in local communities or, for that matter, subdivisions of larger systems that are not territorially based.

Moreover, central legislation sometimes demands coordination at the local level. Something short of this was implied in the antipoverty and Model Cities programs that have been described. Even closer to the idea is West German law, which requires widespread local participation in city planning. Our model suffices to predict relative outcomes of such requirements from one city to the next. In similar vein, certain central planning philosophies seem to assume the impossibility of central coordination and control in large multiorganizational settings, be they circumscribed or comprehensive. Here emphasis is placed on enriching the social environment with resources in such a way that local decisions tend more toward certain general outcomes than toward others. Non-specific financial grants-in-aid to local governments ("revenue sharing," for instance) constitute only one example. This is the epitome of the two-step process already mentioned. The analogy comes to mind that such macrosocial units as local interorganizational complexes may mediate between the external context and smaller social units, much as small groups mediate between large organizations and their members.

Finally, some of our data had to do with the *association* between the availability of local linkage and the correlation between local demand for interorganizational activation and its supply. Where linkage is slight or local demands are few one would expect to operate only on different portions of relevent dimensions, not along different dimensions. The strength with which our theory is supported in the local case may depend on the degree of autonomy enjoyed by the subsystem; it may even drop to zero in certain cases (a doubtful possibility, however, given any interdependence among local organizations, whether based on conflict or mutual need). In such an event, however, we would shift to a more comprehensive macrosocial unit of analysis in order to test the same propositions. Whether or not cities, or even nations, for that matter, only become places where mutually isolated bits of fully externally oriented organizations are located—a doubtful possibility—there will always be some context, however large, in which interorganizational theories such as the one stated and illustrated in this book will apply.

"Integration" by Government and Voluntary Associations or Their Surrogates

The effectiveness of voluntary associations and government in the integration of large, modern social systems has been widely claimed—mainly by social scientists in the United States, to be sure. Yet much of the evidence has come from case studies or from such remote data as the increased civic participation of association members.

What has not been recognized is that the major integrative significance of the two kinds of organizations may be in the linkage they make available among other organizations. Given only one case, that of the United States, not much can be said about the integrative significance of these two kinds of organization for the national system. Yet the tendencies of national headquarters of voluntary associations and grants by federal agencies to emphasize or neglect the same cities, and also to follow concentrations of economic organizations in these respects, at least fulfill certain conditions necessary for these national functions. National organizations seem to contact or to locate near other national organizations that need or are needed by them. The effect of external linkage, measured in terms of government and voluntary associations, on both extralocal flow of (antipoverty) resources and possibly the activation of certain local interorganizational networks (health and welfare councils, Model City programs) provides further, albeit very tenuous, support.

At the local level, both the literature and the comparative findings presented suggest one aspect of external linkage to be that large-scale and diversified municipal government occurs and, given the latter or an older city, that city-wide voluntary associations occur as well. These two organizational types make linkage available within organizationally complex urban settings, the first of them emphasizing the formation of coalitions under conditions of partial conflict among organizations, the second emphasizing the abstractly solidary aspects of interorganizational relations. One or both of these sources of the availability of local linkage appear to have direct effects in all instances of interorganizational activation considered among our 130 cities, save one (Model City status) in which the effect was possibly an indirect one of previously having produced new sources of linkage. In every case (including Model City status) both municipal scale and diversification *and* the extent to which local voluntary associations were uncontested and city-wide affected *the concerting* of nationally defined interorganizational activation with nationally defined levels of need. Taken together, these two organizational sources of linkage make it possible to consider the *fluid* aspects of the community, which classical urban or other typologies do not anticipate, but which current investigation into urban politics suggest.

Cross-National Comparisons. Although the results of our comparative analyses are congruent with what has been written about the effect of government and voluntary association on urban process in the United States, every effort has been made to place their telling linkage-producing characteristics of scale, diversification, decentralization, internal conflict resolution, consensus generation, and visibility into the broader context of organizational and interorganizational theory. By these means, concrete investigations may be extended to include cities with non-Western modes of social organization. For example, Eastern European nations do not have competing political parties and private voluntary associations comparable to those in the United States; but they are likely to contain other kinds of organizations that vary from urban place to urban place as to scale, diversification, visibility, decentralization, the resolution of internal conflict, diffuseness of goals, avoidance of external conflict, and other linkage-producing properties. Such variation should permit attempts to verify, challenge, or to specify the propositions that impelled the present analyses of the 130 largest United States cities.

Empirical Emphases. That the integrative aspects of interorganizational relations have been emphasized in this study of the United States is merely based on the empirical evidence from the cases used that organizations fell short of seeking to destroy one another—not that this is necessarily good or bad.

Social Implications

Clearly, our empirical findings have practical value in helping national policymakers think about when and how to support which communities, and in helping dissidents consider when and how which city is ripe for protest. The findings might even suggest the results of conscious efforts to alter the basic organizational composition of a community or highlight some problems inherent in the shape taken by certain planned communities. But there are even broader issues to be discussed.

Unabashedly speculative and ideologically influenced, to be sure, in the topic selected for discussion, one might consider the implications of a world whose organizational complexity is increasing. Whether gratifying or disturbing, this trend is likely to continue, because the increasing magnitude and complexity of urban life demands organizational means of its implementation and because organizations attempt to expand their domains, even across national boundaries, until they are checked by other organizations, with which they are then likely to enter into issue-specific rivalries or compacts, thereby creating new social organization of the decentralized, coalitional, interorganizational variety. This will mean ever-larger macrosocial units—for example, the world community—that are formed by these organizations.

Our inquiry into organizational barrenness suggests that rigidity and total conflict only occur when one or a few organizations monopolize what little collective life there is within an isolated community and centralize that life in an organizational vacuum. It is under these conditions, our theory lets us guess, that the unorganized mass can develop a consciousness of common fate that is capable of revolutionary organization or capable of revolutionary expression if the organizational means of expression are at hand. We have already suggested that this form of centralization and polarization is not possible in organizationally complex communities characterized by cross-cutting alliance and conflict. Might not the same be said of international communities once they become populated by United Nations organizations, multinational corporations, Interpol, international professional associations, the European Economic Community (EEC), the Organization of Petroleum-Exporting Countries (OPEC), and so forth? Here the political state, generally the only organization capable of forming alliances for purposes of total war, not only is in part itself under international control, but also must compete with international organizations or coalitions of organizations having nonpolitical objectives that transcend or cut across national boundaries—thus weakening military alliances and dampening the forces of total conflict. In the world, as in organizationally dense cities and modern nations, many little conflicts may prevent one big one. Moreover, as nations modernize (that is, develop national organizations and become mass societies) identifications and values tend to refer more to nation than to locality[3] and to become specific in content. As international organizations increase in number and power, a similar process may replace diffuse nationalism by specific and cross-cutting multinational sentiments.

Finally, our analysis of Community Chest campaigns suggests how much organizations can cooperate with one another, and how efficiently, in instances where disparate interests do not intrude. The personally disturbing thought occurs: that similar machinery might be similarly efficient in collecting taxes or mobilizing opinion. But, on an optimistic note, problems such as those of pollution and the depletion of natural resources might prove to affect most organizations in similar fashion; and, once they recognize this collectively, they can provide powerful coordinating machinery for their solution. If, in a democracy, national policy, including the waging of war, depends on the mild attitudes and mild actions of many persons, one can imagine that the actions of any majority of organizations can have an even more resounding impact.

What has been left out is "the crisis of the cities." Theory has not been restricted to cities as macrosocial units here and therefore should not become obsolete, granted even premature speculations by some about the obsolescence of cities. Crime, for example, has both its organizational structure and its organizational adversaries within the multiorganizational setting; its manifestations are more a topic for scandal and mass entertainment than for serious interorganizational studies. Unorganized criminality provides a clientele for enforcement and correction units, much as poverty provides one for welfare agencies. The "flight to the suburbs" and the lower-class character of the central city affect the burdens placed on the city's organizations and diminish their resources. But, if true, this might simply be an indication of, say, greater dependence on extralocally obtained resources and of consequent effects on local solidarity. It might also mean a reduction in the number and strength of voluntary associations as their middle-class members leave. These possibilities alter some of the values of our interorganizational parameters—not necessarily the parameters themselves or their interrelations.

Then again, the urban crisis might exist only to the extent that our image of the city is people—residents or workers—rather than a place where organizations concentrate to conduct affairs of region, nation, or world. This has profound implications, say, for planning places of residence, places of work, and who shall pay

the taxes. To name these implications in detail would be presumptuous, given the current state of our knowledge.

Toward Broader Macrosocial Inquiry

The dynamics of interorganizational relations have been
sketched in bold strokes, and the word *dynamic* is used advisedly.
For the fluid macrounit that organizations form, given their shifting goals, alliances, and conflicts has not been anticipated by such
classic typologies as Gemeinschaft and Gesellschaft, mechanical
and organic solidarity, folk and urban or sacred and secular society,
or integrated and disorganized cities. Whether it is an abstraction
from concrete reality, or description of it, we have added the pluralist idea of a fluid social unit characterized by cross-cutting and ever-
changing lines of partial conflict and partial accord that can alter
the collective as well as the individual interests and values of the
unit's organizations—a type that, unlike all of the others mentioned,
seems based on adaptability to rapidly changing social environment.

Social Relations, Not Necessarily Spatial Relations. In this book
we have emphasized the territorially based unit and subunit, respectively, of nation and city; but our theory is not restricted to such
instances. With advanced means of transportation and communication and the consequently wide dispersal over place and time that
most organizations can effect may mean that geographical propinquity will play less and less of a role in defining the boundaries
of systems and subsystems. Cross-national networks are already
being formed that are more tightly linked than many local federations, for example, and geographically dispersed workers already have been made to constitute office forces via closed-circuit
television.

Organizations, by their very specialized natures, must in-
evitably take one another and relevant populations of people into
account. However, the extent to which geographical dispersion
and propinquity of organizations or of populations will continue
to be salient variables is an open question. What will remain, regardless, are interorganizational pluralism, partial conflict and
accord, decentralization of complex structures, the barriers such
decentralization presents to polarized conflict, the direct effect of

organizationally induced linkage in adapting to change with new interorganizational relations, and its effect on concerting such new relations with "need." Whether or not social space and physical space continue to overlap—in the case of love, they probably will; in that of violence and coercion, perhaps less and less—our macrosocial propositions will still apply, but their further testing is mandatory.

Formal Macrotheory. While we have already provided an informal narrative summary in this chapter, Figures 1 through 4, taken together, provide the full statement of our formal macrotheory in the most concise terms. Although highly interconnected, their merging into a single diagram would create an indigestible complexity, and any verbal recapitulation would either be lengthy and involved or be oversimplified. Thus, I ask the reader to examine the chapter summaries at this point in order to regain the whole picture I have endeavored to paint.

The formal set of propositions, be it noted, has related to one another such key social scientific properties as linkage, organizational complexity, regulation, coordination, consensus, solidarity, stratification, centralization, dialectical conflict, interest, standard, resource, demand—and some new ones as well. Thus it is general social science. The reader is invited to seek the utility of some of the propositions for, say, small group dynamics, *intra*organizational relations, the family, international systems, industrial sociology, and so on, by substituting the appropriate term for *macrosocial unit* and the more general term *actor* for *organization*.

What is particularly pertinent to macrosocial science, where organizations are the actors—and what is a main premise on which these propositions are based—is that where multiple and specialized organizations occur, so does pluralism, accompanied by the interdependence of partial conflict and partial accord that specialization produces. This will not change even if the macrosocial units were fully to be emancipated from spatial relations, nor will the more fundamental claim the macrosocial units are constellations of organizations.

As for the indicators used in conjunction with the formal propositions, it should be kept in mind that both national headquarters of voluntary associations and economic complexity signified both external linkage and organizational complexity. Municipal scale and diversification signified the latter, and possibly also the inverse of centralization. Additionally, this last indicator also signified interorganizational power: the political capacity to make internal linkage available. These ambiguities do not seriously blur the empirical outcomes, however, because each indicator was used in conjunction with others with which it overlapped, and patterns of effects—sometimes along alternate hypothetical paths—were observed in addition to the effects of and on individual variables. And none of the empirical outcomes are in direct contradiction to our formal macrosocial theory, although several required qualification.

More important, we must study, not just posit, the system of links that affects *any entire set of* macrosocial units. Political economy, urban hierarchy, federal democracy, world trade, or class struggle affect ubiquities in, say, system-subsystem relations, nonissues, or legal constraints; these demand comparisons among sets.

Further Inquiry

The formal macrosociology offered in the summaries of Chapters 2 through 5 requires specification of the conditions under which each proposition holds, operational indicators of properties that were unmeasured and additional ones of those that were, and assessment of both the conceptual and the empirical scope of its applicability. To restate the preface, the theory is in such a form that the reader can insert his or her own hypothetical constructs.

More generally, the reader must evaluate this far-ranging set of conclusions regarding interorganizational theory in the light of their "fit" with the literature cited in this book and the comparative analyses that gave it substance; but clearly not everything has been written by way of qualification that should have been written, nor all done by way of empirical analysis that should have been done. Nor may the particular model used always be the only one fitting the materials reported; and certainly one cannot expect the concrete findings and conclusions to hold up invariably, once better indicators of some of the concepts and improved methodologies (see the broader comparisons just noted) come into existence.

The use of such broad, broadly defined properties as "organizations," "linkage," "organizational complexity," and "centralization" has been deliberate. Subcategories of these concepts, consequently more refined definitions, and subsequently further specification of the gross covariations we have explored are sorely needed next steps. But here the "style" has been to provide a bold statement of our formal theory, even at the expense of obvious needs to qualify, rather than to lose the overall picture through inclusion of premature detail.

We have sought to synthesize, for the moment, as many aspects of macrosocial science as came to mind through reading, research, and reflection. A major intent has been to provide points of departure and points to be challenged as well. Every attempt has been made to distinguish between what is fact and what is speculation; the success or failure of these attempts rests on the fit between theory and the analyses of our 130 cities. This book has set an agenda for seeking to understand macrophenomena, has striven to defend its priority, and has provided some of its methodology and implementation. At the very least, it has stated and sought to defend the assertion that whether metropolis, society, or even some larger macrounit (perhaps not even locality-based) is in question, its collective processes of conflict or accord are organization-based processes and should therefore be viewed in interorganizational terms.

Notes

1. Warren, Rose, and Bergunder (1974) implied this on the basis of essential "domain consensus" observed among certain organizations in the handful of Model Cities they studied. But since Model City selections were allegedly made *because of* the city's capacity for coordination, one would also have to discover similar patterns in non-Model Cities in order to substantiate this position. But even at that, how much permanent linkage is much? To answer this, one needs cross-national research.

2. For both the importance of this question and difficulties in addressing it empirically, see, for example, Bachrat and Baratz (1962) and Frey (1971).

3. Suggested by Lerner's (1958) discussion of the passing of traditional society. Also see Shils (1962).

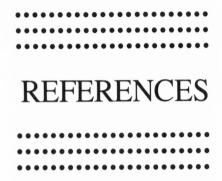

REFERENCES

ABBE, L. M., and BANEY, A. M. *The Nation's Health Facilities: Ten Years of the Hill-Burton Hospital and Medical Facilities Program 1946–1956*. Washington, D.C.: U.S. Government Printing Office, 1958.

Advisory Commission on Intergovernmental Relations. *Fiscal Balance in the American Federal System*. Vol. 1. Washington, D.C.: U.S. Government Printing Office, 1967a.

Advisory Commission on Intergovernmental Relations. Intergovernmental Relations in the Poverty Program. Washington, D.C.: U.S. Government Printing Office, 1967b.

AIKEN, M. "The Distribution of Community Power: Structural Bases and Social Consequences." In M. AIKEN and P. E. MOTT (Eds.), *The Structure of Community Power*. New York: Random House, 1970.

AIKEN, M., and ALFORD, R. R. "Community Structure and Innovation: The Case of Urban Renewal." *American Sociological Review*, 1970, *35*, 650–665.

AIKEN, M., and HAGE, J. "Organizational Interdependence and Intraorganizational Structure." *American Sociological Review*, 1968, *33*, 912–930.

ALFORD, R. R., and LEE, E. C. "Voting Turnout in American Cities." *American Political Science Review*, 1968, *62*, 796–813.

ALFORD, R. R., and SCOBLE, H. "Political and Socio-Economic Characteristics of American Cities." In International City Managers Association, *The Municipal Yearbook 1965.* Chicago: International City Managers Association, 1965.

ALLAN, G. J. B. "Ordinal-Scaled Variables and Multivariate Analysis: Comment on Hawkes." *American Journal of Sociology,* 1976, *81,* 1498–1500.

ALMOND, G. A. "A Comparative Study of Interest Groups and the Political Process." *American Political Science Review,* 1958, *52,* 270–282.

ALMOND, G. A. [Remarks in a symposium]. In H. W. EHRMANN, *Interest Groups on Four Continents.* Pittsburgh: University of Pittsburgh Press, 1960.

ANGELL, R. C. "The Social Integration of American Cities of More than 100,000 Population." *American Sociological Review,* 1947, *12,* 335–340.

BABCHUK, N., and EDWARDS, J. N. "Voluntary Associations and the Integration Hypothesis." *Sociological Inquiry,* 1965, *35,* 149–162.

BABCHUK, N., MARSEY, R., and GORDON, C. W. "Men and Women in Community Agencies." *American Sociological Review,* 1960, *25,* 399–403.

BACHRAT, P., and BARATZ, M. S. "The Two Faces of Power." *American Political Science Review,* 1962, *57,* 947–952.

BALES, R. F. *Interaction Process Analysis: A Method for the Study of Small Groups.* Cambridge, Mass.: Addison-Wesley, 1949.

BANFIELD, E. C. *The Moral Basis of a Backward Society.* New York: Free Press, 1958.

BANFIELD, E. C. *Political Influence.* New York: Free Press, 1961.

BANFIELD, E. C. *Big City Politics.* New York: Random House, 1965.

BANFIELD, E., and WILSON, J. Q. *City Politics.* Cambridge, Mass.: Harvard University Press, 1963.

BANFIELD, E., and WILSON, J. Q. "Power Structure and Civic Leadership." In J. K. HADDEN, L. H. MASOTTI, and C. J. LARSON (Eds.), *Metropolis in Crisis.* Itasca, Ill.: Peacock, 1967.

BARTH, E. A. T. "The Causes and Consequences of Interagency Conflict." *Sociological Inquriy,* 1963, *33,* 51–57.

BEER, S. H. "The Representation of Interests in British Government: Historical Background." *American Political Science Review,* 1957, *51,* 613–650.

BELKNAP, I., and STEINLE, J. G. *The Community and Its Hospitals: A Comparative Analysis.* Syracuse, N.Y.: Syracuse University Press, 1963.

BELL, D. *The Coming of Post-Industrial Society.* New York: Basic Books, 1973.

BERNARD, J. *American Community Behavior.* New York: Dryden, 1949.

BERNARD, J. *American Community Behavior: An Analysis of Problems Confronting American Communities Today.* Rev. ed. New York: Holt, Rinehart, and Winston, 1966.

BERRY, B. J. L. "The Goals of City Classification." In B. J. L. BERRY (Ed.), *City Classification Handbook: Methods and Applications.* New York: Wiley-Interscience, 1972.

BESHERS, J. M. *Urban Social Structure.* New York: Free Press, 1962.

BIDWELL, C. E. "The Young Professional in the Army." *American Sociological Review,* 1961, *26,* 360–372.

BLACK, B. J., and KASE, H. M. "Interagency Co-operation in Rehabilitation and Mental Health." *Social Service Review,* 1963, *37,* 26–32.

BLALOCK, H. M., JR. *Social Statistics.* New York: McGraw-Hill, 1960.

BLALOCK, H. M., JR. "The Problem of Multicollinearity." *Social Forces,* 1963, *41,* 233–237.

BLANKENSHIP, L. V., and ELLING, R. H. "Organizational Support and Community Power Structure of the Hospital." *Journal of Health and Human Behavior,* 1962, *3,* 257–269.

BLAU, P. M. *The Dynamics of Bureaucracy.* Chicago: University of Chicago Press, 1955.

BLAU, P. M. (Ed.) *Approaches to the Study of Social Structure.* New York: Free Press, 1975.

BLAU, P. M., and SCOTT, W. R. *Formal Organizations: A Comparative Approach.* San Francisco: Chandler, 1962.

BLUMER, H. "The Field of Collective Behavior." In R. E. PARK (Ed.), *An Outline of the Principles of Sociology.* New York: Barnes and Noble, 1939.

BLUMER, H. "Public Opinion and Public Opinion Polling." *American Sociological Review,* 1948, *13,* 542–554.

BOLLENS, J. C. (Ed.) *Exploring the Metropolitan Community.* Berkeley, Calif.: University of California Press, 1961.

BOLLENS, J. C., and SCHMANDT, H. J. *The Metropolis.* New York: Harper & Row, 1965.

BONJEAN, C. M., BROWNING, H., and CARTER, L. "Toward Comparative Community Research: A Factor Analysis of United States Counties." *Sociological Quarterly,* 1969, *10,* 157–176.

BOSANQUET, B. *The Philosophical Theory of the State.* London: Macmillan, 1966.

BOULDING, K. E. *The Organizational Revolution: A Study in the Ethics of Economic Organizations.* Chicago: Quadrangle, 1953.

BOULDING, K. E. *Conflict and Defense: A General Theory.* New York: Harper & Row, 1962.

BURGESS, E. W. "The Growth of the City." In R. E. PARK, E. W. BURGESS, and R. D. McKENZIE, *The City.* Chicago: University of Chicago Press, 1925.

BURLING, T., LENTZ, E., and WILSON, R. N. *The Give and Take in Hospitals.* New York: Putnam, 1956.

CAMPBELL, A., GURIN, G., and MILLER, W. E. *The Voter Decides.* Evanston, Ill.: Row Peterson, 1954.

CARTER, L. F. "Inadvertent Sociological Theory." *Social Forces,* 1971, *50,* 12–25.

CASTELLS, M. "Urban Sociology and Urban Politics: From a Critique to New Trends of Research." (M. RENAUD and M. AIKEN, Trans.) Unpublished paper presented to the annual meeting of the American Sociological Association, Montreal, September 1974.

CATTON, W. R., JR. *From Animalistic to Naturalistic Sociology.* New York: McGraw-Hill, 1966.

CLARK, B. R. "Interorganizational Patterns in Education." *Administrative Science Quarterly,* 1965, *10,* 224–237.

CLARK, T. N. *Community Structure and Decision-Making: Comparative Analyses.* San Francisco: Chandler, 1968a.

CLARK, T. N. "Community Structure, Decision-Making, Budget Expenditures, and Urban Renewal in 51 American Communities." *American Sociological Review,* 1968b, *33,* 576–593.

CLARK, T. N. "Community Structure, Decision-Making, Budget Expenditures, and Urban Renewal in 51 American Communities." In C. M. BONJEAN, T. N. CLARK, and R. L. LINEBERRY, (Eds.), *Community Politics: A Behavioral Approach.* New York: Free Press, 1971.

CLARK, T. N. "The Structure of Community Influence." In H. HAHN (Ed.), *People and Politics.* Beverly Hills, Calif.: Sage, 1972.

CLARK, T. N. *Community Power and Policy Outputs: A Review of Urban Research.* Beverly Hills, Calif.: Sage, 1973.

CLARK, T. N. "The Irish Ethic and the Spirit of Patronage." *Ethnicity,* 1975, *2,* 305–359.

COKER, F. W. "The Technique of the Pluralistic State." *American Political Science Review,* 1921, *15,* 186–213.

COKER, F. W. *Recent Political Thought.* New York: Appleton-Century, 1934.

COLEMAN, J. S. *Community Conflict.* New York: Free Press, 1957.

COLEMAN, J. S. "Collective Decisions." *Sociological Inquiry,* 1964, *34,* 166–181.

COLEMAN, J. S. "Community Disorganization." In R. K. MERTON and R. A. NISBET (Eds.), *Contemporary Social Problems.* New York: Harcourt Brace Jovanovich, 1966.

COLEMAN, J. S. "Community Disorganization and Conflict." In R. K. MERTON and R. NISBET (Eds.), *Contemporary Social Problems* (rev. ed.). New York: Harcourt Brace Jovanovich, 1971.

COLLINS, B. E., and RAVEN, B. H. "Group Structure: Attraction, Coalitions, Communication, and Power." In G. LINDZEY and E. ARONSON (Eds.), *The Handbook of Social Psychology.* Reading, Mass.: Addison-Wesley, 1959.

CONANT, R. W. *The Politics of Community Health.* Washington, D.C.: Public Affairs Press, 1968.

CONNERY, R. H.; BACKSTROM, C. H.; FRIEDMAN, J. R.; MARDEN, R. H.; MEEKISON, P.; DEEVER, D. R.; KROLL, M.; McCLESKEY, C.; and MORGAN, J. A., JR. *The Politics of Mental Health: Organizing Community Mental Health in Metropolitan Areas.* New York: Columbia University Press, 1968.

COOLEY, C. H. *Human Nature and the Social Order.* New York: Scribner's, 1910.

CRAIN, R. L., KATZ, E., and ROSENTHAL, D. B. *The Politics of Community Conflict: The Fluoridation Issue.* Indianapolis: Bobbs-Merrill, 1969.

CRAIN, R. L., and VANECKO, J. J. "Elite Influence in School Desegregation." In J. Q. WILSON (Ed.), *City Politics and Public Policy.* New York: Wiley, 1968.

CUTRIGHT, P. "Nonpartisan Electoral Systems in American Cities." *Comparative Studies in Society and History,* 1963, *5,* 218.

CYERT, R. M., and McCRIMMON, K. R. "Organizations." In G. LINDZEY and E. ARONSON (Eds.), *The Handbook of Social Psychology.* Reading, Mass.: Addison-Wesley, 1968.

DAHL, R. A. *Who Governs? Democracy and Power in an American City.* New Haven, Conn.: Yale University Press, 1961.

DAHRENDORF, R. "Out of Utopia: Toward a Reorientation of Sociological Analysis." *American Journal of Sociology,* 1958, *64,* 115–127.

DAHRENDORF, R. *Class and Class Conflict in Industrial Society.* Stanford, Calif.: Stanford University Press, 1959.

DE GRAZIA, S. *The Political Community.* Chicago: University of Chicago Press, 1948.

DERTHICK, M. "Intercity Differences in Administration of the Public Assistance Program: The Case of Massachusetts." In J. Q. WILSON (Ed.), *City Politics and Public Policy.* New York: Wiley, 1968.

DILL, W. R. "Environment as an Influence on Managerial Autonomy." *Administrative Science Quarterly,* 1958, *2,* 409–443.

DODD, S. F., and CHRISTOPHER, S. C. "Products Predict Interaction Where Sums Do Not." *Sociological Inquiry,* 1966, *36,* 48–60.

DUNCAN, O. D. "From Social System to Ecosystem." *Sociological Inquiry,* 1961, *31,* 140–149.

DUNCAN, O. D., and REISS, A. J., JR. *Social Characteristics of Urban and Rural Communities.* New York: Wiley, 1950.

DUNCAN, O. D., and SCHNORE, L. F. "Cultural, Behavioral, and Ecological Perspectives in the Study of Social Organization." *American Journal of Sociology,* 1959, *65,* 132–153.

DUNCAN, O. D.; SCOTT, W. R.; LIEBERSON, S.; DUNCAN, B. D.; and WINSBOROUGH, H. H. *Metropolis and Region.* Baltimore, Md.: Johns Hopkins University Press, 1960.

DURKHEIM, E. *The Division of Labor in Society.* (G. SIMPSON, Trans.) New York: Free Press, 1933. Originally published in 1893; new preface added in 1902; translated in 1933.

DURKHEIM, E. "Pragmatism and Sociology." In K. H. WOLF (Ed.) *Essays on Sociology and Philosophy.* New York: Harper Torch Books, 1964. Originally published 1914.

DYE, T. R. "Urban School Segregation: A Comparative Analysis." *Urban Affairs Quarterly,* 1968, *4,* 141–165.

DYE, T. R., and MACMANUS, S. A. "Predicting City Government Structure." *American Journal of Political Science,* 1976, *20,* 257–271.

"Economic Opportunity Act of 1964, Public Law 88-452." In *United*

States Statutes at Large. Vol. 78, Washington, D.C.: U.S. Government Printing Office, 1964.

EISENSTADT, S. N. "Sociological Aspects of Political Development in Under-Developed Countries." *Economic Development and Cultural Change,* 1957, *5,* 289–307.

EISENSTADT, S. N. *Essays on Comparative Institutions.* New York: Wiley, 1965.

EISENSTADT, S. N. "Transformation of Social, Political, and Cultural Orders in Modernization." In S. N. EISENSTADT (Ed.), *Comparative Perspectives on Social Change.* New York: Little, Brown, 1968.

ELLING, R. H., and HALEBSKY, S. "Organizational Differentiation and Support." *Administrative Science Quarterly,* 1961, *6,* 185–209.

ELLING, R. H., and LEE, O. J. "Formal Connections of Community Leadership to the Health System." *Milbank Memorial Fund Quarterly,* 1966, *44,* 294–306.

ELLIOTT, W. Y. *The Pragmatic Revolt in Politics.* New York: Macmillan, 1928.

EMERY, F. E., and TRIST, E. L. "The Causal Texture of Organizational Environment." *Human Relations,* 1965, *18,* 21–32.

Encyclopedia of Associations. Vol. 2., [Geographic and Executive Index.] Detroit: Gale, 1961.

ENGEL, G. V. "The Effects of Bureaucracy on the Professional Autonomy of the Physician." *Journal of Health and Social Behavior,* 1969, *10,* 30–41.

ETZIONI, A. *Modern Organizations.* Englewood Cliffs, N.J.: Prentice-Hall, 1964.

ETZIONI, A. *The Active Society: A Theory of Societal and Political Processes.* New York: Free Press, 1968.

EVAN, W. M. "The Organization-Set: Toward a Theory of Interorganizaational Relations." In J. D. THOMPSON (Ed.), *Approaches to Organizational Design.* Pittsburgh, Pa.: University of Pittsburgh Press, 1966.

EYESTONE, R., and EULAU, H. "City Councils and Policy Outcomes: Developmental Profiles." In J. Q. WILSON (Ed.), *City Politics and Public Policy.* New York: Wiley, 1968.

FOLLETT, M. P. *The New State.* New York: Longmans Green, 1918.

FORM, W. H. "The Place of Social Structure in the Determination of

Land Use: Some Implications for a Theory of Urban Ecology." *Social Forces,* 1954, *32,* 317–323.

FORM, W. H., and MILLER, D. C. *Industry, Labor, and Community.* New York: Harper, 1960.

FORM, W. H., and NOSOW, S. *Community in Disaster.* New York: Harper & Row, 1958.

FOWLER, I. A. "Local Industrial Structures, Economic Power, and Community Welfare." *Social Problems,* 1958, *6,* 41–51.

FREEMAN, L. C. *Patterns of Local Community Leadership.* New York: Bobbs-Merrill, 1968.

FREEMAN, L. C., FARARO, T. J., BLOOMBERG, W., and SUNSHINE, M. H. *Metropolitan Decision-Making.* Syracuse, N.Y.: Syracuse University Press, 1962.

FREEMAN, L. C., and WINCH, R. F. "Societal Complexity: An Empirical Test of a Typology of Societies." *American Journal of Sociology,* 1957, *62,* 461–466.

FREY, F. W. "Comment: On Issues and Nonissues in the Study of Power." *American Political Science Review,* 1971, *65,* 1081–1101.

FRIEDEN, B. J., and MORRIS, R. *Urban Planning and Social Policy.* New York: Basic Books, 1968.

FRIEDMAN, J. J. "Structural Constraints on Community Action: The Case of Infant Mortality Rates." *Social Problems,* 1973, *21,* 230–245.

FRIEDMAN, J. J. "Community Action on Water Pollution." *Human Ecology,* in press.

FULLER, R. C., and MYERS, R. R. "The Natural History of a Social Problem." *American Sociological Review,* 1941, *6,* 320–329.

FURNISH, B. "Conditions Influencing the Persistence of Certain Types of Urban Voluntary Associations." Unpublished doctoral dissertation, University of Southern California at Los Angeles, 1975.

GALBRAITH, J. K. *American Capitalism: The Concept of Countervailing Power.* Boston: Houghton Mifflin, 1952.

GALBRAITH, J. K. *The Affluent Society.* Boston: Houghton Mifflin, 1958.

GALLE, O. R. "Occupational Composition and Metropolitan Hierarchy: The Inter- and Intra-Metropolitan Division of Labor." *American Journal of Sociology,* 1963, *68,* 260–269.

GALLUP, G. H. *A Guide to Public Opinion Polls.* (2nd ed.) Princeton, N.J.: Princeton University Press, 1948.

GAMSON, W. A. "The Fluoridation Dialogue: Is It an Ideological Conflict?" *Public Opinion Quarterly,* 1961, *25,* 526–537.

GAMSON, W. A. "Rancorous Conflict in Community Politics." *American Sociological Review,* 1966, *31,* 71–81.

GARDINER, J. A. "Police Enforcement of Traffic Laws." In J. Q. WILSON (Ed.), *City Politics and Public Policy.* New York: Wiley, 1968.

GERTH, H., and MILLS, C. W. *Character and Social Structure.* New York: Harcourt Brace Jovanovich, 1953.

GIBBS, J. P., and MARTIN, W. T. "Urbanization, Technology, and the Division of Labor: International Patterns." *American Sociological Review,* 1962, *27,* 667–677.

GILBERT, C. "The Study of Community Power: A Summary and a Test." In S. GREER, D. L. McELRATH, D. W. MINAR, and P. ORLEANS (Eds.), *The New Urbanization.* New York: St. Martin's Press, 1968.

GIST, N. P., and FAVA, S. F. *Urban Society.* New York: Crowell, 1964.

GLAZER, N. *American Judaism.* Chicago: University of Chicago Press, 1957.

GLAZER, N. "The Renewal of Cities." In The Editors of *Scientific American,* (Eds.), *Cities.* New York: Knopf, 1966.

GLAZER, N. "Dilemma of Housing Policy." In D. P. MONYIHAN (Ed.), *Toward a National Urban Policy.* New York: Basic Books, 1970.

GOLDHAMER, H. *Some Factors Affecting Participation in Voluntary Associations.* Chicago: University of Chicago Press, 1942.

GOLDHAMER, H. "Some Factors Affecting Participation in Voluntary Organizations." in E. W. BURGESS and D. J. BOGUE (Eds.), *Contributions to Urban Sociology.* Chicago: University of Chicago Press, 1964.

GORDON, R. A. "Issues in Multiple Regression." *American Journal of Sociology,* 1968, *73,* 592–616.

GOULDNER, A. W. "Reciprocity and Autonomy in Functional Theory." In L. GROSS (Ed.), *Symposium on Sociological Theory.* New York: Harper & Row, 1959.

GREENSTONE, J. D., and PETERSON, P. E. "Reformers, Machines and the War on Poverty." In J. Q. WILSON (Ed.), *City Politics and Public Policy.* New York: Wiley, 1968.

GREER, S. *Governing the Metropolis.* New York: Wiley, 1962.

GREER, S. "The Governance of the Central City." In J. K. HADDEN, L. H. MASOTTI, and C. J. LARSON (Eds.), *Metropolis in Crisis: Social and Political Perspectives.* Itaska, Ill.: Peacock, 1967.

GREER, S., and ORLEANS, P. "The Mass Society and Parapolitical Structure." *American Sociological Review,* 1962, *27,* 634–646.

GRUSKY, O., and MILLER, G. A. *The Sociology of Organizations: Basic Studies.* New York: Free Press, 1970.

GUETZKOW, H. "Relations Among Organizations." In R. V. BOWERS (Ed.), *Studies on Behavior in Organizations: A Research Symposium.* Athens, Ga.: University of Georgia Press, 1966.

GUILFORD, J. P. *Fundamental Statistics in Psychology and Education.* New York: McGraw-Hill, 1950.

GUTTENBERG, E. Z. "The Tactical Plan." In M. M. WEBBER, J. W. DYCKMAN, D. L. FOLEY, A. Z. GUTTENBERG, and C. B. WURSTER (Eds.), *Explorations in Urban Structure.* Philadelphia: University of Pennsylvania Press, 1964.

HADDEN, J. K., and BORGATTA, E. F. *American Cities: Their Social Characteristics.* New York: Rand McNally, 1965.

HADDEN, J. K., MASOTTI, L. H., and LARSON, C. J. *Metropolis in Crisis.* Itasca, Ill.: Peacock, 1967.

HAGE, J., and AIKEN, M. *Social Change in Complex Organizations.* New York: Random House, 1970.

HAGE, J., and DEWAR, R. "The Prediction of Organizational Performance: The Case of Program Innovation." Paper presented at the annual meeting of the American Sociological Association, Denver, Colorado, September 1971.

HAHN, H. "Voting in Canadian Communities." *Canadian Journal of Political Science,* 1968, *1,* 462–469.

HANSON, R. C. "Predicting a Community Decision." *American Sociological Review,* 1959, *24,* 662–671.

HARBISON, F. H., and COLEMAN, J. R. *Goals and Strategy in Collective Bargaining.* New York: Harper, 1951.

HASLEY, W. D., and WIRT, F. M. *The Search for Community Power.* Englewood Cliffs, N.J.: Prentice-Hall, 1968.

HATT, P. K., and REISS, A. J. *Cities and Society: The Revised Reader in Urban Sociology.* New York: Free Press, 1957.

HAUSER, P. M. "Urbanization: An Overview." In P. M. HAUSER and L. F. SCHNORE (Eds.), *The Study of Urbanization.* New York: Wiley, 1965.

HAUSER, P. M., and SCHNORE, L. F. *The Study of Urbanization.* New York: Wiley, 1965.

HAWLEY, A. H. *Human Ecology.* New York: Ronald Press, 1950.

HAWLEY, A. H. "Community Power and Urban Renewal Success." *American Journal of Sociology,* 1963, *68,* 422–431.

HAWLEY, A. H. "Reply to Straits." *American Journal of Sociology,* 1965, *71,* 82–84.

HAWLEY, A. H. *Urban Society: An Ecological Approach.* New York: Ronald Press, 1971.

HAWLEY, A. H. "Comment on Williams' 'The Ecological Approach in Measuring Community Power Concentration'." *American Sociological Review,* 1973a, *73,* 390–393.

HAWLEY, A. H. "Ecology and Population." *Science,* 1973b, *179,* 1196–1201.

HAWLEY, A. H., and DUNCAN, O. D. "Social Area Analysis: A Critical Appraisal." *Land Economics,* 1957, *33,* 337–345.

HAWLEY, A. H., and ZIMMER, B. G. *The Metropolitan Community: Its People and Government.* Beverly Hills, Calif.: Sage, 1970.

HAWLEY, W. D. "Election Systems, Community Power, and Public Policy: The Partisan Bias of Nonpartisanship." In W. D. HAWLEY and F. M. WIRT (Eds.), *The Search for Community Power.* (2nd ed.) Englewood Cliffs, N.J.: Prentice-Hall, 1974.

HOBBES, T. *Leviathan.* Oxford, England: James Thornton, 1881. Originally published 1651.

HOMANS, G. C. *The Human Group.* New York: Harcourt Brace Jovanovich, 1950.

HOMANS, G. C. *Social Behavior: Its Elementary Forms.* New York: Harcourt Brace Jovanovich, 1961.

HOOVER, E. M., and VERNON, R. *Anatomy of a Metropolis.* Garden City, N.Y.: Doubleday, 1962.

HORTON, J. E., and THOMPSON, W. E. "Powerlessness and Political Negativism: A Study of Defeated Local Referendums." *American Journal of Sociology,* 1962, *67,* 485–493.

"Hospitals." *Journal of the American Hospital Association:* Guide Issue, August 1961 (Whole Issue).

HUNTER, F. *Community Power Structure.* Chapel Hill: University of North Carolina Press, 1953.

HUNTER, F. *Top Leadership, USA.* Chapel Hill: University of North Carolina Press, 1959.

HUNTER, F., SCHAFFER, R. C., and SHEPS, C. G. *Community Organization: Action and Inaction.* Chapel Hill: University of North Carolina Press, 1956.

HUNTINGTON, S. P. "Political Modernization: America vs. Europe." *World Politics,* 1966, *28,* 391–408.

HYMAN, H. H., and WRIGHT, C. R. "Trends in Voluntary Association Membership of American Adults: Replication Based on Secondary Analysis of National Sample Surveys." *American Sociological Review,* 1971, *36,* 191–206.

ISARD, W. *Location and Space-Economy.* New York: Wiley, 1956.

JAMES, W. *A Pluralistic Universe.* New York: Longmans Green, 1909.

JIOBU, R. M. "Integration and Conflict: Initial Perspectives on Urban Race Riots." Unpublished doctoral dissertation, University of Southern California, Los Angeles, 1970.

JIOBU, R. M. "City Characteristics, Differential Stratification, and the Occurrence of Interracial Violence." *Social Science Quarterly,* 1971, *51,* 508–520.

JIOBU, R. M. "City Characteristics and Racial Violence." *Social Science Quarterly,* 1974, *54,* 52–64.

KALLEN, H. M. *Cultural Pluralism and the American Idea.* Philadelphia: University of Pennsylvania Press, 1956.

KARIEL, H. S. *The Decline of American Pluralism.* Stanford, Calif.: Stanford University Press, 1961.

KASARDA, J. D. "The Impact of Suburban Population Growth on Central City Service Functions." *American Journal of Sociology,* 1972, *77,* 1111–1124.

KASS, R. "A Functional Classification of Urban Communities." *Demography,* 1973, *10,* 427–444.

KATZ, E., and LAZERSFELD, P. F. *Personal Influence.* New York: Free Press, 1955.

KAUFMAN, H. F. "Toward an Interactional Concept of Community." *Social Forces,* 1959, *38,* 9–17.

KIM, J. O. "Multivariate Analysis of Ordinal Variables." *American Journal of Sociology,* 1975, *81,* 261–298.

KLUCKHOHN, F. R., and STRODTBECK, F. L. *Variations in Value Orientations.* Evanston, Ill.: Row, Peterson, 1961.

KORNHAUSER, W. *The Politics of Mass Society.* New York: Free Press, 1959.

LABOVITZ, S. "The Assignment of Numbers to Rank Order Categories." *American Sociological Review,* 1970, *35,* 515–524.

LADINSKY, J. "Careers of Lawyers, Law Practice, and Legal Institutions." *American Sociological Review,* 1963, *28,* 47–54.

LAMPARD, E. E. "Historical Aspects of Urbanization." In P. M. HAUSER and L. F. SCHNORE (Eds.), *The Study of Urbanization.* New York: Wiley, 1965.

LAMPARD, E. E. "The Evolving System of Cities in the United States: Urbanization and Economic Development." In H. S. PERLOFF and L. WINGO, JR. (Eds.), *Issues in Urban Economics.* Baltimore, Md.: Johns Hopkins University Press, 1968.

LANCASTER, H. O., and HAMBDAN, M. A. "Estimation of Correlation Coefficient in Contingency Tables with Possibly Nonmetrical Characters." *Psychometrica,* 1964, *29,* 383–391.

LANDECKER, W. S. "Types of Integration and Their Measurement." *American Journal of Sociology,* 1951, *56,* 332–340.

LANE, R. E. *Political Life.* New York: Free Press, 1959.

LATHAM, E. *The Group Basis of Politics.* Ithaca, N.Y.: Cornell University Press, 1952.

LAUMANN, E., and PAPPI, F. "New Directions in the Study of Community Elites." *American Sociological Review,* 1973, *38,* 212–230.

LAUMANN, E., VERBRUGGE, L., and PAPPI, F. "A Casual Modelling Approach to the Study of a Community Elite's Influence Structure." *American Sociological Review,* 1974, *39,* 162–174.

LAWRENCE, P. R., and LORSCH, J. W. "Differentiation and Integration in Complex Organizations." *Administrative Science Quarterly,* 1967a, *12,* 1–47.

LAWRENCE, P. R., and LORSCH, J. W. *Organization and Environment: Managing Differentiation and Integration.* Cambridge, Mass.: Harvard University Press, 1967b.

LEISERSON, A. "Pluralism." In J. GOULD and W. L. KOLB (Eds.), *A Dictionary of the Social Sciences.* New York: Free Press, 1964.

LENSKI, G. E. "Status Crystallization: A Non-Vertical Dimension of Social Status." *American Sociological Review*, 1954, *19*, 405–413.

LERNER, D. *The Passing of Traditional Society: Modernizing the Middle East.* New York: Free Press, 1958.

LEVINE, S., and WHITE, P. E. "Exchange as a Conceptual Framework for the Study of Interorganizational Relationships." *Administrative Science Quarterly*, 1961, *5*, 583–601.

LEVINE, S., WHITE, P. E., and PAUL, B. D. "Community Interorganizational Problems in Providing Medical Care and Social Service." *American Journal of Public Health*, 1963, *53*, 1183–1195.

LEVY, M. J. *Modernization and the Structure of Society.* Princeton, N.J.: Princeton University Press, 1966.

LIEBERSON, S. "An Empirical Study of Military-Industrial Linkages." *American Journal of Sociology*, 1971, *76*, 562–584.

LIEBERSON, S., and ALLEN, I. L. "Location of National Headquarters of Voluntary Associations." *Administrative Science Quarterly*, 1963, *8*, 316–338.

LIEBERT, R. "Municipal Functions, Structure and Expenditures: A Reanalysis of Research." *Social Science Quarterly*, 1974, *54*, 765–783.

LINCOLN, J. R. "Power and Mobilization in the Urban Community: Reconsidering the Ecological Approach." *American Sociological Review*, 1976, *41*, 1–15.

LINEBERRY, R. L., and FOWLER, E. P. "Reformism and Public Policies in American Cities." *American Political Science Review*, 1967, *61*, 701–716.

LIPPMAN, W. *The Public Philosophy.* Boston: Little, Brown, 1955.

LIPSET, S. M. *Political Man.* New York: Doubleday, 1960.

LIPSET, S. M., LAZARSFELD, P. E., BARTON, A. H., and LINZ, J. "The Psychology of Voting: An Analysis of Voting Behavior." In G. LINDSEY (Ed.), *Handbook of Social Psychology.* Reading, Mass.: Addison-Wesley, 1954.

LITWAK, E., and HYLTON, L. F. "Interorganizational Analysis: A Hypothesis on Coordinating Agencies." *Administrative Science Quarterly*, 1962, *6*, 395–420.

LONG, N. E. "The Local Community as an Ecology of Games." *American Journal of Sociology*, 1958, *63*, 251–261.

MacGILLIVRAY, L. A. "Municipal Power Distribution and Municipal Change." Unpublished doctoral dissertation, University of North Carolina, Chapel Hill, 1973.

MANIHA, J., and PERROW, C. "The Reluctant Organization and the Aggressive Environment." *Administrative Science Quarterly,* 1965, *10,* 238–257.

MARCH, J. G. (Ed.) *Handbook of Organizations.* Chicago: Rand McNally, 1965.

MARGOLIS, J. "The Demand for Urban Public Services." In H. S. PERLOFF and L. WINGO (Eds.), *Issues in Urban Economics.* Baltimore, Md.: Johns Hopkins University Press, 1968.

MARRIS, P., and REIN, M. *Dilemmas of Social Reform: Poverty and Community Action in the United States.* New York: Atherton, 1969.

MARX, K., and ENGELS, F. "Manifesto of the Communist Party" (Preface to the English edition of 1888). In L. F. FEUER (Ed.), *Marx and Engels.* New York: Doubleday, 1959. Originally published 1888.

McDILL, E. L., and RIDLEY, J. C. "Status, Anomia, Political Alienation and Political Participation." *American Journal of Sociology,* 1962, *68,* 205–213.

McKENZIE, R. D. *The Metropolitan Community.* New York: McGraw-Hill, 1933.

MERTON, R. K. *Social Theory and Social Structure.* New York: Free Press, 1968.

MEYER, W., and BROWN, N. C. "The Process of Bureaucratization." *American Journal of Sociology,* in press.

MEYERSON, M., and BANFIELD, E. C. *Politics, Planning and the Public Interest: The Case of Public Housing in Chicago.* New York: Free Press, 1955.

MICHELS, R. *Political Parties.* New York: Free Press, 1958. Originally published in 1915.

MILLER, G. A. "Professionals in Bureaucracy: Alienation Among Industrial Scientists and Engineers." *American Sociological Review,* 1967, *32,* 755–767.

MILLER, P. T. *Community Health Action: A Study in Community Contrast.* East Lansing: Michigan State University Press, 1953.

MILLER, W. B. "Inter-Institutional Conflict." *Human Organization,* 1958, *17,* 20–23.

MILLS, C. W. *The Power Elite.* New York: Oxford University Press, 1956.

MINAR, D. W., and GREER, S. *The Concept of Community.* Chicago: Aldine, 1969.

MOE, E. O. "Consulting with a Community System: A Case Study." *Journal of Social Issues,* 1959, *15,* 28–35.

MORLOCK, L. L. "Business Interests, Countervailing Groups, and the Balance of Influence in 91 Cities." In W. D. HAWLEY and F. M. WIRT (Eds.), *The Search for Community Power.* (2nd ed.) Englewood Cliffs, N.J.: Prentice-Hall, 1974.

MORRIS, R. "Basic Factors in Planning for the Coordination of Health Services—Part 1." *American Journal of Public Health,* 1963a, *53,* 248–259.

MORRIS, R. "Basic Factors in Planning for the Coordination of Health Services—Part 2." *American Journal of Public Health,* 1963b, *53,* 462–472.

MORRIS, R., and REIN, M. "Emerging Patterns in Community Planning." In *Social Work Practice* [1963]. New York: Columbia University Press, 1963. Also published in B. J. FRIEDEN and R. MORRIS (Eds.), *Urban Planning and Social Policy* (New York: Basic Books, 1968).

MOTT, P. E. *The Organization of Society.* Englewood Cliffs, N.J.: Prentice-Hall, 1965.

MOTT, P. E. "The Role of the Absentee-Owned Corporation in Changing Community." In M. AIKEN and P. E. MOTT (Eds.), *The Structure of Community Power.* New York: Random House, 1970.

MOYNIHAN, D. P. *Maximum Feasible Misunderstanding: Community Action in the War on Poverty.* New York: Free Press, 1969.

MUMFORD, L. *The Culture of Cities.* New York: Harcourt Brace Jovanovich, 1938.

NAGEL, E. *Logic Without Metaphysics.* New York: Free Press, 1956.

National Center for Health Services Research and Development. *Focus: Health Services and Mental Health Administration.* No. 5 (Summer). Rockville, Md.: U.S. Public Health Service, 1970.

NELSON, H. J. "A Service Classification of American Cities." *Economic Geography,* 1955, *31,* 189–210.

NETZER, D. "Federal, State and Local Finance in a Metropolitan Context." In H. S. PERLOFF and L. WINGO, JR. (Eds.), *Issues in*

Urban Economics. Baltimore, Md.: Johns Hopkins University Press, 1968.

NOLTING, O. F., and ARNOLD, D. S. (Eds.) *The Municipal Year Book, 1963.* Chicago: International City Managers' Association, 1963.

PARETO, V. *Vilfredo Pareto: Selections From His Treatise.* (J. LOPREATO, Ed.,) New York: Crowell, 1965. Originally Published in 1916.

PAPPENFORT, D. H. "The Ecological Field and the Metropolitan Community: Manufacturing and Management." *American Journal of Sociology,* 1959, *64,* 380–85.

PARK, R. E. "Community Organization and the Romantic Temper." *Social Forces,* 1925, *3,* 675–677.

PARK, R. E. "Human Ecology." *American Journal of Sociology,* 1936, *42,* 1–15.

PARK, R. E. "Symbiosis and Socialization: A Frame of Reference for the Study of Society." *American Journal of Sociology,* 1939, *45,* 1–25.

PARK, R. E. *Human Communities.* New York: Free Press, 1952.

PARSONS, T. *The Social System.* New York: Free Press, 1951.

PARSONS, T. "Suggestions for a Sociological Approach to the Theory of Organizations—I." *Administrative Science Quarterly,* 1956, *1,* 5–19.

PARSONS, T. "'Voting' and the Equilibrium of the American Political System." In E. BURDICK and A. J. BRODBECK (Eds.), *American Voting Behavior.* New York: Free Press, 1959.

PARSONS, T. *Structure and Process in Modern Societies.* New York: Free Press, 1960.

PARSONS, T. "An Outline of the Social System." In T. PARSONS, E. SHILS, K. D. NAEGELE, and J. R. PITTS (Eds.), *Theories of Society.* New York: Free Press, 1961.

PARSONS, T. *Sociological Theory and Modern Society.* New York: Free Press, 1967.

PARSONS, T. "On the Concept of Value-Commitments." *Sociological Inquiry,* 1968, *38,* 135–160.

PARSONS, T. "Higher Education as a Theoretical Focus." In H. TURK and R. L. SIMPSON (Eds.), *Institutions and Social Exchange: The Sociologies of Talcott Parsons and George C. Homans.* Indianapolis: Bobbs-Merrill, 1971a.

PARSONS, T. *The System of Modern Society*. Englewood Cliffs, N.J.: Prentice-Hall, 1971b.

PARSONS, T., and BALES, R. F. *Family, Socialization and Interaction Process*. New York: Free Press, 1955.

PARSONS, T., BALES, R. F., and SHILS, E. A. *Working Papers in the Theory of Action*. New York: Free Press, 1953.

PARSONS, T., and SMELSER, N. J. *Economy and Society: A Study in the Integration of Economic and Social Theory*. New York: Free Press, 1956.

PELLEGRIN, R. J., and COATES, C. H., "Absentee-Owned Corporation and Community Power Structure." *American Journal of Sociology*, 1956, *61*, 413–419.

PERROW, C. "The Analysis of Goals in Complex Organizations." *American Sociological Review*, 1961, *26*, 854–866.

PERRUCCI, R., and PILISUK, M. "Leaders and Ruling Elites: The Interorganizational Bases of Community Power." *American Sociological Review*, 1970, *35*, 1040–1057.

PHILBRICK, A. K. "Principles of Areal Functional Organization in Regional Human Geography." *Economic Geography*, 1957, *33*, 299–336.

PITKIN, H. F. *The Concept of Representation*. Berkeley: University of California Press, 1967.

POLLOCK, J. K. (Chairman). [Symposium on] "The Over-All Effects of Pressure Groups on Political Consensus and Decision Making—Results of a Comparative Study of Pressure Groups for the Advancement of Political Theory." In H. W. EHRMANN (Ed.), *Interest Groups on Four Continents*. Pittsburgh, Pa.: University of Pittsburgh Press, 1960.

POLSBY, N. W. "How to Study Community Power: The Pluralist Alternative." *Journal of Politics*, 1960, *22*, 474–484.

QUINN, J. A. *Human Ecology*. Englewood Cliffs, N.J.: Prentice-Hall, 1950.

RAMSÖY, O. *Social Groups as System and Subsystem*. New York: Free Press, 1963.

REID, W. "Interagency Coordination in Delinquency Prevention and Control." *Social Service Review*, 1964, *38*, 418–428.

REIN, M. "Social Planning: The Search for Legitimacy." In D. P. MOYNIHAN (Ed.), *Toward a National Urban Policy*. New York: Basic Books, 1970.

RIECKEN, H. W., and HOMANS, G. C. "Psychological Aspects of Social Structure." In G. LINDSEY (Ed.), *Handbook of Social Psychology.* Vol. 2. Reading, Mass.: Addison-Wesley, 1954.

ROBINSON, W. S. "The Statistical Measure of Agreement." *American Sociological Review,* 1957, *22,* 17–25.

ROETHLISBERGER, F. J., and DICKSON, W. J. *Management and the Worker: An Account of a Research Program Conducted by the Western Electric Company, Hawthorne Works, Chicago.* Cambridge, Mass.: Harvard University Press, 1939.

ROGERS, D. *The Management of Big Cities: Interest Groups and Social Change Strategies.* Beverly Hills, Calif.: Sage, 1971.

ROSENTHAL, D. B., and CRAIN, R. L. "Structure and Values in Local Political Systems: The Case of Fluoridation Decisions." *Journal of Politics,* 1966, *28,* 169–196.

ROSSI, P. H. "Power and Community Structure." *Midwest Journal of Political Science,* 1960, *4,* 390–401.

ROSSI, P. H. "The Organizational Structure of an American Community." In A. ETZIONI (Ed.), *Complex Organizations.* New York: Holt, Rinehart and Winston, 1961.

ROSSI, P. H., and CUTRIGHT, P. "The Impact of Party Organization in an Industrial Setting." In M. JANOWITZ (Ed.), *Community Political Systems.* New York: Free Press, 1961.

ROSTOW, W. W. *The Dynamics of Soviet Society.* New York: Norton, 1953.

SAYRE, W. S., and KAUFMAN, H. *Governing New York City: Politics in the Metropolis.* New York: Russell Sage Foundation, 1960.

SAYRE, W. S., and POLSBY, N. W. "American Political Science and the Study of Urbanization." In P. M. HAUSER and L. F. SCHNORE (Eds.), *The Study of Urbanization.* New York: Wiley, 1965.

SCHNORE, L. F. "The Myth of Human Ecology." *Sociological Inquiry,* 1961, *31,* 128–139.

SCHNORE, L. F. *The Urban Scene.* New York: Free Press, 1965.

SCHNORE, L. F., and ALFORD, R. R. "Forms of Government and Socioeconomic Characteristics of Suburbs." *Administrative Science Quarterly,* 1963, *8,* 1–17.

SCHNORE, L. F., and LAMPARD, E. E. "Social Science and the City: A Survey of Research Needs." In L. F. SCHNORE and

H. FAGIN (Eds.), *Urban Research and Policy Planning.* Beverly
Hills, Calif.: Sage, 1967.

SCHOTTLAND, C. I. "Federal Planning for Health and Welfare." In *The Social Welfare Forum [1963].* New York: Columbia University Press, 1963.

SCHULZE, R. O. "The Bifurcation of Power in a Satellite City."
In M. JANOWITZ (Ed.), *Community Political Systems.* New
York: Free Press, 1961.

SEARS, D. O. "Political Behavior." In G. LINDSEY and E.
ARONSON (Eds.), *The Handbook of Social Psychology.* Reading, Mass.: Addison-Wesley, 1969.

SEELEY, J. R., JUNKER, B. H., JONES, R. W., JR., JENKINS,
N. H., HAUGH, M. T., and MILLER, I. *Community Chest.*
Toronto, Canada: University of Toronto Press, 1957.

SELZNICK, P. *TVA and the Grass Roots.* Berkeley: University of
California Press, 1949.

SELZNICK, P. *The Organizational Weapon: A Study of Bolshevik
Strategy and Tactics.* New York: McGraw-Hill, 1952.

SHILS, E. A. *The Torment of Secrecy.* New York: Free Press, 1956.

SHILS, E. A. "The Theory of Mass Society." *Diogenes,* 1962, *39,*
45–66.

SHILS, E. A., and JANOWITZ, M. "Cohesion and Disintegra-
tion in the Wehrmacht in World War II." *Public Opinion Quarterly,* 1948, *12,* 280–315.

SILLS, D. L. *The Volunteers: Means and Ends in a National Organization.* New York: Free Press, 1957.

SIMMEL, A. "A Signpost for Research on Fluoridation Conflicts:
The Concept of Relative Deprivation." *Journal of Social Issues,*
1961, *17,* 26–36.

SIMMEL, G. *Sociologie: Untersuchungen uber die Formen der Vergesell-
schaftung.* Leipzig: Dundker und Humblot, 1908.

SIMMEL, G. *The Sociology of Georg Simmel.* (K. H. WOLFF, Trans.)
New York: Free Press, 1950. Originally published in 1908.

SIMPSON, R. L. "Imperative Control, Associationalism, and
the Moral Order." In H. TURK and R. L. SIMPSON (Eds.),
*Institutions and Social Exchange: The Sociologies of Talcott Par-
sons and George C. Homans.* Indianapolis: Bobbs-Merrill, 1971.

SIMPSON, R. L., and GULLEY, W. H. "Goals, Environmental

Pressures, and Organizational Characteristics." *American Sociological Review*, 1962, *27*, 344–351.

SJOBERG, G. "The Rural-Urban Dimension in Preindustrial, Transitional, and Industrial Societies." In R. E. L. FARIS (Ed.), *Handbook of Modern Sociology*. Chicago: Rand McNally, 1964.

SJOBERG, G. "Theory and Research in Urban Sociology." In P. M. HAUSER and L. F. SCHNORE (Eds.), *The Study of Urbanization*. New York: Wiley, 1965.

SMITH, J., and HOOD, T. "The Delineation of Community Power Structures by a Reputational Approach." *Sociological Inquiry*, 1966, *36*, 3–14.

SMITH, P. A. "The Games of Community Politics." In W. D. HAWLEY and F. M. WIRT (Eds.), *The Search for Community Power*. Englewood Cliffs, N.J.: Prentice-Hall, 1968.

SMITH, R. A. "Community Power and Decision Making: A Replication and Extension of Hawley." *American Sociological Review*, 1976, *41*, 691–705.

SOWER, C., HOLLAND, J., TIEDKE, K., and FREEMAN, W. "The Death of the Health Council—An Analysis of Formal Organization." In C. SOWER, J. HOLLAND, K. TIEDKE, and W. FREEMAN, *Community Involvement: The Webs of Formal and Informal Ties that Make for Action*. New York: Free Press, 1957.

STARBUCK, W. H. "Organizational Growth and Development." In J. G. MARCH (Ed.), *Handbook of Organizations*. Chicago: Rand McNally, 1965.

STEIN, M. R. *The Eclipse of Community*. New York: Harper & Row, 1960.

STINCHCOMBE, A. L. "Social Structure and Organizations." In J. G. MARCH (Ed.), *Handbook of Organizations*. Chicago: Rand McNally, 1965.

STINCHCOMBE, A. L. *Constructing Social Theories*. New York: Harcourt Brace Jovanovich, 1968.

STRAITS, B. C. "Community Adoption and Implementation of Urban Renewal." *American Journal of Sociology*, 1965, *71*, 77–82.

STRAUSS, A. L. *Images of the American City*. New York: Free Press, 1961.

SUMNER, W. G. *Folkways.* Boston: Ginn, 1906.

TERREBERRY, S. "The Evolution of Organizational Environments." *Administrative Science Quarterly,* 1968, *12,* 590–613.

THEODORSON, G. A. (Ed.) *Studies in Human Ecology.* New York: Harper & Row, 1961.

THEODORSON, G. A., and THEODORSON, A. G. *A Modern Dictionary of Sociology.* New York: Crowell, 1969.

THOMPSON, J. D. *Organizations in Action.* New York: McGraw-Hill, 1967.

THOMPSON, J. D., and McEWEN, W. J. "Organizational Goals and Environment." *American Sociological Review,* 1958, *23,* 23–31.

THOMPSON, W. R. *A Preface to Urban Economics.* Baltimore, Md.: Johns Hopkins University Press, 1965.

TONNIES, F. *Community and Society.* (C. P. LOOMIS, Trans. and Ed.) New York: Harper & Row, 1957.

TRUMAN, D. B. *The Governmental Process.* New York: Knopf, 1951.

TURK, H. "Social Cohesion Through Variant Values: Evidence from Medical Role Relations." *American Sociological Review,* 1963, *28,* 28–37.

TURK, H. "An Inquiry into the Undersocialized Conception of Man." *Social Forces,* 1965, *43,* 518–521.

TURK, H. "Comparative Urban Studies in Interorganizational Relations." *Sociological Inquiry,* 1969, *38,* 108–110.

TURK, H. "Interorganizational Networks in Urban Society: Initial Perspectives and Comparative Research." *American Sociological Review,* 1970, *35,* 1–19.

TURK, H. "Task and Emotion, Value and Charisma: Theoretical Union at Several Levels." In H. TURK and R. L. SIMPSON (Eds.), *Institutions and Social Exchange: The Sociologies of Talcott Parsons and George C. Homans.* New York: Bobbs-Merrill, 1971a.

TURK, H. "Hospital Mergers as Interorganizational Events in a Community Setting." In D. B. STARKWEATHER (Ed.), *Proceedings of the Conference on Analysis of Hospital Mergers.* Washington, D.C.: National Center for Health Services Research and Development, 1971b.

TURK, H. "Comparative Urban Structure from an Interorganizational Perspective." *Administrative Science Quarterly,* 1973a, *18,* 37–55.

TURK, H. *Interorganizational Activation in Urban Communities: Deductions from the Concept of System.* Arnold and Caroline Rose Monograph Series. Washington, D.C.: American Sociological Association, 1973b.

TURK, H. "The Policy Outputs and Conflicts of Large Communities from an Interorganizational Viewpoint." *Sociological Focus,* 1975, *8,* 111–123.

TURK, H. "An Interorganizational View of Pluralism, Elitism, Conflict, and Policy Outputs in Large Communities." In R. L. LIEBERT and A. W. IMERSHEIM (Eds.), *Power Paradigms and Community Research.* London: Sage, 1977.

TURK, H., and LEFCOWITZ, M. J. "Towards a Theory of Representation Between Groups." *Social Forces,* 1962, *40,* 337–341.

TURK, H., and SIMPSON, R. L. (Eds.) *Institutions and Social Exchange: The Sociologies of Talcott Parsons and George C. Homans.* New York: Bobbs-Merrill, 1971.

TURK, H., SMITH, J., and MYERS, H. P. "Understanding Local Political Behavior: The Role of the Older Citizen." In I. H. SIMPSON and J. C. McKINNEY (Eds.), *Social Aspects of Aging.* Durham, N.C.: Duke University Press, 1966.

TURK, T. G. "The Allocation of Support to Urban Organizations: Hill-Burton Funding of General Hospitals in Large Cities." Unpublished doctoral dissertation, University of California at Los Angeles, 1970.

UDY, S. H. "Administrative Rationality, Social Setting, and Organizational Development." *American Journal of Sociology,* 1962, *68,* 299–308.

UDY, S. H. "The Comparative Analysis of Organizations." In J. G. MARCH (Ed.), *Handbook of Organizations.* Chicago: Rand McNally, 1965.

United Community Funds and Councils of America. [Bibliographies of Reports and Manuals, published annually] New York: United Community Funds and Councils of America, [1961–1969].

United Community Funds and Councils of America. "Listing of Campaign Data." In United Community Funds and Councils of America, *The Director*. New York: United Community Funds and Councils of America, 1966.

U.S. Bureau of the Census. *U.S. Census of Manufactures, 1954*. Washington, D.C.: U.S. Government Printing Office, 1954.

U.S. Bureau of the Census. *U.S. Census of Manufactures, 1958*. Washington, D.C.: U.S. Government Printing Office, 1958.

U.S. Bureau of the Census. *Census of the Population: 1960 Number of Inhabitants, United States Summary*. Washington, D.C.: U.S. Government Printing Office, 1961.

U.S. Bureau of the Census. *County and City Data Book, 1962*. Washington, D.C.: U.S. Government Printing Office, 1962a.

U.S. Bureau of the Census. *Census of the Population: 1960 General Social and Economic Characteristics, United States Summary*. Washington, D.C.: U.S. Government Printing Office, 1962b.

U.S. Bureau of the Census. *County and City Data Book, 1967*. Washington, D.C.: U.S. Government Printing Office, 1967.

U.S. Department of Health, Education and Welfare. *Fluoridation Census*. Bethesda, Md.: U.S. Department of Health, Education and Welfare, 1967.

U.S. Department of Health, Education and Welfare. *Hill-Burton Project Register*. Washington, D.C.: U.S. Department of Health, Education and Welfare, 1968.

U.S. Housing and Home Finance Agency. *Fourteenth Annual Report*. Washington, D.C.: U.S. Government Printing Office, 1960.

U.S. Office of Economic Opportunity. *Poverty Program Information as of 1 April, 1966*. Washington, D.C.: U.S. Office of Economic Opportunity, 1966.

VERNON, R. "External Economies." In M. EDEL and J. ROTHENBERG (Eds.), *Readings in Urban Economics*. New York: Macmillan, 1972.

VIDICH, A.J., and BENSMAN, J. *Small Town in Mass Society: Class, Power and Religion in a Rural Community*. Garden City, N.Y.: Anchor Books, 1958.

VON BERTALANFFY, L. *General System Theory: Foundations Development Applications*. New York: Braziller, 1968.

WALTON, J. "Differential Patterns of Community Power Structure." In T.N. CLARK (Ed.), *Community Structure and Decision-Making: Comparative Analyses*. San Francisco: Chandler, 1968.

WARNER, W. L., and LOW, J. D. *The Social Life of a Modern Community.* New Haven, Conn.: Yale University Press, 1941.

WARREN, R. L. "Toward a Reformulation of Community Theory." *Human Organization,* 1956, *15,* 8–11.

WARREN, R. L. *The Community in America.* Chicago: Rand McNally, 1963.

WARREN, R. L. "Introduction to [section on] 'The Community's Vertical and Horizontal Patterns.'" In R. L. WARREN (Ed.), *Perspectives on the American Community.* Chicago: Rand McNally, 1966.

WARREN, R. L. "Interaction of Community Decision Organizations: Some Basic Concepts and Needed Research." *Social Service Review,* 1967a, *41,* 261–270.

WARREN, R. L. "The Interorganizational Field as a Focus of Investigation." *Administrative Science Quarterly,* 1967b, *12,* 396–419.

WARREN, R. L. "Toward a Non-Utopian Model of the Community." *American Sociological Review,* 1970, *35,* 219–228.

WARREN, R. L. *Truth, Love, and Social Change.* Chicago: Rand McNally, 1971.

WARREN, R. L. and HYMAN, H. H. "Purposive Community Change in Consensus and Dissensus Situations." In T. N. CLARK (Ed.), *Community Structure and Decision-Making: Comparative Analysis.* San Francisco: Chandler, 1968.

WARREN, R. L., ROSE, S. M., and BERGUNDER, A. F. *The Structure of Urban Reform: Community Decision Organizations in Stability and Change.* Lexington, Mass.: Heath, 1974.

WEBBER, M., DYCKMAN, J. W., FOLEY, D. L., GUTTENBERG, A. Z., WURSTER, C. B. (Eds.), *Explorations in Urban Structure.* Philadelphia: University of Pennsylvania Press, 1964.

WEBER, M. *The Theory of Social and Economic Organization.* (A. M. HENDERSON and T. PARSONS, Trans.) New York: Free Press, 1947. Originally published 1922.

WEBER, M. *The Protestant Ethic and the Spirit of Capitalism.* (T. PARSONS, Trans.) New York: Scribner, 1958. Originally published 1904.

WEBER, M. *The City.* New York: Free Press, 1958. Originally published 1921.

WEIL, A. P. "An Investigation of the Preconditions and Effects of Mergers Among Hospitals in the United States as Perceived by Hospital Administrators." Unpublished masters thesis, University of Iowa, 1969.

WIEBE, G. D. "Responses to the Televised Kefauver Hearings: Some Social Psychological Implications." *Public Opinion Quarterly,* 1952, *16,* 179–200.

WILENSKY, H. L. *Industrial Society and Social Welfare.* New York: Russell Sage Foundation, 1958.

WILLIAMS, J. M. "The Ecological Approach in Measuring Community Power Concentration: An Analysis of Hawley's MPO Ratio." *American Sociological Review,* 1973, *38,* 230–242.

WILLIAMS, O. P. "Life-Style Values and Political Decentralization in Metropolitan Areas." In T. N. CLARK (Ed.), *Community Structure and Decision-Making: Comparative Analysis.* San Francisco: Chandler, 1968.

WILLIAMS, O. P., and ADRIAN, C. R. "The Insulation of Local Politics under the Nonpartisan Ballot." *American Political Science Review,* 1959, *43,* 1052–1063.

WILLIAMS, O. P., HERMAN, H., LIEBMAN, C. S., and DYE, T. *Suburban Differences and Metropolitan Policies: A Philadelphia Story.* Philadelphia: University of Pennsylvania Press, 1965.

WILSON, J. Q. "Planning and Politics: Citizen Participation in Urban Renewal." *Journal of the American Institute of Planners,* 1963, *29,* 242–249.

WILSON, J. Q. "Innovation in Organization: Notes Toward a Theory." In J. D. THOMPSON (Ed.), *Approaches to Organizational Design.* Pittsburgh, Pa.: University of Pittsburgh Press, 1966a.

WILSON, J. Q. *Urban Renewal: The Record and the Controversy.* Cambridge, Mass.: M.I.T. Press, 1966b.

WILSON, J. Q. "Introduction: City Politics and Public Policy." In J. Q. WILSON (Ed.), *City Politics and Public Policy.* New York: Wiley, 1968.

WILSON, J. Q., and BANFIELD, E. C. "Public-Regardingness as a Value Premise in Voting Behavior." *American Political Science Review,* 1964, *58,* 876–887.

WILSON, J. Q., and BANFIELD, E. C. "Letter to the Editor." *American Political Science Review,* 1966, *60,* 998–999.

WILSON, R. N. *Community Structure and Health Action.* Washington, D.C.: Public Affairs Press, 1968.

WINSBOROUGH, H.H., FARLEY, W.R., and CROWDER, N.D. "Inferring an Hierarchy from Flow Data." Paper presented at the annual meetings of the American Sociological Association, Miami Beach, September 1966.

WIRTH, L. "The Scope and Problems of the Community." *Publications of the Sociological Society of America,* 1933, *27,* 61–73.

WIRTH, L. "Urbanism as a Way of Life." *American Journal of Sociology,* 1938, *44,* 1–24.

WOLFINGER, R. and FIELD, J.O. "Letter to the Editor." *American Political Science Review,* 1966, *60,* 1000.

WOLFINGER, R., and FIELD, J.O. "Political Ethos and the Structure of City Government." In T.N. CLARK (Ed.), *Community Structure and Decision-Making: Comparative Analysis.* San Francisco: Chandler, 1968.

WRIGHT, C.R., and HYMAN, H.H. "Voluntary Association Membership of American Adults: Evidence from National Sample Surveys." *American Sociological Review,* 1958, *23,* 284–294.

ZIPF, G.K. *Human Behavior and the Principle of the Least Effort.* Reading, Mass.: Addison-Wesley, 1949.

Appendix

••••••••••••••••••••
••••••••••••••••••••
••••••••••••••••••••••

TERTIARY DATA FOR
VERIFICATION AND
FURTHER ANALYSES

••••••••••••••••••••
••••••••••••••••••••••
•••••••••••••••••••••

FIGURE A. Descriptions, Sources, and Summary Measures of All Indicators that Appear on Tables 1 through 25

TABLES A–D. Zero-Order Interrelationships Among All Indicators that Appear on Tables 1 through 25

Figure A. Descriptions, Sources, Overall and Regional Means, and Probability of Regional Differences of All Indicators.

Indicator Reported on Tables 1–25	Year(s) Measured	Description[a]	Source of Indicator or Source of Computed Data	Mean Rank[a] of Cities (Proportion Having): All Cities and by Region						Probability of Regional Differences[b]
				All	NE	ENC	W	SW	SE	
Age of City	N/A	Number of censuses since first having 50,000 inhabitants	U.S. Bureau of the Census (1961)	65.5	36.0	57.5	74.0	92.0	77.0	<.001
Economic Complexity	1963	Expert diversification plus bank deposits (details in Chapter Two)	U.S. Bureau of the Census (1967) U.S. Bureau of the Census (1962a)	65.5	36.5	81.0	74.0	73.5	67.0	<.001
Industrialization	1958	Per capita value added by manufacturing	U.S. Bureau of the Census (1962a)	65.5	39.5	28.0	84.0	100.0	82.5	<.001
Private Schools	1960	Percent elementary pupils in private schools	U.S. Bureau of the Census (1962a)	65.5	24.5	46.0	71.5	95.5	103.0	<.001
Foreign Stock	1960	Percent native-born of foreign parent(s)	U.S. Bureau of the Census (1962a)	65.5	20.5	62.5	58.5	95.5	110.0	<.001
Nonwhite	1960	Percent nonwhite	U.S. Bureau of the Census (1962a)	65.5	80.5	68.5	85.5	59.0	22.0	<.001
Democratic Vote	1960	Percent Democratic in county's two-party Presidential vote	U.S. Bureau of the Census (1962a)	65.5	41.5	66.0	72.5	82.5	71.5	<.01
National Headquarters of Voluntary Associations	1960	Number of such headquarters	Encyclopedia of Associations (1961)	65.5	60.5	61.5	59.5	79.0	74.0	>.30
National Headquarters Relative to Population Size	1960	Voluntary associations headquarters rank minus population rank	Encyclopedia of Associations (1961) U.S. Bureau of the Census (1961)	65.5	51.5	63.0	63.5	83.0	74.5	<.10
Municipal Scale and Diversification	1960	Number employed and budget diversification (details in Chapter Two)	U.S. Bureau of the Census (1962a, 1962b)	(.28)	(.55)	(.25)	(.20)	(.06)	(.28)	<.01
City-Wide Associations	1960	Knowledgables' reports (Chapter Two)	Mail, early 1961	(.58)	(.48)	(.50)	(.69)	(.47)	(.72)	>.10

Variable	Year	Measure (description)	Source							Significance
Prestige-Based Hospital Support	1947–1968	Stratified Hill-Burton (H-B) funding (Chapter Three)	"Hospitals" (1961) Hill-Burton Register (1968)	65.5	65.5	78.5	64.5	62.5	56.5	>.40
"Reform" Government	1962	City manager, nonpartisan and at-large election (Chapter Three)	Nolting and Arnold (1963)	(.55)	(.24)	(.29)	(.77)	(.65)	(.76)	<.001
Population Size	1960	Number of inhabitants	U.S. Bureau of the Census (1961)	65.5	74.5	64.0	61.5	61.5	65.0	>.60
Population Density	1960	Persons per square mile	U.S. Bureau of the Census (1962a)	65.5	29.0	53.0	77.0	104.0	77.5	<.001
(In-) Migration	1960	Percent in different county five years before	U.S. Bureau of the Census (1962a)	65.5	104.5	89.0	41.5	37.5	50.0	<.001
(Median) Education	1960	School years completed by Age 25+	U.S. Bureau of the Census (1962a)	65.5	92.5	75.0	30.0	53.0	83.0	<.001
Poverty	1959	Percent families with incomes under $3,000	U.S. Bureau of the Census (1962a)	65.5	72.0	91.5	88.5	35.0	22.0	<.001
Crude Death Rate	1960	Deaths per 1000 inhabitants	U.S. Bureau of the Census (1962a)	65.5	37.5	70.0	70.0	102.5	62.2	<.001
Per Capita Education Expenditures	1960	Municipal expenditures for education	U.S. Bureau of the Census (1962a)	65.5	34.5	83.0	86.5	84.5	42.5	<.001
Per Capita Welfare Expenditures	1960	Municipal expenditures for welfare	U.S. Bureau of the Census (1962a)	65.5	32.5	73.0	74.0	88.0	69.5	<.001
Per Capita Health and Hospital Expenditures	1960	Municipal expenditures for health and hospitals	U.S. Bureau of the Census (1962a)	65.5	39.5	73.5	74.5	74.5	69.5	<.001
Fluoridation	1966	Low fluoridation conflict (Chapter Three)	U.S Department of Health, Education, and Welfare (1967)	(.38)	(.31)	(.58)	(.26)	(.29)	(.52)	<.05
Per Capita Federal Poverty Fund	1964–1966	All kinds of antipoverty dollars	U.S. Office of Economic Opportunity (1966)	65.5	42.5	65.5	74.5	84.5	66.5	<.01
CAA-Sponsored NYC Project	1964–1966	Complex antipoverty network of organizations	U.S. Office of Economic Opportunity (1966) U.S. Dept. of Labor Files	(.29)	(.45)	(.21)	(.06)	(.06)	(.32)	<.01
NYC not CAA-Sponsored	1964–1966	Elementary antipoverty network	U.S. Office of Economic Opportunity (1966), U.S. Department of Labor Files	(.33)	(.28)	(.38)	(.37)	(.41)	(.24)	>.60

Figure A. Descriptions, Sources, Overall and Regional Means, and Probability of Regional Differences of All Indicators (Continued).

Indicator Reported on Tables 1–25	Year(s) Measured	Description[a]	Source of Indicator or Source of Computed Data	Mean Rank[a] of Cities (Proportion Having): All Cities and by Region						Probability of Regional Differences[b]
				All	NE	ENC	W	SW	SE	
Number of General Hospitals	1960	Short-term, nonprofit hospitals: public and private	"Hospitals" (1961)	65.5	72.5	72.5	55.0	71.0	61.5	>.20
Hospital Council	1969	City had hospital (cooperation among hospitals)	List provided by American Hospital Association	(.35)	(.31)	(.50)	(.37)	(.18)	(.36)	>.20
Urban Renewal	1959	Urban renewal status (details in Chapter Four)	U.S. Housing and Home Finance Agency (1960)	65.5	40.5	68.0	72.0	102.5	57.5	<.001
Model City	1967	In first wave of Model Cities	Los Angeles Times November 17, 1967	(.32)	(.48)	(.25)	(.34)	(.12)	(.32)	>.10
Broad Health and Welfare Planning Reports	1961–1969	Comprehensive report by health and welfare council	United Community Funds and Councils of America	(.33)	(.34)	(.38)	(.40)	(.24)	(.24)	>.50
Per Capita Community Chest Revenue	1966	Per capita dollars raised in annual campaign	United Community Funds and Councils of America	65.5	58.5	36.5	76.0	78.5	78.0	<.001
NUMBER OF CITIES				130	29	24	35	17	25	
Decentralization of Decision Making	1967	Participation in four actual community decisions (details in Chapter Three)	Clark (1971)	18.5	9.0	14.5	21.5	29.0	24.5	<.02
NUMBER OF CITIES				36	8	6	13	2	7	

[a] All per capita rates used number of inhabitants in 1960 as the base. This tends to depress the magnitudes of regression coefficients involving such standardization in the cases of variables measured before or after that year. Mean ranks (1 = "highest") are rounded to the nearest half due to computer imprecision in calculating this table.

[b] Two-tailed probability using chi-square, based on the Kruskal-Wallis H statistic for ranked data and on 2×5 contingency for dichotomous data.

Table A. Product-Moment Intercorrelations (r) and their Estimates[a] among All Indicators Reported on Tables 1–25 (N = All 130 Cities), Rounded to Two Decimal Places, with Decimal Points Removed.

	1	2	3	4	5	6	7	8	9	10	11	12	13	14	15	16	17	18	19	20	21	22	23	24	25	26	27	28	29	30	31	32
1 Age of City		52	44	63	38	14	33	69	20	66	04	08	−44	54	60	−66	−44	−04	65	32	46	36	24	40	54	08	56	53	56	52	37	37
2 Economic Complexity	52		22	14	04	17	02	60	29	39	−05	04	−15	36	33	−28	−13	10	43	15	18	19	28	19	25	−03	49	37	34	34	33	31
3 Industrialization	44	22		48	36	−02	12	17	27	39	−10	−10	−41	−03	48	−71	−46	−33	21	35	21	17	20	21	31	02	11	11	11	12	11	47
4 Private Schools	63	14	48		71	−29	42	28	18	42	−07	01	−54	14	59	−66	−28	−40	48	20	31	06	14	29	19	05	14	−01	29	28	05	29
5 Foreign Stock	38	04	36	71		−49	48	17	21	20	−20	−10	−31	01	06	−49	−11	−47	37	29	31	06	14	32	30	13	48	43	46	25	18	04
6 Nonwhite	14	17	−02	−29	−49		05	19	−12	20	08	−16	−00	−36	−33	58	39	67	07	−11	−27	−15	−09	06	−23	05	06	−01	−00	−14	19	−03
7 Democratic Vote	33	02	12	42	48	05		12	05	36	−08	05	−28	08	40	−41	−27	−34	28	21	30	13	38	37	05	77	−07	02	−01	14	−03	04
8 National Headquarters of Voluntary Associations	69	60	17	28	17	19	12		38	64	08	38	−26	71	35	−24	−41	−08	38	16	30	25	22	31	38	05	69	69	35	43	46	25
9 National Headquarters Relative to Population Size	20	29	27	18	21	−12	05	38		23	−12	−00	−33	08	09	−16	−04	−23	23	30	15	01	01	12	−10	06	77	82	32	63	10	04
10 Municipal Scale and Diversification	66	39	39	42	20	20	36	64	23		08	−02	23	45	51	−60	−16	−16	39	62	15	61	01	60	38	−23	77	52	43	48	22	29
11 City-Wide Associations	04	−05	−10	−07	−20	08	−08	08	−12	08		08	02	08	03	04	02	14	09	07	15	−08	−01	08	60	−23	−07	02	00	−14	−21	−06
12 Prestige-Based Hospital Support	08	04	−10	01	−10	−16	05	38	−00	−02	08		02	57	03	03	02	20	17	−09	62	19	−01	06	45	08	11	07	−06	07	−19	−28
13 "Reform" Government	−44	−15	−41	−54	−31	−00	−28	−26	−33	23	02	02		−20	−37	39	39	20	−34	−11	−27	01	−08	−24	−26	−23	03	−14	07	−22	−21	−06
14 Population Size	54	36	−03	14	01	−36	08	71	08	45	08	57	−20		20	−12	−04	10	56	03	48	31	21	22	16	14	82	67	24	54	38	07
15 Population Density	60	33	48	59	06	−33	40	35	09	51	03	03	−37	20		−54	−38	20	56	03	33	33	25	38	38	−00	17	18	34	46	06	17
16 (In-) Migration	−66	−28	−71	−66	−49	58	−41	−24	−16	−60	04	03	39	−12	−54		67	−39	−60	−28	−15	−24	−18	−34	−52	−06	−12	−17	−41	−22	−16	−39
17 (Median) Education	−44	−13	−46	−28	−11	39	−27	−41	−04	−16	02	02	39	−04	−38	67		−50	−60	−39	−31	−15	−18	−34	−54	−08	−04	−00	−34	−14	08	−13
18 Poverty	−04	10	−33	−40	−47	67	−34	−08	−23	−16	14	20	20	10	20	−39	−50		10	24	05	19	−02	06	23	02	30	16	37	34	17	18
19 Crude Death Rate	65	43	21	48	37	07	28	38	23	39	09	17	−34	56	56	−60	−60	10		24	32	56	11	36	36	02	38	37	38	34	17	00
20 Per Capita Education Expenditures	32	15	35	20	29	−11	21	16	30	62	07	−09	−11	03	03	−28	−39	24	24		56	33	26	36	45	−12	03	21	38	21	03	07
21 Per Capita Welfare Expenditures	46	18	21	31	31	−27	30	30	15	15	15	62	−27	48	33	−15	−31	05	32	56		44	12	32	48	−00	21	11	29	43	38	07
22 Per Capita Health and Hospital Expenditures	36	19	17	06	06	−15	13	25	01	61	−08	19	01	31	33	−24	−15	19	56	33	44		12	30	37	−00	25	19	29	46	21	14
23 Fluoridation	24	28	20	14	−09	−09	38	22	13	01	−01	−01	−08	21	25	−18	−18	−02	11	26	12	12		14	13	08	20	36	32	27	−03	25
24 Per Capita Federal Poverty Funding	40	19	21	29	32	06	37	31	12	60	08	06	−24	22	38	−34	−34	06	36	36	32	30	14		61	12	32	35	42	46	17	09
25 CAA-Sponsored NYC Project	54	25	31	19	30	−23	05	38	−10	38	60	45	−26	16	38	−52	−54	23	36	45	48	37	13	61		−1.	21	24	30	13	03	09
26 NYC Not CAA-Sponsored	08	−03	02	05	13	05	77	06	05	−23	−23	08	−23	14	−00	−06	−08	02	02	−12	−00	−00	08	12	−1.		13	63	26	13	13	03
27 Number of General Hospitals	56	49	11	14	48	06	−07	69	77	77	−07	11	03	82	17	−12	−04	30	38	03	21	25	20	32	21	13		63	24	48	38	09
28 Hospital Council	53	37	11	−01	43	−01	02	69	82	52	02	07	−14	67	18	−17	−00	16	37	21	11	19	36	35	24	63	63		34	42	45	29
29 Urban Renewal	56	34	11	29	46	−00	−01	35	32	43	00	−06	07	24	34	−41	−34	37	38	38	29	29	32	42	30	26	24	34		52	18	22
30 Model City	52	34	12	28	25	−14	14	43	63	48	−14	07	−22	54	46	−22	−14	34	34	21	43	46	27	46	42	13	48	42	52		19	17
31 Broad Health and Welfare Planning Reports	37	33	11	05	18	19	−03	46	10	22	−21	−19	−06	38	−21	−16	08	−15	17	03	21	21	−03	17	18	38	45	18	19			26
32 Per Capita Community Chest Revenue	37	31	47	29	04	−03	04	25	04	29	10	−06	07	−28	17	−39	−13	18	00	07	14	25	10	09	09	03	09	29	22	17	26	

[a] Biserial r (r_b) where one variable is continuous and the other is a dichotomous representation of a continuous variable and tetrachoric r (r_t) where both variables are such representations.

Table B. Product-Moment (r), Point-Biserial, and Phi Intercorrelations[a] among All Indicators Reported on Tables 1–25 (N = All 130 Cities), Rounded to Two Decimal Places, with Decimal Points Removed.

	1	2	3	4	5	6	7	8	9	10	11	12	13	14	15	16	17	18	19	20	21	22	23	24	25	26	27	28	29	30	31	32
1 Age of City		52	44	63	38	14	33	69	20	49	03	08	−35	54	60	−66	−44	−04	65	32	46	36	19	40	39	08	56	41	56	40	28	37
2 Economic Complexity	52		22	48	04	17	02	60	29	29	−04	04	−12	36	33	−28	−13	10	43	18	28	19	21	19	18	−03	49	29	27	26	26	31
3 Industrialization	44	22		48	36	−02	12	17	27	30	−08	−08	−33	−03	48	−71	−46	−33	35	21	28	17	15	21	21	23	02	26	09	09	04	47
4 Private Schools	63	48	48		71	−29	42	28	31	31	−05	01	01	14	59	−66	−28	−40	48	20	33	06	11	32	19	12	02	19	04	04	29	29
5 Foreign Stock	38	04	36	71		−49	48	17	21	−12	07	04	−10	20	06	−12	−04	−08	07	19	16	29	14	−07	29	14	04	03	19	03	04	29
6 Nonwhite	14	17	−02	−29	−49		05	−06	−10	05	02	17	17	−01	−26	31	06	−20	08	13	16	30	14	10	29	11	−09	02	11	10	26	−03
7 Democratic Vote	33	02	12	42	48	05		38	17	27	−00	−13	−01	20	−08	−38	−24	−16	56	21	14	25	38	27	05	14	23	18	35	33	03	04
8 National Headquarters of Voluntary Associations	69	60	17	28	17	−06	38		17	38	05	07	−00	71	40	−04	−33	−23	28	19	16	25	40	31	18	06	23	18	20	29	16	25
9 National Headquarters Relative to Population Size	20	29	27	31	21	−10	17	17		17	38	05	31	28	06	08	−08	16	23	42	15	30	36	31	09	05	07	18	11	19	13	24
10 Municipal Scale and Diversification	49	29	30	31	−12	05	27	38	17		05	−02	−00	35	38	−32	−24	−22	29	47	30	26	01	12	36	37	−10	−07	38	10	08	04
11 City-Wide Associations	03	−04	−08	−05	07	02	−00	05	38	05		05	17	−11	−11	04	01	11	19	−07	06	15	−01	08	11	34	−12	02	09	11	08	00
12 Prestige-Based Hospital Support	08	04	−08	01	04	17	−13	07	05	−02	05		17	07	20	03	03	−04	01	−16	−09	03	−06	07	17	05	−06	05	12	05	02	08
13 "Reform" Government	−35	−12	−33	01	−10	17	−01	−00	31	−00	17	17		−01	20	03	67	−38	−16	20	19	48	16	20	31	−37	−06	−04	17	−13	−16	−06
14 Population Size	54	36	−03	14	20	17	20	71	28	35	−11	07	−01		20	−54	−54	46	16	56	31	27	−15	−34	36	33	17	14	34	36	41	17
15 Population Density	60	33	48	59	06	−26	−08	40	06	38	−11	20	20	20		−60	−60	09	10	56	19	48	−28	−37	33	−00	31	08	24	34	29	07
16 (In-) Migration	−66	−28	−71	−66	−12	31	−38	−04	08	−32	04	03	03	−54	−60		67	−60	−16	−28	−34	−31	16	−13	−11	06	−28	−24	−08	−13	−11	−13
17 (Median) Education	−44	−13	−46	−28	−04	06	−24	−33	−08	−24	01	03	67	−54	−60	67		−39	−50	−34	−39	31	−02	−14	−04	17	−13	−41	−34	00	29	−39
18 Poverty	−04	10	−33	−40	−08	−20	−16	−23	16	−22	11	−04	−38	46	09	−60	−39		10	07	09	05	−14	02	−34	−08	12	00	−03	00	−11	−13
19 Crude Death Rate	65	43	35	48	07	08	56	28	23	29	19	01	−16	16	10	−16	−50	10		24	32	33	20	−02	36	30	12	09	12	26	06	18
20 Per Capita Education Expenditures	32	18	21	20	19	13	21	19	42	47	−07	−16	20	56	56	−28	−34	07	24		56	33	20	15	36	32	03	08	38	16	33	00
21 Per Capita Welfare Expenditures	46	28	28	33	16	16	14	16	15	30	06	−09	19	31	19	−34	−39	09	32	56		44	34	34	36	56	34	08	37	03	08	07
22 Per Capita Health and Hospital Expenditures	36	19	17	06	29	30	25	25	30	26	15	03	48	27	48	−31	31	05	33	33	44		09	15	36	30	27	14	35	16	14	14
23 Fluoridation	19	21	15	11	14	14	10	10	36	01	−01	−06	16	−15	−28	16	−02	−14	20	20	34	09		11	07	05	09	22	25	19	−02	19
24 Per Capita Federal Poverty Funding	40	19	21	32	−07	10	25	38	31	12	08	07	20	−34	−37	−13	−14	02	−02	15	34	15	11		44	12	15	30	21	10	13	10
25 CAA-Sponsored NYC Project	39	18	21	19	29	36	38	31	09	36	11	17	31	36	33	−11	−04	−34	36	36	36	36	07	44		−38	13	30	11	02	02	07
26 NYC Not CAA-Sponsored	08	−03	23	12	14	06	27	18	05	37	34	05	−37	33	−00	06	17	−08	02	32	56	30	05	12	−38		13	11	07	26	15	13
27 Number of General Hospitals	56	49	02	02	04	05	14	06	07	−10	−12	02	−06	17	03	−12	−13	12	30	03	34	27	09	15	13	13		49	26	37	28	20
28 Hospital Council	41	29	26	19	03	07	23	23	18	−07	02	12	−04	14	34	−00	−41	00	12	08	08	14	22	30	30	11	49		49	14	28	22
29 Urban Renewal	56	27	09	04	19	02	18	18	11	38	09	05	17	34	08	−24	−34	−03	09	38	37	35	25	21	11	26	26	49		40	14	13
30 Model City	40	26	09	04	03	11	35	20	19	10	11	12	−13	36	24	−08	00	00	12	16	03	16	19	10	26	07	37	14	40		11	20
31 Broad Health and Welfare Planning Reports	28	26	04	29	04	10	03	16	13	08	08	05	−16	41	34	−13	29	−11	26	33	08	14	−02	13	02	15	28	28	14	11		20
32 Per Capita Community Chest Revenue	37	31	47	29	29	26	04	25	24	04	00	08	−06	17	07	−11	−39	−13	18	00	07	14	19	10	07	13	20	22	13	20	20	

[a]These two are the coefficients conventionally used in multiple regression analyses that include dummy variables. Association is underestimated wherever the latter represent underlying continua, but analyses based on the above matrix are also reported throughout the book to satisfy the skeptical reader. Significance is conservatively assessed on the basis of this table as follows: Critical values for the .20, .10, .05, and .01 levels (two-tailed) are, respectively, .12, .15, .18, .23 for product-moment r; .11, .15, .17, .22 for point-biserial r; .10, .15, .17, .22 for *phi*.

Table C. Product-Moment Intercorrelations (r) and their Estimates[a] among All Indicators Reported on Tables 1–25 (N = the 36 Cities in Common with the Clark-NORC Study), Rounded to Two Decimal Places, with Decimal Points Removed.

	1	2	3	4	5	6	7	8	9	10	11	12	13	14	15	16	17	18	19	20	21	22	23	24	25	26	27	28	29	30	31	32
1 Age of City		69	35	-00	60	36	12	51	73	26	75	-32	-24	-53	47	67	-64	-41	06	53	51	45	48	20	31	30	43	63	67	63	49	43
2 Economic Complexity			-00	14	-07	23	02	60	10	53	-02	-03	-04	56	37	-29	-17	34	44	26	28	31	15	07	16	34	73	72	30	45	31	31
3 Industrialization				46	23	23	37	15	14	27	-38	-51	-61	03	-15	-54	-31	30	-31	26	34	33	41	-01	37	06	07	53	26	21	21	52
4 Private Schools					75	-39	24	59	24	32	-25	-25	-64	-01	-36	-64	-24	-41	39	51	03	27	25	15	03	25	55	72	53	41	21	57
5 Foreign Stock						-58	08	41	-14	27	08	-23	-36	-01	-23	-16	-31	33	46	-01	08	16	18	-04	16	08	18	41	21	22	28	35
6 Nonwhite							-02	24	-14	00	-25	-10	14	29	09	16	-12	55	-05	21	21	08	26	21	59	00	29	35	26	17	01	-05
7 Democratic Vote								15	29	48	-01	29	-51	-08	48	-24	-31	-24	25	31	33	38	14	04	48	14	-23	16	04	37	01	41
8 National Headquarters of Voluntary Associations									27	74	-10	27	-09	00	-14	-07	-28	13	06	34	21	36	18	20	14	28	59	81	67	57	44	41
9 National Headquarters Relative to Population Size										06	-17	-14	-15	-11	49	16	-07	16	01	06	18	08	18	16	06	22	24	59	28	28	10	01
10 Municipal Scale and Diversification											06	46	56	15	-10	10	06	01	21	53	13	19	12	-15	06	22	64	74	28	46	44	45
11 City-Wide Associations												06	56	62	73	31	18	37	-33	33	-04	-04	13	19	-30	27	07	04	00	14	-23	06
12 Prestige-Based Hospital Support													46	-04	-27	-14	14	21	33	04	04	-04	-28	-10	-17	06	00	14	-28	-61	07	-41
13 "Reform" Government														-31	-15	31	93	-16	21	-25	25	-10	-03	-22	-25	-32	-27	-44	-05	-30	-14	-71
14 Population Size															25	-16	-21	18	28	24	18	13	34	44	09	05	-25	-27	49	-05	18	26
15 Population Density																-42	-19	-13	49	43	31	50	22	21	21	25	-32	-25	27	29	35	38
16 (In-) Migration																	74	06	-50	-50	-42	-28	-26	-30	-69	04	49	46	40	16	-14	-63
17 (Median) Education																		-40	38	-38	-30	-12	-19	-41	-27	-25	-29	40	-61	-41	-30	-33
18 Poverty																			27	07	07	23	-20	49	25	-27	14	-28	-05	07	-15	-23
19 Crude Death Rate																				29	16	20	13	-01	17	-32	04	15	40	25	-09	28
20 Decentralization of Decision-Making																					32	45	18	45	14	48	46	40	16	22	03	28
21 Per Capita Education Expenditures																						58	22	02	27	18	24	40	18	22	42	41
22 Per Capita Welfare Expenditures																							48	18	28	49	24	15	27	30	18	30
23 Per Capita Health and Hospital Expenditures																								22	28	-04	32	13	10	56	29	12
24 Fluoridation																									-04	-43	33	59	22	22	37	40
25 Per Capita Federal Poverty Funding																										61	07	18	10	53	23	14
26 CAA-Sponsored NYC Project																											14	40	32	10	26	-01
27 Number of General Hospitals																												79	34	39	17	38
28 Hospital Council																													38	26	42	67
29 Urban Renewal																														62	28	50
30 Model City																															01	40
31 Broad Health and Welfare Planning Reports																																40
32 Per Capita Community Chest Revenue																																

[a]Biserial r (r_b) where one variable is continuous and the other is a dichotomous representation of a continuous variable and tetrachoric r (r_t) where both variables are such representations. Items 20–26 label the variables differently than on Tables A and B owing to the removal of "NYC NOT CAA-SPONSORED" and inclusion of "DECENTRALIZATION OF DECISION-MAKING."

Table D. Product-Moment (r), Point-Biserial, and Phi Intercorrelations[a] among All Indicators Reported on Tables 1–25 (N = the 36 Cities in Common with the Clark-NORC Study), Rounded to Two Decimal Places, with Decimal Points Removed.[b]

	1	2	3	4	5	6	7	8	9	10	11	12	13	14	15	16	17	18	19	20	21	22	23	24	25	26	27	28	29	30	31	32
1 Age of City																																
2 Economic Complexity	69																															
3 Industrialization	35	-00																														
4 Private Schools	60	14	46																													
5 Foreign Stock	36	-07	23	75																												
6 Nonwhite	12	23	07	-39	-58																											
7 Democratic Vote	51	02	37	64	59	-02																										
8 National Headquarters of Voluntary Associations	73	70	15	24	08	24	15																									
9 National Headquarters Relative to Population Size	26	10	14	32	41	-14	29	27																								
10 Municipal Scale and Diversification	59	14	22	38	30	09	37	57	05																							
11 City-Wide Associations	-25	-02	-41	-29	-20	11	-00	-08	05	-07																						
12 Prestige-Based Hospital Support	-24	-03	-38	-25	-25	00	-22	-15	-14	-08	05																					
13 "Reform" Government	-42	-49	-51	-29	-41	-39	-41	-07	-11	-07	38	37																				
14 Population Size	47	56	03	-01	-23	33	-08	70	49	49	02	-04	02																			
15 Population Density	67	37	39	64	47	-08	46	52	29	57	26	-15	-24	25																		
16 (In-) Migration	-64	-29	-54	-59	-33	-12	-56	-24	-07	-25	26	30	-24	-16	-42																	
17 (Median) Education	-41	-17	-31	-24	03	-36	-31	-10	16	-24	14	14	59	-21	-19	74																
18 Poverty	06	34	-42	-41	-57	55	-24	09	-28	17	17	33	-59	28	-13	-40	-40															
19 Crude Death Rate	53	44	-04	39	33	11	25	31	06	31	-19	04	-36	17	04	-50	-38	27														
20 Decentralization of Decision-Making	51	26	27	53	45	-05	31	34	18	29	-26	-29	-42	18	43	-50	-48	27	29													
21 Per Capita Education Expenditures	45	28	26	34	21	21	25	21	08	21	-11	-03	-30	13	31	-42	-30	07	16	32												
22 Per Capita Welfare Expenditures	48	31	41	51	46	-04	38	36	21	36	-04	-44	-05	16	50	23	-10	-22	45	58	58											
23 Per Capita Health and Hospital Expenditures	20	15	-01	03	08	21	20	18	13	31	23	34	18	13	-03	08	13	34	-03	45	22	48										
24 Fluoridation	24	13	29	21	-01	12	11	27	13	07	41	-13	-25	17	09	34	17	-03	13	01	14	17	17									
25 Per Capita Federal Poverty Funding	30	07	16	25	16	06	-17	13	07	26	36	-12	-30	21	30	-41	-48	20	17	45	14	34	27	28	-03							
26 CAA-Sponsored NYC Project	30	24	21	00	-13	12	04	38	26	15	-12	13	05	26	25	-17	-03	13	14	34	14	34	22	-17	43							
27 Number of General Hospitals	63	73	-06	15	02	17	04	81	61	52	17	00	01	61	27	-25	-27	38	34	38	28	24	10	26	07	10						
28 Hospital Council	52	56	05	11	-26	04	12	52	30	36	-08	11	-03	60	31	-37	-41	15	15	12	14	12	48	14	07	10	61					
29 Urban Renewal	63	30	34	55	41	04	57	28	10	36	-08	06	10	30	27	-44	-05	34	35	28	24	40	22	17	32	26	61	30				
30 Model City	38	35	17	19	17	14	34	08	32	25	13	26	13	18	26	08	13	25	24	13	22	10	23	43	26	38	13	16	48			
31 Broad Health and Welfare Planning Reports	33	24	16	03	-12	21	01	25	34	31	-17	-26	-25	31	46	-24	-11	03	13	14	13	22	21	13	16	25	13	25	21	00		
32 Per Capita Community Chest Revenue	63	31	52	57	35	-05	41	43	18	35	-33	-16	-57	26	38	-63	-33	-23	41	41	25	30	12	31	39	67	32	30	39	30	30	

aThese two are the coefficients conventionally used in multiple regression analyses that include dummy variables. Association is underestimated wherever the latter represent underlying continua, but analyses based on the above matrix are also reported throughout the book to satisfy the skeptical reader. Significance is conservatively assessed on the basis of this table as follows: Critical values for the .20, .10, .05, and .01 levels (two-tailed) are, respectively, .22, .28, .33, and .42 for product-moment r, point-biserial r, and phi.

bItems 20–26 label the variables differently than on Tables A and B owing to the removal of "NYC NOT CAA-SPONSORED" and inclusion of "DECENTRALIZATION OF DECISION-MAKING."

AUTHOR INDEX

265

SUBJECT
INDEX

A

Activation, interorganizational, 137, 199–204, 211–212. *See also:* Formal relations among organizations; Interorganizational networks; Interorganizational relations; Linkages

Activity, 29

Adaptation, 74, 84. *See also* Systems

Age of city, 46–48, 49, 62, 84, 93, 109, 126, 258, 261, 262, 263, 264

Alternative models, 214–221

Antipoverty funds, 77–82, 195–196. *See also* War on Poverty

Antipoverty networks, 28; need for activation of, 196–197; prediction of, 149–153. *See also* War on Poverty

Associations. *See* Voluntary associations

B

Banking activity, 39–40, 92

Beta, 21

Blacks. *See* Nonwhites

Boundedness, degree of, 18

Business associations, 41–42

Businesses, linkage of, 142–143

Bureaucracies, 59

C

Capacity, for interorganizational activation, 27–28, 136–184, 185–186, 189, 199–204, 209–210, 212–213

Centralization, of the macrosocial unit, 97–112, 129; and antipoverty networks, 151; conflict and, 97–98; consensus and, 9–10, 102–103; decision making, and interorganizational, 122–128; defined, 97; and dialectical conflict, 95, 113, 129–131; and health planning reports, 170; and health services delivery, 158; interorganizational bases of, 128–132; of macrosocial unit, 97–98, 128–132, 209; and organizational complexity, 98, 102–